CW01095713

DUNPECKHAM

Johnny Mack was born in Peckham, South-East London an only child to loving but strict parents. Although a bright and shrewd boy, he did not enjoy school – and school did not really enjoy him! He soon found out quickly that he had no choice but to join in the dodgy world of wheeling, dealing, ducking and diving which was all around him, getting involved in armed robbery, violence and drugs. He often tried to make a living in other ways - cab driving, running an illegal club frequented by infamous villains – but the easy money always beckoned as he tried to make a life for himself, his wife Carol and his children. In this, his first book, he tells his story with no holds barred from his childhood and to when reality bites and he must choose between his old life and his family.

DUNPECKHAM

Johnny Mack

DUNPECKHAM

Olympia Publishers
London

www.olympiapublishers.com
OLYMPIA PAPERBACK EDITION

A CIP catalogue record for this title is
available from the British Library.

ISBN: 978-1-905513-50-5

First Published in 2008

Olympia Publishers
60 Cannon Street
London
EC4N 6NP

Printed in Great Britain

So many people have helped and encouraged me to get this book this far and to all of them, I extend a huge thank you. But I would especially like to mention:

Ken Irons, for getting me started on the writing in the first place; to Carol and the kids for all their support and love through the years; to Graham Gauntlett and Seija Chowdhury for their brilliant graphics and to my secretary, Carol Trow.

Chapter One

PECKHAM SE15

I'm known as Johnny Mack. Peckham, in South London, was where I was born in the 1950s. I am an only child, Mum having lost two boys prematurely. Mum, all four feet eleven inches of her, was a quick-tempered little Irish woman who took no prisoners. Where she was strong-willed and dominant, my old man, on the other hand, was quiet and reserved unless pushed. He was also mechanically gifted and good with his hands, a trait I obviously inherited from him as I have always enjoyed making and repairing things.

My old man was away working as a steel erector most of the time so it was Mum's domineering influence that I was subject to most in my younger years; to be honest I was shit-scared of her, as were most people. My first memory of fear was when I started school at four. I remember being left crying at the school gates by my Mum; after she'd left I had to run the gauntlet of all the older kids in the playground who were shoving me and laughing and taking the piss – it was more like an initiation. Mum had decided that this school would be better for me to attend rather than the local one (it had a bad reputation and she considered it too rough), but it meant I had to walk four miles every day to get there. Mum had to start work at eight in the morning, so I was put out of the front door every day at 7.30 am and left to make my own way.

If I got on the wrong side of her, Mum could dish it out. She had an old carpet sweeper instead of a hoover, and when I got out of line she would unscrew the handle and give me a fucking good hiding with it – we had the only carpet sweeper that could go round corners, because the handle got quite bent from all this use. Mum had quite a reputation on the estate for being very fierce in spite of her small stature. I remember her knocking out this big fat Turkish bird with a tin of carrots and then beating her old man round the head with a leg of lamb when he tried to pull her off. She chased that cunt all round the estate hitting him with it and that was our fucking Sunday dinner! All this was down to me really, because these women would come to our flat and complain about me getting up to no good round the estate, and fighting with their kids and so on, but Mum didn't want to lose face and would always take my side, even if I was in the wrong. Mum was also of the Old School when it came to bringing me up.

When I got to the age where I wanted to start wearing fashionable gear like the other kids – Levi jeans and stuff like that – she wouldn't have any of it. She'd say that they were too expensive, then give me a lecture on how she went to school with cardboard boxes on her feet and then take me to charity shops or somewhere like that and I'd be given these cheap old things to wear. I remember ripping a pair of cheap jeans on purpose once, thinking that she might buy me some decent ones, but she wasn't having any of it and wouldn't buy me any more. So as a kid I had just the two pairs of trousers given to me by a neighbour, some German leather lederhosen shorts which I wore to school (I used to tell the other kids I wore them because I didn't feel the cane in them) and, believe it or not, a pair of beige riding jodhpurs, which I'd wander round the estate in, making out to the other kids that I was having riding lessons.

Another thing with my mother was that I was made to eat my grub up, whether I liked it or not. Or at least if I didn't eat it I'd go without. But it was all good grub, stuff I'd want today such as greens and proper vegetables and everything – none of your junk food. But where Mum was very domineering and a complete nutter she always wanted things her own way. I would resent this and try to fight back wherever I could. In fact I've got to admit that right up until I was in my thirties I didn't really like Mum. I loved her as a mother and I respected her, but the clash of personalities was always there.

Dad, as I mentioned, would be away working a lot of the time. Mum, as I said also worked, holding down a job at a suitcase factory, where she was well thought of for her hard work and no-nonsense attitude. When Dad came home every other weekend, or sometimes just once a month (I'm sure he felt safer working away), Mum would have a list of what I'd got up to all ready for him. But he just wanted to relax and didn't want to get too involved. I can't say I blamed him. The old man wasn't one to show me too much affection, but when I was a kid he would take me down the toy shop after he'd been to the pub and had a few pints down him. He'd always buy me something – he was good like that.

We lived on the Pelican Estate which was later to become part of the infamous North Peckham Estate. My favourite pastime as a kid was to wander around the bomb sites left over from World War II and collect all sorts of scrap material, incendiary devices, bicycle frames, you name it, I would bring it home and work on it in the bike shed we had been allocated by the council. I'd paint up the old bikes and sell them. I'd make scooters out of wood using old bearings as wheels and sell them to other kids, making good use of the old man's tools although, officially, I wasn't allowed to touch them. This boosted my threepence a day pocket money.

I remember the first time I stole something was when I nicked a board game out of Jones and Higgins store. I was with another nipper who was older than me who was always nicking stuff. Afterwards we went to an old bombed out house near the estate which we would use to hide out in sometimes. I can remember this occasion and the two of us opening up the game. To be honest the game itself didn't really mean much to me – it was the sheer excitement and buzz that came from nicking it. We both got caught for it and we both got a good hiding from our parents, but I couldn't resist the thrill it brought and, needless to say, I carried on doing it.

Once during the summer holidays I can remember going into the Catholic church with some other kids and nicking the collection box. The priest caught us as we were running down the street and he was just putting put me in the back of his Ford Poplar car when Mum came along the road. By the way Mum, was a Catholic, although Dad was Protestant. Anyway, the upshot was the priest took pity on me because he could see how I was shit-scared of Mum, and he told her he wouldn't report me to the police – if I attended Catechism. So I ended up going to Catechism and attending Sunday Mass and eventually got confirmed. That priest, Father Clements, was very good to me and he never once mentioned the incident again. Unfortunately his influence wasn't enough to keep me on the straight and narrow – nobody's was, if I'm to be honest.

High rise tower blocks were springing up all over the show in our area at the time to cater for the population increase. I remember Crane House going up, all the buildings on the 'Pelican' being named after birds, such as Gannet, Heron, Tern etc. Two gangs formed on my estate. One was made up of the 'local kids', and the other was those who had been brought into the area. I had no credibility whatever with either gang as I was a meek kid, bullied at school, and with no idea how to fight. This meant that, without protection, both gangs would pick on me pretty well every time they saw me.

So, not only was I getting bashed at school, I would also regularly cop a good kicking on the streets around my home. I was so timid I was even scared of fireworks. Mind you, that didn't stop me from doing 'penny for the guy' outside the pubs with my made up Guy Fawkes, also, in my defence, it has to be said that most of the gang members on both sides were older than me. The new gang had a leader called Dave Ryall – more about him later. Fights with the new mob would often occur at 'the pit'. This was a local play area – a sand pit originally, but someone had nicked all the sand and sold it, so it was just 'the pit' after that. Mum could see the pit from our top floor flat and would roar out the window to me across the estate when my dinner was ready.

Sometimes I'd run home to Mum when the new gang members gave me a bashing. I was always coming in crying with a black eye, bruising or cuts but wouldn't tell Mum how or who I'd got it from. When the old man came home Mum would tell him about it, but his attitude was that he didn't want a wimp for a son. If I came home crying, he'd make me go back outside again and tell me to give the same back to whoever had hit me. What he didn't seem to appreciate however was that these kids were about four or five years older than I was. I suppose there were about fifty or so kids altogether that would scrap and run riot around the estate. Eventually the new gang invited me to join their lot permanently but I was always a stubborn kid and refused.

I lived at a four storey block called Tern House, on the top floor. Next door to us lived a geezer called Tony Banbridge. Tony, who lived there with his Dad, must have been in his twenties then and I looked on him like the older brother I wished I'd had. Tony was later to marry gang leader Charlie Richardson's daughter. When I was about thirteen I remember working with him on old man Richardson's stall (Charlie's Dad) at the foot of Westminster Bridge selling post cards and ornaments to the tourists – Tony would get hold of all sorts of dodgy gear.

He was always a tearaway and getting into trouble but Mum used to love him and wouldn't hear a word said against him and sometimes I would get jealous for that reason. Often the Old Bill would turn up looking for Tony and he would climb out of the window at the back of his place – sometimes just wearing a towel if he'd just been in the bath or whatever, and he'd come into our place at the back and beg Mum to let him hide out. Although Mum was straight as a die she would always help Tony. She also loved his Dad, who was getting on a bit and was as deaf as a post, and she would help him out wherever she could; she was good like that. In the end, although Tony was a key figure in my childhood, we fell out after he wrongly accused me of trying to skank him over some jeans I was selling for him from his stall. We were sitting in his Jag arguing when he lost it and punched me in the eye, and remember, I was still only a teenage kid. He damaged it so badly I had to have stitches (still have the scar today). I was so pissed off and upset I didn't know what to do; I'd always more or less idolised the guy – he was my hero. In the end my sorrow turned to rage and I set my mind on killing the cunt with a four-ten shotgun I'd got indoors hidden in my fishing case. Luckily it never came to that and I just stabbed him instead and that was the end of our friendship and, although I know he later regretted what he did, we never spoke again.

But all this was in the future, one day Tony saw me come up upstairs to my flat after another kid had been giving me a good hiding. He called me over and gave me a lump of wood. He then told me to wait and hide for this kid (one of the gang leaders) and, as the kid went past, smash him across the back of the head with the tool; he was always good at giving advice. I went back downstairs, hid out in the block until this kid came back for his tea and, as he passed by, I jumped out from my hiding place, and smashed him across the nut. He went down like a sack of shit but that wasn't enough for me. I then jumped on him, kicking him, and carried on laying into him with the tool until my arms started to ache, even then I didn't want to stop, but remember being dragged off him screaming. It was the first time I had experienced this rush of adrenalin-fuelled rage that had come over me. It wasn't to be the last. By the way, the kid's name was Dave Ryall – the gang leader I mentioned before.

News of the fight reached my school, Denmark Hill; I was hauled in front of the headmaster and was expelled because they would not tolerate violence inside or outside the class room. As far as I was concerned though, I'd been done a favour because no longer did I have to walk four miles every day to the place and another bonus was that my new school, Oliver Goldsmith, had a lot of the 'old' gang members as pupils there and, needless to say, my reputation had gone up quite a lot with them as a result of that fight. Where I'd always been 'out', I was now definitely 'in'. Although I'd hurt Ryall quite badly I felt no remorse because he was a racist bastard and he'd hurt me plenty of times, frequently calling me an "Irish bastard". Racism was common in the area due mainly, I believe, to the competition for accommodation. Those regarded as 'outsiders' were hated. 'No Blacks' or 'No Irish' were signs that were still well in people's minds in the capital. Maybe, just maybe, it had been this release of an 'outsider's' frustrations that had made me feel so good when I whacked Ryall.

But I don't think that I could have survived the harsh environment I'd been brought up in if I had remained the loner I started out as; to be honest, I think if I had tried to 'fight fair' as my parents always urged me to, I would just not have coped. You had to have an edge out there on the streets.

It was about this time that I took up boxing. One day a big kid from the Thomas Carlton School came by our school to pick up his younger brother. This kid was about fourteen, I guess I was about eleven or so. The kid's younger brother was younger than me and I quite liked him and used to make sure he was alright at school and didn't get bullied. Anyway, whether it was due to the young kid being late out of school or, more likely, because the older kid resented having to pick him up, the older one started to give him a good hiding in the playground in front of everyone and made him cry. When I saw this I went ape-shit! I steamed into the big kid and gave him a right mullering. I wouldn't lay off him, raining punches, and in the end the school caretaker had to pull me off him. For this I had to leave the school or get expelled, although I was almost due to leave and go to secondary school anyway. It was a shame though, because my motive in attacking the boy seemed, to me at least, to be a good one. I would often befriend some of the younger kids, probably because I knew what it was like to be left on your own with bigger kids ready to pick on you all the time. It was the same with animals; I've always liked them and can't stand seeing them ill-treated. Perhaps I just missed not having brothers and sisters and needed someone or something to relate to in that way.

The other kids in the local gang all went to Peckham Manor secondary school but Mum had heard it was rough and I ended up at another school, a secondary modern, William Penn, in North Dulwich. I actually settled in quite well there. I was in Ruskin house, I remember, and loved doing the woodwork and metalwork. I was crap at maths though and, to be honest, couldn't really understand the Pakistani maths teacher we had, a Mr Kumar. After about six months I began to start asserting myself with the other kids and putting myself about. I'd started getting more into the boxing at the Fisher Club in Bermondsey and could use myself a bit. You had to be a bit tough and resolute if you wanted to survive at the Fisher because when you first joined (and this happened to me) you'd get put in the ring with someone who was well above your class. You'd take a boxing lesson that you'd never forget and the trainer would just say "See you again Monday, then," knowing that those who *did* return, at least had the balls for the game; it was as quick and simple as that.

Anyway, as mentioned, I started to put myself about and started to bully the other kids who I knew were shit-scared of me. Not just for the sake of it, but to bump up my pocket money. I would spend my return fare money and my one shilling dinner money I was given, and then threaten and intimidate the other kids into handing over theirs to me. They would also bring me in salmon sandwiches and Mars bars to order. It was pure extortion I know, but I did it. The other kids must have been glad that I wasn't there as often as I should have been, because I'd bunk off school regularly. Some of the older lads had started doing burglaries. I'd listen to them, well impressed, and watch them flash the cash. One of the older kids, Johnny Salter, took a shine to me and took me on a trip to Sussex. We got on the train but didn't pay the fare, as it was easier in those days than it is now to avoid it, and ended up breaking into a couple of mansions. We got away with silverware, and the like, which we sold to a geezer who would take this stuff from us kids but regularly rip us off, then sell the goods on with a nice profit. The most we'd ever get given for our stuff would be about fifty quid or so – that amount to me at the time was like a win on the lottery. Johnny Salter is dead now, killed off in the end by skag (heroin) so I was told; more about him later though.

Eventually I was called into school, with Mum, about the bullying. Naturally I'd kept all the details from her and she just wouldn't believe that I was guilty of it; as I said before, she could not lose face to anyone. The housemaster, a Mr Oleman, dealt with the complaint. Oleman, a big guy, didn't like me and the feeling was mutual - we'd crossed swords before. Anyway, on this occasion, I refused to be given the cane by him and, after two other masters tried to put me over a chair, I went berserk in the office, sent one of them flying, and rushed out of school. I was later called before the head, a horrible bastard called Richardson (no relation to our local big time gangster). Richardson and some of the other teachers, possibly due to Mum's intervention, decided on a lenient course of action. I would be put on the school camping trip to Guernsey in the hope that this would somehow straighten me out and curb my wicked and evil ways. Mum was happy with this proposition, probably because she wouldn't see the back end of me for a few weeks.

Mum gave me the ten pounds pocket money required, and this I handed over to Mr Oleman who had to look after the money on behalf of all the other kids on the trip as well. The trip proved pretty eventful as far as I was concerned. I got involved with the daughter of the local farmer, whose farm we were staying on, and ended up shagging her. We were supposed to help the farmer pick tomatoes but I used to slope off on the quiet to see her. She was a lovely girl, a college student, quite well spoken and everything. She had never met cockney boys like us before and seemed fascinated by us. Not that that was my first sexual experience. I'd lost my virginity at eleven in a lift, in transit somewhere between the first and eighth floors. It must have been either a case of premature ejaculation or else lifts were a lot slower in those days. Either way I remember getting the job done.

We camped out in tents on this field just outside St Peters Port, about a dozen of us to a tent, with no ground sheets. After a couple of days of really hot weather it really pissed down with rain and we got flooded. I had the bright idea of digging drainage ditches round our row of tents to let the water drain away. It worked. The other tents got flooded, so the kids had to be evacuated to the local school. We, on the other hand, carried on as normal and took a trip into the local town. I would always dress smartly, now that I was a bit older and wanted to pull, but never wore a school tie or badge or anything that would signify I was still at school. Instead I had a black blazer, Prince of Wales check trousers, and real smart shoes. I also looked and acted older than my years and had no trouble getting served in this nice little pub that we found in the town. After a pleasant little session, these other kids and I decided to head back for the camp site. To our surprise no one was there; they had all been evacuated because of the rain.

We went into the marquee and all this dinner the others had been cooking was there. There was roast chicken all laid out, a right feast. I went into Oleman's tent and found this stash of brandy. Of course we started drinking it and when the teachers came back we were paralytic, and there were chicken bones scattered all over the show. We were taken back to the local school where all the other kids were and Oleman put me in a stinking basement with no windows, full of solid fuel for the central heating. I was locked in there all night with no food. I resented this, but in hindsight I can see that there was little chance of me being undernourished, with all that roast chicken inside me. When Mr Oleman discovered that his brandy had been drunk my ten pounds pocket money mysteriously disappeared. When I mentioned the subject to him he stalled and said, "I'll sort it out for you tomorrow". This happened several times.

Over the next few days Mr Oleman organised a fishing competition; whoever brought in the most fish on the day in question would win a prize of five pounds, to be presented at this fish supper. It didn't matter what you caught, as long as it was edible. I got thinking about this so some other kids and I found this little bay with a line of lobster pots and I threw my line over them with a big fucking brick on the end and started to pull. The floats were coming in and we started to bring in spider crabs and lobsters which, of course, we were nicking from the fishermen. We had to get some sacks off of the farmer so that we could put them all in. Of course, the other kids all had small catches and we staggered in to the camp with all these sacks. Oleman was furious. "Where did you get that?" he wanted to know, obviously unwilling to believe that we had played by the rules. When the question of our five pound prize cropped up he didn't want to commit himself. The more he flannelled and made excuses, the more I got the hump. Finally I kicked off.

When this happened some of the other kids had been cooking; next thing, the tables went one way, the boiling water went the other, and there were crabs everywhere. I picked up a bench and tried to hit Oleman with it. I was jumped on by all the teachers, but would only quieten down once I had been given the fiver. After that, they took me back to the local school again. By my reckoning I was still owed five pounds but, there again, I'd drunk Oleman's brandy, so I figured we were all square. The next day we went home. I really expected the shit to hit the fan and Mum to be called to the school again but, amazingly, nothing happened.

Another master I did not get along with was our English master, Mr Kingston. Again the feeling was mutual. One day I brought a Malaysian machete into school. Not with any bad intentions in mind, but because it was something I'd picked up from a bomb site (it was probably brought back from the Second World War) and I just wanted to get it sharpened up because I liked it. Anyway, I was in the English class with this machete wrapped up in newspaper beside me, having sharpened it up earlier in the metal work lesson. Mr Kingston had a habit of clipping kids round the head when they made mistakes in class and I fucking hated it when he done that. Sure enough, it came to my turn to pronounce this word, or whatever it was we were doing, and, as often was the case, I made a complete balls up of it; English was never my best subject. Kingston smacked me hard round the ear hole. It's always the blow you don't see coming that does the most damage and for a moment I was stunned and in some pain; next thing I knew I was chasing the fucker round the classroom with a sharpened machete, slashing the furniture into pieces with it. Other teachers, alerted by the noise, came running in; we had a gym teacher, a Pakistani, who was quite a fit guy. He and the others managed to get the weapon off of me and I was dragged into the housemaster's office. They tried to get me over the table to hit me with a length of rubber, which we knew as 'the conveyor belt' (an implement that some smart arse, who was probably into sado-masochism, had it cut round to make it more effective). They were hitting me on the back, on the arse, on the legs. I just went fucking mental; I chinned the English master, Kingston, sending him flying, and ended up storming out.

Later there was a phone call to my Mum, and I finished up getting expelled from the school. Looking back, it would be hard to deny that I was a tearaway and, at times, a right evil bastard at the school. But it wasn't the whole story. One of the teachers, a Polish guy called Mr Polanski, I found I could respect; he had a cane which was the longest I've seen, like the sort you use for runner beans. He'd put long words on the board – like 'chrysanthemum' for example – and you'd have to pronounce and spell them correctly. If you didn't, he hardly had to move himself to clout you with this long cane. But you knew what to expect with him, you knew what the deal was, and that was something I could respect. In the end I'd get the words right, which was what he was after. I still feel grateful to Mr Polanski for his upfront teaching methods. It was the smarmy, devious bastards like Kingston who got up my nose.

Eventually I ended up at Thomas Carlton, a mixed school, after getting expelled from William Penn. That was the theory anyway, because, to be fair, I'd bunk off so much I was hardly ever there. At this time I'd adopted the skinhead mode of dress – boots, braces, and the works. At weekends I'd go out fly pitching, selling from a suitcase at Rye Lane. (Where Mum worked at a suitcase factory there was never a shortage of them!). I'd go to a wholesale warehouse in Camberwell Green, get, say, twelve quids worth of stock, shove it in the case, and go straight up to Rye Lane, where I'd stand outside Woolworths doorway and flog the gear. I'd learn the trade by watching the other traders and after seeing how they did it, I'd knock out socks, handkerchiefs, tinsel, anything. My old man had taught me to drive by then, so I'd drive all over the place, although officially of course I was under age.

But looking older than my years was never a problem for me. Working with the traders had given me a nice line in patter, and my profits would be spent on clothes. I'd go into Leslie Andrews tailors, in Rye Lane, and order a made-to-measure suit and other expensive gear. Ridiculous as it may seem, I'd buy an old banger. I remember one old Vauxhall in particular, and I'd actually drive into school. When I met Carol, my missus, at fifteen, I had a Mark II Zephyr.

The selling from a suitcase was known as 'fly pitching', as I have already mentioned. You had to keep a keen eye out for the Old Bill and as soon as you spotted a helmet you'd shut your case. I got really good at it after a while; I was earning more than my old man earned, by just working Saturdays. One crazy thing I did was to enlist the services of an old dosser from the local doss house. For a pound note I'd get him to stand absolutely still, like a statue, close to my pitch outside Woolworths, just so I could get the punters' attention. People would always stop and look, mystified, thinking what the fuck's all this about, is he real or what, and then I would jump in with my spiel. I'd knock out boxes of eight games (snakes and ladders, draughts etc), "There you are, ladies and gentlemen, you don't get *one*, you don't get *two*, you get *eight*. All for one pound!" and I'd slam the box down on the case dramatically, like I'd seen the other traders do. People would flock around me the more noise I made. They could get their Chrismas presents for relations, neighbours, what have you, all on the cheap, they loved it. Then I'd go back to the wholesaler for more stock and start the circus all over again.

There were of course, established traders operating who, naturally, began to resent my fly pitching skills. I remember two families in particular, the Butchers and the Carters, as being among the more influential of these traders. One day one of these traders came over and accused me of nicking goods off his truck; it was completely untrue, I hadn't been near his fucking truck, and didn't need to anyway, the way I was shifting my gear. He was just a jealous cunt trying to cause problems, so I stood my ground.

At weekends I'd spend my money in the pubs, drinking and rubbing shoulders with much older people, a right Jack the Lad. If there was a problem with any of the other trader families it would usually end in violence. I remember waiting outside the pub for this older bloke, who was the head of this family that I was in dispute with. Remembering the sound advice from Tony Banbridge a few years earlier, I whacked him from behind and took his legs away before he could react. Then I gave him a fucking good hiding with a bit of pipe. It seemed strange to me to hear this bloke, who was something of a hard man, respected and even feared by many, yelping and crying out for mercy like a gutless bastard on the deck. Mind you I guess it was only to be expected when you really think about it - I suppose I would have done it myself, if I believed it. Naturally this incident didn't go down too well with the rest of his family and remember, I had no real back up at this time because I'd finished with the school gangs and had not yet got involved heavily in the real gangland. How I actually survived this period I'm not too sure, because there were always very similar incidents that I got involved in that could have landed me in deep shit.

If I'm honest, I think I'd have to say that the fact that Tony Banbridge was my neighbour and mentor counted for a lot. He was, after all, a 'face' with the necessary influence to be able to smooth these things over. Incidentally, Banbridge later went off to America for a while. He did well for himself importing Mercedes cars from Germany and Jaguars from the UK. At one time he used to get me to sell snide 'Mickey Mouse' watches which I'd buy from him for sixteen pounds and sell off for twenty-five pounds down at the docks. But that's another story for later.

Chapter Two

THE GREAT DIAMOND HEIST

I left school – I suppose you could say by mutual consent – at fourteen. I was hardly ever there anyway so it seemed the most sensible thing all round. I picked up an old Thames Trader 15 CWT truck and started working for myself. I did a bit of 'totting', mainly with scrap metal. There were lots of sites about still, with houses being pulled down making way for housing estates, and I'd search for things like cast iron baths, copper, and lead. I did actually get pulled by the Old Bill for not having a licence but just gave a moody name and changed the plates on the truck and carried on.

I also carried on with the boxing, Monday and Thursday nights, and boxed for the Queen Ann club in Vauxhall as well as the Fisher. My trouble was that I easily got frustrated and lost my temper in the amateur ring, never a good thing, although it didn't hurt me when I later switched to unlicensed prize fighting. At the club I'd often find myself up against taller geezers who would use their long reach to out-point me. Me being shorter, thicker set and more of a street fighter, I would try to get inside and rough them up, but I found this wearing on my patience, I'm afraid. By temperament I was definitely more suited to the 'anything goes' stuff, as opposed to being restricted to the Queensberry rules.

Through my love of cars I got involved with a geezer called Gordon, who was twenty-eight and a bit of a so-called character. He lived on our estate and worked as a mechanic, not in a garage, but he would duck and dive and do roadside repairs and the like. I was quite good with car engines myself, as my old man had been a mechanic originally in his younger years and had taught me enough to get by. So Gordon and I teamed up and started working together. At weekends we'd pick up girls, managing to impress them by driving flash cars like Jaguars, for example, but, needless to say, the cars actually belonged to our customers. I didn't realise it at the time but Gordon had some serious mental problems and, underneath it all, was one very fucked up geezer.

Another friend at that time was a geezer from the boxing club called Tony. He was sixteen, a couple of years older than me, and I'd known him at school. He was tall, lean, good-looking and a promising young boxer. He was a bit of a babe-magnet and always seemed to have a bird on his arm. More importantly he worked at a Hatton Garden diamond sorting company. Tony would sometimes tell me things about his firm, like for instance how they counted the uncut stones he worked with – they'd do them in twos and threes. Little things like that, he'd come out with.

Now that Tony Banbridge was in America, I guess Gordon started to become my older brother figure. Mum would get on to me about where I'd been, who I was with, why was I out all hours, and I'd always have to say I'd been out with Gordon, although I kept schtum about what we got up to. Anyway, one day I told Gordon about Tony and his job at Hatton Garden. Later on I introduced Tony to him and they discussed whether there was any prospect of Tony getting any stones out of the company without getting sussed. It happened that there was a possibility. Apparently the security guards would sometimes let Tony out to go and put their bets on for them – crucially bypassing their security sensor, or whatever they had as security there.

One day, quite out of the blue, Tony phoned me excitedly and asked me to meet him at Blackfriars. When I got there he told me he'd been out at lunchtime to place some bets for the security guys, then handed me a little brown sack with a string top that you could pull tight. Inside the sack were uncut diamonds, about two hundred of them, an opaque yellow-brownish colour which looked to the naked eye much like crack cocaine. Tony and I took them to Gordon's flat at Kingfisher House on the Pelican, the estate where I lived. His dark dodgy eyes lit up and his drawn, grimy face wrinkled with pleasure when he saw what we brought him.

What happened next was straight out of an *Only Fools and Horses* sketch with Gordon as Rodney, the plonker. He took one of the stones into his kitchen, put it on the stainless steel worktop and started to smash it with a fucking lump hammer. If I saw it now I'd think to myself 'What the fuck are we dealing with here?', but remember, I was just a naïve kid then. Gordon was smashing away as hard as he could and the stone was flying about the kitchen from wall to wall. He completely destroyed the kitchen unit but only gave up when he couldn't find the stone which, for all I knew, had flown out of the fucking window.

When Tony saw what this fucking idiot was doing, he screamed, "What the fuck are you playing at? You can't break diamond, you cunt, it's the hardest thing going." If Tony Banbridge had been around I'd have got Tony to go to him for advice and I'm sure he'd have put us in touch with someone who knew what they were doing, that could help us move the stuff. As it happened, Gordon contacted a 'face', a famous fence who known as 'Little Legs'. Little Legs was about forty, a small guy, as his name suggested; he usually wore a crombie coat and tinted glasses and he had this habit of putting his thumb and forefinger at right angles and pressing them to his forehead as though protecting himself from sunlight. And he would constantly be saying, "Oh my Gawd, Oh my Gawd," – especially when talking about money. He was a cross between the actor Joe Peschi and the singer Roy Orbison

His impressive, three-storey house in Peckham was immaculate. When I went there with Gordon, he had fake Persian rugs, vases, Louis XIV clocks, and the like, all around the gaff. You only had to look at the place and it somehow screamed out 'villain' at you. I kept quiet because I knew that I was getting into pretty heavy company now; what I didn't know was that Little Legs was a middle man who acted for a well-known London villain (and for this reason he shall not be named). Looking back on this episode in my life, I often think that, if I'd been a grown man rather than just a kid when it happened, I'd be rich and living on the Costa because these stones were actually valued later in court at a quarter of a million quid.

Anyway, a meeting was arranged for later that day by Little Legs with some potential buyers in this minicab office (which was really a front for organised crime) in Peckham High Street. When we attended it I again kept very quiet; this was a bit of an effort really because I could see the way that things were going when Gordon was persuaded by the 'faces' to hand over the stones with some bollocks about getting them cut and polished. I was dead against that from the start, but what could I do? Tony was told about it afterwards and reluctantly went along with the decision. After all, he was as much out of his depth as I was. Of course, none of us knew the true value of the stones until much, much later as I already mentioned.

But our next job now was to get the merchandise to the faces, as agreed. Tony showed me how to count the diamonds in a special way using matchsticks and we filled up probably eight to ten Bryant and May matchboxes with them. Another meet had been arranged at the minicab firm for us to hand them over, so we had them hidden in the car boot and parked up opposite the cab firm on the main road. Believe it or not, just as Gordon was getting them out, ready to take them into the meeting, the wanker dropped a box; some spilled out of one of the boxes onto the pavement and out into the road. Right there in the middle of fucking Peckham High Street! It was dark and we had to rely on the street and shop lights, and there we were, like fucking idiots, Gordon, Tony, and me, running around, dodging the traffic, picking up everything from pebbles to rat shit, desperately trying to recover the stones. What a fucking fiasco. We managed to get them all but one. Where that one went I'll never know – maybe a rat swallowed it, or perhaps it just rolled away and eventually some road sweeper had a right result.

We went into the minicab office and handed the boxes over to the faces. I'll always remember the sight of them all being stacked on top of one another and being bound with tape. Then it was a case of, "We'll be in touch" and out we came, empty-handed. Further meets with the faces then had to be conducted by Gordon because Tony could just not afford to be seen associating with us. Even though the stones had not yet been reported missing, it would have been too dangerous for him.

Gordon was about the worst person possible to have to rely on, a real slippery cunt. The day after we handed the stones to the faces, I was up in his flat when the phone rang. He told me to take a walk down the road to the corner of Lyndhurst Way and Peckham High Street, where the Peckham Girls' School was, and said to me just wait there. This I did, and soon a geezer I'd never seen before came walking along, not a care in the world, then shoved a rolled up newspaper under my arm, quickly said, "See you tomorrow", and carried on walking. I assumed the newspaper must contain some sort of payment because of the weight. When I got back to Gordon's flat and unrolled it, we counted out four grand. Tony turned up while we were counting it – I remember it was now evening time and he'd just finished work.

Anyway, we were told by Gordon that the four grand was supposed to be a first instalment. The faces were supposed to be getting the stones cut, and paying us a bit at a time as things went along. Or, as I saw it, when it suited them, because I'd been sceptical all along.

Gordon's idea was that we didn't go mad with the money as this would attract too much attention. He would keep the main part of the money and we (Tony and I) would take a couple of hundred quid apiece. Although our end, to start with, appeared very slim, it all has to be taken in context. After all, my old man's wage at that time was, maybe, forty-five quid a week, so a couple of hundred sounded nice.

The next night there was the same performance at the street corner with me returning with the rolled up newspaper, only this time we copped for eight grand. This went on for three or four days then things went suddenly quiet. Meantime Gordon went out and bought a Bentley (wanker). Tony, Gordon and I started to eat out in a steak house owned by some local 'bubbles' (Greeks) most nights and we certainly did not stint ourselves and ended up with our own table. At about this time one of Tony's mates came to hear about our little secret and wanted to 'come in' on the scam. What he could offer beggars belief as the stones were already gone and apart from that, he was a sneaky little untrustworthy cunt! But we wouldn't have any of it and told him to fuck off. His name was Eugene and he was relative of a future big time boxing promoter called Frank, who, of course, was highly influential in the career of one of our British world champions.

Now that our lifestyles had begun to improve a bit it seemed unfair to Tony and me that Gordon should be the one who was getting nearly all the perks. After all, we liked cars as well. So Gordon invested in a Lincoln Continental, which I drove, and a brand new

Mark II Cortina for Tony. Now we felt better! I well remember a day out in Margate that we had when Gordon brought his mum and sister. We were there with a couple of girls we'd brought along, all of us travelling in style. This sort of thing went on for a while until the money started to dry up. There was also another unwelcome development that really started to put the mockers on everything: Gordon's girlfriend went and got the hots for Tony and before long he was giving her one.

It was difficult to sympathise with Gordon though, because although he was always a character and a bit 'different', I later learned that he really had some pretty heavy mental problems. And these apparently involved not being able to sexually satisfy a woman and, far worse, a liking for practicing violence on them. He had been regularly giving his girlfriend a beating, and her kids, by a previous marriage; they were all shit-scared of the evil bastard. He'd punish those poor kids by doing things like making them stand, naked, in front of an open window on a freezing winter's night if they had wet the bed, really scabby things like that. Maybe if I'd been a bit older at the time I would have picked up on some of the telltale signs. But that's the way it goes.

Another couple of meetings with Little Legs came and went. I sussed that we were being palmed off now, when we were told that things needed to cool down because the authorities were starting to take notice of us and our lifestyles. The stones had been noticed missing but they were not sure if it was theft because their security was so tight. So it was most important no one rocked the boat or arouse suspicion. Soon after I went to Gordon's flat. As I passed his kitchen window I just happened to spot him talking to another geezer inside. I did not ring his doorbell but kept on walking because I had recognised this geezer as the Old Bill! I waited until he had left before going in to Gordon's. "What the fuck was he doing here, he's Old Bill?" I shouted. He tried to palm me off with some old bollocks, but it turned out that some of our main fears had been realised. The authorities certainly were on to us. Our new-found wealth had attracted attention. Tony had been 'drawn in' to the plot by his regular visits to Gordon's flat, visits that didn't always coincide with Gordon being at home because, remember, he was just as pre-occupied with giving Gordon's girlfriend a seeing-to.

However at this stage the stones had still not been officially reported as missing. Gordon decided to bribe a bookmaker into giving him a moody betting slip which 'proved' that he had won eleven grand on a bet and he had this mounted in a frame and hung on the wall in his flat. It later came out that he'd also given his copper friend, or at least offered him, one of the stones as a bribe. Don't ask me where it came from or how he got it. It may have been the one missing from the mad night in Peckham High Street, which he could have picked up. On the other hand it might have been the one that got lost in the kitchen, I just don't know. But I remember the newspaper reports of the case stating later that the copper had been offered a stone.

The truth was that Gordon had somehow persuaded Tony not to involve me in some of the decisions that they were now making, and I was kept out of the picture a bit. I did keep on about the money though and where it was going. I was picking up my end of the take in hundreds, while Gordon always copped for thousands. One day my mum found a stash of money under the carpet in my room (she would have made a great detective). I wouldn't tell her where it came from. She also found a shotgun in the cupboard in my fishing case. It was a four-ten bolt action, not a sawn-off, and I told her that it was an air rifle; she promptly told me to get rid of it.

After Gordon's attempted bribery episode we were all put on 'obbo' (observation); of course, I didn't realise this at the time. One weekend a meet was arranged with the faces, at the Lord Lyndhurst pub in Lyndhurst Way, Peckham. Gordon and I went in the Lincoln Continental and we parked up outside. When we entered the pub there was no one to be seen. None too pleased; we came back outside and got back into the car effing and blinding. We had been due another payment and I remember thinking that we'd been well and truly ripped off.

I was complaining to Gordon when, suddenly, this geezer pops up from the back seat brandishing this enormous, fuck-off knife. Gordon all but shit himself, I've never seen a grown man so petrified.

We were told not to look round but the mirrors were so big in these cars that I could see the guy anyway. He spoke in what was obviously a fake accent, a moody Scots one, he then threatened Gordon verbally. At that point I started to say something, then a gun appeared and was pushed into the back of my head, and I was told to, "Keep my fucking mouth shut," and he assured us that we'd get paid, "When it's safe." I reckoned that the details of the attempted bribery had somehow got out and that, as a result, the faces were starting to get very edgy. Incidentally, I was later told that this little scene in the car had been my first meeting with a geezer who used to be muscle for the Krays and Richardsons. What I can say for certain is that Gordon wasn't the only one who was scared shitless that day.

Shortly after, Tony and Gordon were both arrested, and held for questioning. Beginning to feel the pressure a bit, I came clean and confessed to my old man everything that had happened. He was shocked and couldn't believe what I had got involved in. He told me that the best thing I could do was to keep my head down, avoid arousing any suspicion, and the best way of achieving this was to get a job, any job, he said, it didn't have to be a good one. So I took an unskilled local job at Magnet Joinery, working in the warehouse, which paid eleven quid a week. This was so little to me that I used to chuck my pay packet on the sideboard unopened and almost forget about it. Shortly after, I was walking up Lyndhurst Way towards Rye Lane when an S-type Jaguar pulled up alongside me; you could smell my arse for fear a mile away. In those days Jags tended to be driven around the manor only by villains. In the back I saw a guy I recognised from the meeting when we handed the diamonds over. I have since become convinced that this was none other than a well-known villain; as mentioned earlier, he shall remain nameless. I was invited to join the three men in the car – they said they just wanted a little chat. I was panicking a bit but kept a brave face and realised even then that they could have had me on 'obbo' as part of a plan to get to Tony and silence him. After all, they couldn't really go banging on his door, him living right in the middle of a housing estate.

I got in the car. They explained that they needed to get Tony away for a time until the heat was off. They said it had been arranged for him to go down to the coast and that he'd no need to worry as they'd shack him up in a nice flat with a bird and everything. It was about a ten-minute drive to Tony's place and during this time I was patronised with things like, "We know you're sound, son" and "You're a good boy, there's no need for you to worry." I was a bit more wised up than they thought though. They parked near Tony's place and sent me off to get him. I could have just fucked off! But I knew that I must do the right thing by Tony. Okay, I realised that, under Gordon's influence, he'd probably ripped me off a bit because I never did find out the full details of who got exactly what from the stones, but I still respected him and didn't want to see him get hurt.

I made sure no one was following me as I approached his place by going through a maze of alleyways. The guys in the car thought I was gullible enough to believe what they'd said, but I was still scared because I knew only too well that, if they had reason to suspect any sort of double cross, then I'd very soon be in deep shit. And also they knew where I lived – and there were my parents to think about. I knocked on the door and Tony's dad answered. I didn't know the man but very quickly let him know exactly what the score was, and how a trip to the coast was in the offing for Tony. He instantly picked up on what I was saying. It was as though he could read my mind. "Thanks son, you've really done me a favour," he said. Then I disappeared as quickly as I could – I knew the estate like the back of my hand and could travel from one side to the other without walking on the road at all.

All this aggro, of course, was really down to Gordon and his idea of dealing with a cozzer, a man I regarded as sheer filth. As far as I'm concerned even his own kind couldn't have thought that much of him because he never got promoted, to my knowledge, in all his time as a copper. Years later, on another case, I remember him coming out to Dorking, with a big fucking smirk on his face, to arrest me. I couldn't take the bastard at any price.

One night I came home from work about six o'clock and my mum was waiting for me. "Your mates are here," she announced. Inside was some pretty heavy Old Bill from Scotland Yard. They then proceeded to tell me everything I'd done for the last seven weeks –

where I'd been, what I'd eaten, what I paid for it, the works. They said as far as arrests went they weren't interested in me – they wanted the big fish. Dad was away at the time and Mum told me I had to tell them the truth, but I refused. The coppers must have been there for a good couple of hours but, in any case, I couldn't really help them because I didn't really know who the big fish were. I was just a kid and it would be a long while before I moved up the gangland ladder, and started to mix with the 'faces'. The coppers searched our place and even took all the plug sockets out of the wall. Obviously there must have been stones missing.

The case went to court and Gordon got 'nutted off' by playing on his low IQ, or whatever. He was assessed as having a mental age of about fourteen. He only got about four years. Tony got a right result by only getting Borstal training of six months to two years. The others were weighed off with eights and nines (years), I believe it was, but I'm not sure now about Stanley (Little Legs). Certainly I remember seeing the full details all reported in the London Evening Standard at the time. At the Old Bailey Gordon turned queen's evidence. I can remember when he did get out the saucy bastard had the cheek to return back to the same area and act as though nothing had happened. One day I saw him lying underneath a car, working on it. There was a toolbox nearby so I took a big screwdriver and plunged it straight through his leg. I'd never heard anyone scream so much. I also had an air rifle and, when he pulled himself out from under the car, I shot him in the head with it and scarpered. After all, the bastard had skanked me. He disappeared and I never knew what happened to him after that. For all I know he could be holding up a motorway somewhere (God willing) after having turned a grass against that lot.

After the trial my old man gave me the option of working with him or move out. At that time he used to get up early to work at Vauxhalls in Dunstable doing steel erecting, trunking and other steel work. It suited me down to the ground. Then I met my Carol, when just short of my sixteenth birthday. I remember she bought me a shirt for my sixteenth birthday – the first time I'd received a present from a girl. She was two years older than me and already married but separated, although she hadn't been for long. We met in the Magdella

Pub in East Dulwich. I had changed since my skinhead days and now favoured the more long-haired, mullet type of style. I was earning about forty-five or fifty quid a week working with the old man, and this was good money considering our digs were all paid for. At the time I was actually dating another girl, a lovely looking bird who a lot of other geezers would have given their right arm to have taken out. But her problem was that she was a bit clingy, and I wasn't into that at all and dumped her.

This particular night in the Magdella I was with a mate called Alan, who was on the run from the army at the time. He was about eighteen or nineteen, a funny guy who was a real good laugh – in a pain-in-the-arse sort of way. Anyway, I noticed this lovely blonde bird (Carol) over the other side of the pub in a black polo neck jumper, a brown leather jacket, black trousers, and brown slip-on shoes. She was with another bird. My ploy was to go over and start chatting up the other bird first. I asked her if she wanted a drink and she said she'd like a vodka and tonic. I thought fuck that, I wasn't that well off for cash this night as I'd been spending heavily that week, so I gradually worked my way round to Carol instead of going straight up to the bar and ordering. She took a lot more persuading than her mate did but eventually settled for a pineapple juice, which was much more suitable to my financial situation.

Carol and I got on very well just chatting in the pub; I was smitten really from the word go. Afterwards we went to a burger bar, the four of us. Carol's mate, who was with Alan, was a bit up herself, I thought – she had this posh way of talking and this attitude as though her shit didn't stink. Carol was the opposite, much more down to earth. She told me she was married but that her husband had pissed off and left her. He was older than she was, maybe six or seven years older. While we were in the burger bar, Alan started to get up to some of his favourite tricks. One of these was to take the onion out of his burger and stick it up his nose so that you could just see the end of it protruding out. This was the main trouble with the geezer, especially when you were trying to pull – he was a decent looking bloke but this weird sense of humour he had would always put the women right off.

Anyway, he got the elbow from this other bird, like he always did, but I walked Carol back to her place.

I told her I was twenty-eight and had a kid, just to try and give the impression that I was more worldly and more mature than I really was. We ended up just literally talking the whole night.

The next day I had to put a new clutch in my Zephyr, and I remember doing the job even though I hadn't slept all night. And that same evening I was back round Carol's bed-sit, having brought a small bottle of vodka and a bottle of lime with me. We sat and talked again and we listened to Elton John records. Her mum and dad lived directly next door, and there was a window in the dividing wall she could tap on, and dinners would get passed through, and so on – a cosy little arrangement, really. Anyway, I carried on seeing Carol, and I just knew that she was the girl for me – even though I was just a kid really, and not the mature bloke I wanted her to think I was. It was several months before I had the courage to tell her my real age, and when I did she wouldn't believe me – I had to take her home to my mum to confirm it.

Unfortunately for my old man, a teenager in love isn't always the ideal person to have as an employee. I had problems concentrating on my job now and would start to dream of Carol back in London. I'd drive backwards and forwards from Peterborough (where I'd ended up working with the old man, after Dunstable and Luton) to Peckham at weekends just so I could be with her, even for a couple of hours. The old man would be there at work wanting some tool or other passing to him and I would be away with the fairies. We fell out to a degree and he sacked me. Soon after, I got my own tools, lied about my age, and found myself another job working nearer home at the Wembley conference centre as a fitter.

I'd work long hours at the centre. I took a mate called Mitch with me; he had been working on the job at Vauxhalls. I coped with the job by blagging my way through, and by getting help from one or two of the older fitters, who didn't mind advising me if I came up against something entirely new that I didn't know about. I picked up a lot like this and was able to use it to good advantage when later working all over Europe. But this was after I'd started to go straight-many, many years later. And that again is another story!

When Carol fell pregnant with our first daughter, Lynsey, we moved in together in a bed-sit in Peckham. Mum, as a Catholic, didn't like that because Carol was still married. Carol's husband was a bloke in his middle to late twenties, a bit of a gambler, and he didn't know about me. He ran off with another bird, called Marie, and, the front of the fucker! then wrote to Carol to say he couldn't make up his mind whether he wanted her or this Marie. He seemed to just assume that Carol would have him back if he wanted to come. Eventually he decided he did want to come back, and turned up at the door with a suitcase one day. I answered it. The confrontation was short, none too sweet, and that was the last we saw of him. They got divorced but it was to be another five years before we got married. Other things were to get in the way before that happened.

Chapter Three

BORSTAL

After a while I got fed up with doing the fitting and gave it the elbow. A couple of easy jobs with friends followed, doing deliveries, as I tried my best to stay away from crime. Then I got involved with a Turkish family called the Hassans. At William Penn school I had known Hassan Ali, who had been a major bully – worse than me to be fair. We always referred to them, or any Cypriots, as 'Bubbles' (bubble and squeak, to rhyme with Greek) even though, in fact, the Hassans were Turkish Cypriots. Me, Hassan, and one of his brothers went on a massive spree all over Surrey, Sussex and Kent. Every night we were out in a stolen car. We robbed garages, warehouses, all types of commercial premises. It all ended up one night in a big car chase when the Old Bill put up a roadblock in Dorking. We had a safe in the back of this Mark II Cortina estate. I should explain that this was one of the older safes made during the war when there was a shortage of metal. They were not totally secure – the back would be mild steel plate which we would 'peel'. We did this by first getting an electric sander to remove the paint at the back to expose the hidden rivets, and then putting in a coal chisel to literally peel off the back of the safe.

Back to the car chase, it was about three in the morning when we hit the roadblock doing about ninety, me driving and the two bubbles in the back with the safe, in the estate part. We turned off the carriageway on two wheels and screeched into this cul-de-sac. It was just like a scene out of the *Dukes of Hazzard*. I turned off into this housing estate and ended up in someone's car port. I tried to leg it through a load of brambles and got cut to fucking ribbons and ended up hiding in a chicken coop. The police dogs found me and tore into me. The chickens were going mad and the farmer came out with a shotgun thinking there was a fox loose. The coppers kicked the living shit out of me. I couldn't walk to the van, they had to drag me. The Alis were rounded up. The younger one, Eddie Ali, decided to grass on all the jobs we had done. He even told them I had been with them on days that I hadn't been with them at all.

I managed to get bail. With Carol pregnant, us living in a £1.80-a-week-bed-sit with no bath, no hot water, a shared toilet and only a bar fire, I had to do something. I started going out on my own doing a bit of work, as I didn't trust anyone any more. One day I nicked a Corsair V4 with a slipping clutch (fucking typical). I got as far as Vauxhall on my way out into the Home Counties and a patrol car started to follow me as the Corsair had been reported stolen. Then followed a nine-mile chase around the one way system at Vauxhall – I had to keep my foot on the gas otherwise I'd have lost all acceleration due to the dodgy clutch. After I got nicked the Old Bill told me that he'd been so shit-scared he couldn't radio in his position. I'd been going down one-way streets the wrong way and all sorts. Anyway I eventually crashed into a shop front, got out, and legged it, right into a dead-end street. The Old Bill were right behind me so I stopped and chinned one copper, and his mate didn't want to know, but then the SPG (Special Patrol Group) turned up. They got out of their van, and true to form, battered me with truncheons, boots, and fists (fucking animals); a whole arm of the leather coat I was wearing came off in the struggle. I was then thrown in the back of the van face down and was given more SPG hospitality and taken to Lambeth police station where I was given such a pasting that I could barely move for about a day and a half. When the sergeant came in for his shift, I think it was on the Monday, he looked at the state of me and panicked, told the arresting coppers to get me out of the fucking place. The bastards took me two miles down the road, kicked me out of the van, and then re-arrested me. This was to cover them. So now, as far as officialdom was concerned, I'd only just been brought in – and therefore I couldn't have sustained my injuries at the police station, could I…?

Eventually I ended up in Ashford remand centre, whilst awaiting sentence, which was a terrible place. I didn't see daylight for three months as I was working in the laundry, which felt like it was underground because no light got through the dingy, frosted windows. Finally, after attending Tower Bridge Magistrate's Court and several other courts, I was due for sentencing at Chichester Crown Court. Mum and the old man came down to see me get weighed off. There were about fifty charges, relating mostly to the burglaries and a few assaults on police. The judge stated that his intention was to send me to prison for a long time because I was a "menace to society". That's when I heard the word 'Borstal' mentioned; I was fucking relieved. It could have been a lot worse, as I had terrorized the best part of the south of England.

I was taken from the eerie, centuries-old, grey stone cells of Chichester Crown Court up to Wormwood Scrubs by taxi with two screws. I needed to go there, basically, for assessment. It was the first time I'd seen the Scrubs apart from on TV. I remember going through the gates and on through to reception. The Borstal assessment centre was on B wing, and I stayed there for two weeks so they could decide whether I'd be going to an open or a closed Borstal. My old man's last words to me at Chichester, in an effort to make sure I buckled down and didn't make matters worse than they already were, were, "Remember: yes sir, no sir, three bags full, sir!" He knew this would be the most sensible approach if I wanted to get out as quickly as possible, and this was exactly the attitude that I adopted when I went in. I was issued with my kit, and then I went up onto the landings of this Victorian prison – dirty and foul smelling. I was on the 'fours' – the top landing – in a corner cell and was sharing with this fat, ginger kid. He was in for shoplifting and I remember him sitting there, crying his eyes out. We, as newcomers, were called SAPS.

I gave the "yes sir, no sir" treatment to all the staff for the two weeks assessment period I spent at the Scrubs. Fortunately it paid off and I was sent to an open, rather than closed, Borstal. The place was called Holesley Bay. It was near Ipswich, close to Woodbridge US airbase. The first thing I had to do there was to go through the eight week induction period. The sentence passed on me was the usual Borstal one of minimum six months, maximum two years. (It was entirely down to the 'con' concerned how much time he actually served between these parameters. If he was prepared to be obedient and cooperative and follow the programme then he could expect full remission six to eight months).

I was in a dormitory with about twenty other geezers. There were no fences, remember, this was an 'open' establishment. I began to feel quite at ease in my surroundings. Then came a bombshell in the form of a 'Dear John' from Carol. I think her sister and her dad had a lot to do with it but of course I only had myself to blame, considering what I had put her through. I'd only seen my daughter Lynsey once and that was at Ashford remand centre. I well remember how I first learned about her birth. One of the screws at Ashford (a real asshole) just put his head round the door of the cell and told me I was a father and quickly shut the door. Carol could have had a boy, girl, or triplets for all I knew and I had to wait all night wondering if everything had gone alright and she was okay. Mind you, I'd tried to play on the aspect of Carol being pregnant when attending the various court cases of course, and there is only so much you can get away with.

The first eight weeks at Holesley Bay were devoted to assessment. The regime was quite strict in the sense that they tried their best to physically wear you out, in the hope that this would keep you out of trouble. Circuit training was the order of the day and I became pretty fit. They had a matron there who was really more of a social services type of woman, and we would be encouraged to talk over any problems we had with her. I kept out of trouble pretty well during this induction period but things started to change when I was moved to the main population Cosford unit.

At Cosford you were allocated work. Another important difference was that they had an inmates' committee in operation. The head of this committee, or the 'Daddy' as he was known, was a guy of twenty-one. The committee paid me a visit and explained that they would be taking twenty pence out of my earnings every week. (Inmates were paid in ten pence pieces for the work they did, whether for working in the fields, on the new prison they were building, or, as in my case, in the boiler house). Anyway, when they asked for the twenty pence I told them to fuck off.

Soon the aggravation started. I was very careful always to leave my room clean and spotless, because this was part of the programme, but now, when I came back from work I'd find it in shit state, stuff chucked around everywhere. I was attacked in the showers. They grabbed hold of me and tried their best to sling me into a bath that had been filled with shit and piss. The normal practice was to then use a yard broom to scrape down your body so that it became scratched and subsequently infected with all the shit. I totally flipped. I hurt one geezer big time and he had to be taken to an outside hospital for treatment. I actually knocked his back teeth out and heard he was eating through a straw for a long time.

For this I got banged up in the "chokey" (solitary) block – an old underground bomb shelter. The routine there was pretty Spartan. There was no talking allowed; you had three boards to sleep on the floor, a table that pulled out from the wall, and a chair. You were not allowed to lie down on your boards when in the cell, you had to stand, walk, or sit on the chair. The only book you were allowed was the Bible, the governor being a devout Christian. At night you had to fold your kit in a precise way and then put it over the chair, which was then put outside your door. You could either wear pyjamas at night or go naked. I preferred to go naked as I couldn't stand having to wear clothes others had worn. The same went for underpants – I'd wear and wash my own usually but of course in the chokey-block you didn't have the washing facilities, so I'd go without.

On my first night in the chokey I heard this kid next door wailing and I could make out what sounded like screws shouting at him. The next night the same thing happened again and I began to wonder what was going on. After a while it seemed pretty obvious to me that someone was trying to make him do something he didn't want to do, and, by the sound of it, they were getting away with it. And it didn't take too much imagination to realise that what he didn't want to do, was to grant sexual favours to these animals. Just who these animals were I wasn't sure but I had my suspicions. And, regretfully, I was soon to find out for myself in the worst possible way.

In the morning I'd have to come out of my cell and run along a red line to go and get my grub, which I would put on a tray. When I'd collected it I had to bring it back by walking on a yellow line as per instructions. You were allowed about an hour to have your breakfast, tidy up your cell and get yourself ready for work. I had an old horsehair mattress which had to be put outside the cell every morning and I'd then get a bucket of water, a bar of carbolic soap and a scrubbing brush and clean out and tidy the cell, so that it was back to its original state of bare boards, table, chair, and Bible. Then I'd have to run out and take my tray back. I soon got used to the regime. However, a couple of days later my little routine was thrown out a bit because I received an early morning call. But this was a strictly unscheduled one.

It must have been about five am when my cell door burst open. Two chokey screws, a flash sadistic bastard Yorkshireman, and one we knew as "Queer Lurch" (because of his size) appeared. They both grabbed me – remember I slept in the nude – and it was clear what they wanted from me. I went fucking ape-shit. I'm not sure how, but I remember wrestling "Lurch" out of the cell and slamming the inward- opening cell door shut. But this was not before I'd grabbed hold of the chair which was outside the cell, the one my clothes were left on overnight. Now it was just me and the sadistic bastard in my cell. I smashed the chair against the wall and had a piece of it in either hand ready to batter the "nonce". "Come on then you fucking cunt," I roared and he cowered down in the corner pleading with me not to attack him. I could hear "Lurch" outside the cell and he obviously had no idea what to do. Both he and sadistic bastard were in the shit and they knew it. They had no business in my cell at that time and certainly no screw should have been inside my cell with the keys – it could have led to a hostage situation. All the screws wore 'civvies' in Borstal then and the keys were not so securely attached to them as they would be now.

I calmed down gradually and let the pathetic, snivelling toad talk me into letting him out of the cell. Were there any repercussions? Not a fucking thing. Nothing was said at all. All day I had expected to be put on governor's report. When the governor did make his regular afternoon visit and kit-check, the two of them stood behind him. The governor said to me: "Well Mack, any problems?"

"No sir, everything's correct sir."

"Are you reading your Bible?" he wanted to know.

"Yes sir, I'm reading my Bible." You had to be that way. I had no problems respecting their authority until somebody started taking the piss by making up their own rules. That's when I would flip.

I lost a month's remission for beating the con in the shower and a week in the chokey. I could have made my defence better but that would have involved grassing up members of the inmates committee and I didn't want that, did I, although the staff would have loved it. I wasn't prepared to go down that road. Before leaving the chokey-block I was treated very well by the two nonce screws. I had cigarettes coming in, although smoking was not allowed, and I even remember getting given a lager, which was most unusual. I was to go into the chokey again five or six times (mostly for fighting – I remember breaking another con's jaw) but I was always treated with respect after that.

As mentioned, I had a job in the boiler house and one little scam I had going was to 'buy' my ten pence pieces, the only currency we were allowed, from the civilian boiler man. He would give me seventy pence worth for every quid I gave him. So, if the old man came in to visit me, he'd bring say, ten pounds in one pound notes, and I could then buy ten pences off the boiler man with it because, remember, visitors weren't allowed to bring any ten pences into the Borstal.

When I got back on Cosford unit the inmates' committee asked me to join them. If they didn't know before that I could use myself a bit, then they certainly knew now. Within a couple of months I was the chairman – the 'Daddy'. Many of the screws there had been in the service a long time and were looking to wind down a bit. They weren't looking for unnecessary aggro and tended to let us run the unit much as we liked, but within reason of course. As a committee we were there, officially, to help run and organise inmates' activities, such as snooker, football, rugby and so on. In reality though, we just used the situation to extort money from them. If any inmates caused problems likely to upset the smooth running of the unit, or, more importantly, the smooth running of the committee, then these people would be quietly pulled aside and warned by the committee, in no uncertain terms, that their continued good health depended on them changing their ways.

I started playing rugby and was made captain of the prison team. The governor was a very keen enthusiast of the game – no, make that a fanatic. Me and the other players would receive extra meat and extra fruit to keep us happy and, of course, to keep our strength up for matches. The only real cloud on the horizon, and to me of course it was an enormous one, was the difficult relationship I had with Carol. I had still only ever seen my eldest daughter, Lynsey once. She was on my mind constantly. We had this P.O. (Personnel Officer) called Mr Shellcock. He was interested in criminal psychology and liked to talk to me about various things. I think it was because I behaved like a sweet, reasonable guy most of the time, but could fly off the handle very quickly when upset, that he saw me as a perfect case study, and used me for the project work he was involved in. He wanted to know what made me tick. I found I could talk to him quite easily. He knew I had problems, the main one of course being that I wanted Carol and Lynsey back in my life. Mr Shellcock said he was going to arrange a special visit for me.

It was organised for Carol and Lynsey to be picked up at the local probation office in Peckham and brought to the prison for a supervised visit. Shellcock was present. He wanted to see if the visit would have a positive effect on my behaviour because, although I played rugger and was the governor's favourite, and also had the unit under control, I was still apt to go round chinning people. Thankfully the visit was a success and Carol and I began to get back on track. I can't say we got back together because there was the small matter of my return to freedom to be sorted out first.

I began to get regular visits from this probation officer because, when I did finally get released, I would have to go on a supervision order for two years. I don't think he really wanted me to get out too soon because the snaky bastard used to visit my Carol late at night, say about 10pm or later, at the bed-sit we had. I always had the feeling he wanted to get over-familiar with her – remember, she was a lovely looking girl. I heard recently that he died of cancer. He was a horrible bastard in my opinion but, to be fair, I must admit that he was good at understanding people, and he had me off to a tee.

In the morning when I'd finished work I'd sometimes go to church with Tom, a civvie, who was the altar boy. The reason I always picked him out was because he had access to the priest's wine, and I had become quite partial to a nice drop of claret. I'd usually nick some and replace it with water but I'm sure Tom must have been fully aware what went on. There were not many of us Catholics, mostly it was CofE, plus some other religions. The CofE vicar was a complete hypocrite in my opinion – more of him later.

One day I was in the queue for my grub and this screw called Boynton was chatting to me. He was a big geezer and coached the rugger team (real nice geezer). He said to me, "You know what you're going to end up as, don't you Mack? An armed robber that's how you'll finish up, mark my words."

I told him: "No sir, I'm getting rehabilitated now, sir."

He wouldn't have any of it; he knew I was talking bollocks. "Mack," he said, "you *will be* an armed robber."

As it turned out, he knew me better than I did. But that was all in the future. There was something else to come along now, right out of the blue, which was to occupy my time and thoughts.

I was given instructions one afternoon to collect three pounds and fifty pence out of my personal cash the following morning. (We were encouraged to save our money and I had a bit put by – in any case money was not a big problem for me bearing in mind the various little scams I was operating at the time). I was also told I'd have to collect my civilian clothes from reception the following morning – and then report. So, next morning I got my chitty and took it to reception where I was given the three pounds fifty and a box containing my 'civvies.' There were five or six other lads at reception with me and I was thinking to myself 'What the fuck's going on here?' I decided to keep schtum.

Soon a white transit van backed up to the reception building steps. A screw then stepped out from behind the reception desk and announced: "Right you lot, in you get." In the van was this young woman with long hair, and a stripy jumper, and she was holding a guitar. I'm thinking 'what the fuck is this?' The screws just walked off when we were all safely inside. Next thing the van starts up and we're driving along the country lanes un-supervised when out comes this woman's guitar and she starts singing 'Bye bye, Miss American pie'. I couldn't keep quiet any longer. There's a black inmate sitting next to me. I said, "What the fuck's all this about then?" He said, "It's the Christian week, and we're all going on a Christian holiday." I couldn't believe it. "Christian week? What the fuck are you talking about?"

It turns out that we're to be part of this annual festival attended by Christians from all over the UK held at this holiday centre place they've rented at a place called North Swaftham, in Norfolk.

We arrived in the evening and it didn't take too long to settle in. There were four of us to a big room. It was all carpeted out. I remember I had a duvet, something I'd never possessed in my life. And when you went down for your food, there were no screws or anything. After asking around I soon found out that I was the only Catholic, the rest of the lads were CofE and had been put on the list by the CofE vicar to attend along with me. I couldn't understand why me, but I wasn't about to make too much of a fuss. If I had known then how anti-Catholic the CofE vicar was (something that I was soon to learn) then I'd have been even more mystified.

What made me soon forget about any religious considerations, or anything else come to that, was a sudden marvellous thought that I had. We were in Norfolk! And Great Yarmouth is in Norfolk! And Great Yarmouth was where Carol was staying on holiday with her parents and sister, and my daughter Lynsey, at that very time!

That first evening we were taken down to the local pub, where my three pounds fifty didn't last too long. I sat on a step outside the pub with this Christian bird that was with us, the one with the guitar, and we got talking. She asked how things were going and I told her great – I liked the nice, relaxed atmosphere and the kind people who were running the show, also the great food and accommodation. But I mentioned about the problems I'd had with the family and told her how my wife and daughter were staying only about fifteen or so miles away, on their holidays.

Unbelievably, the next morning, the woman came to me with this big smile and said "We're going to Great Yarmouth to see your wife and daughter!" She had this Morris 1000 car, and soon we were on our way. I knew the address of the caravan site Carol and Lynsey were at because we had been writing to each other regularly. When we arrived we went straight to reception. We were told they weren't in but had probably gone to the beach nearby, and to try there. I began to panic a bit. There were so many people about. What if we couldn't find them? We looked around the beach for ages without success.

My companion said we should try the pier, but they weren't there either. She suggested we pray. I agreed and we both asked for God's help in finding her (I always had faith). Eventually though, we had to give up the search and the woman said, "Let's leave a note for them at the site and come back tomorrow."

Then, as we were driving back, I suddenly spotted them. I said, "Stop, stop," and when she pulled in to the kerb I leaped out.

Carol's sister spotted me first and said, "Oh my God, he's escaped!"

I said "No, I'm on a Christian week."

Carol's old man looked at me very dubiously "Christian week... you?" He'd never really liked me.

Anyway, the Christian lady gave me time to talk to Carol, but we couldn't stay too long because, remember, we'd spent a lot of time trying to find them on the beach, and the surrounding area, and we had to be back at the Christian centre for the evening. But, by the way, it wasn't only a talk I managed to fit in, because thankfully Carol and I later managed a 'quickie' in the back of the caravan while her family were still talking in the front.

I also pleaded my case to my Christian lady that I hadn't really had as much time as I would have liked to see Carol, and she said not to worry because we'd come back tomorrow. What a result, I thought! And the best bit was we actually came back every day of the week! She'd drop me off in the morning at the caravan camp, go back and spend the day at the centre, and then come back and collect me at midnight. I was in seventh heaven!

When the week was over and I got back to the Borstal, I barely had time to change my gear before one of the screws said "Mack, get your kit and get down to the block." This meant the chokey-block. I spent that night in the familiar surroundings – without having a clue as to why I'd been put there. Next day, round comes the governor on his afternoon inspection. Behind him is the CofE vicar who demands to know how I've been put on the list for the Christian holiday week. "You're a Catholic," he stormed. I said I hadn't asked to go; I'd just done what I'd been ordered to by the screws. My temper was starting to rise and I started to get a bit abusive. The screws rushed forward and reprimanded me saying, "You can't talk to him like that," and so on. I calmed down a little and said, "I'm sorry, sir perhaps it was God's will."

Then the grilling started. The vicar said, "You were at a holiday resort every day at Yarmouth?"

"Yes sir, I was. The very kind lady took me there every day and it helped my relationship with my common-law wife." This touched another raw nerve.

"COMMON LAW WIFE?"

I said "Yes sir, common-law wife – with a child" (I was thinking 'If you'd let me out of here, I'd *get* married.') It came out about us not being able to find Carol on the beach, and how we'd said a prayer.

"YOU prayed?" he said. To me it seemed as though the man thought only his own religion capable of doing such a thing.

The governor was much more low key. He said, "We'll have to consider this matter. I don't know how you came to be on the list. And it's not as though there are two people named Mack." That was true, but if *he* didn't know then I'm bloody sure I didn't have a clue. In the end I had to put it all down to a bit of help from above! Anyway, in the meantime, I'm stuck there in the chokey. On the Sunday I'm doing nothing in particular when the door opens, the sadistic bastard and Lurch are standing there. "Mack, you've got a couple of visitors," I'm told. Then in comes the bird from the Christian organisation with this other geezer.

"John, what's been happening?" she wants to know.

"I don't know. It seems like I'm being penalised for being a Catholic."

"But John, you can be Catholic, Methodist or anything. You don't have to be any particular faith to be a Christian."

I said, "Well tell them that, not me." Anyway her guitar soon came out, and we all sat there together singing, with the screws outside the cell listening.

They let me out after the week and there was no more punishment to follow. I told the Catholic priest about what had happened and he said, "It's God's fate." He also said, "Take no notice of that ridiculous clergyman (I remember these words well), he's totally prejudiced." It wasn't as though the two men were friends or really worked much together anyway, because the vicar lived on the Borstal grounds whereas the priest came in from outside – there were not enough Catholic cons to justify his permanent presence there.

Serving my time and running the unit was no particular hardship for me in the months that followed. I had a nice easy job – I managed to get out of the boiler house and into the unit's clothing store, which meant I had nice clean clothes every day. Some of the lads used to do tailoring, and I would get them to work on my gear, putting in pleats and all that kind of stuff. It was nice to make yourself look presentable for when you had a visit. I tried to knuckle down to 'earn my dates' for early release. All this was worked out on a points system whereby, for example, you'd get four points for a spotless room, and so on. It turned out however that another lucky break meant that I picked up some 'bonus points' from an unexpected source.

One day this nice-looking bird of about eighteen came into the unit. If it hadn't been I was a family man I could definitely have thought of giving her one. Anyway, she sat next to me, said "hello" and introduced herself. "I'm from CSV," (community service volunteers) she said. "We are doing this project. I chose to come into this place – other volunteers help out in hospitals, mental institutions and so on."

I couldn't believe it. I said, "Are you barmy or something? Coming in this place with all this lot?" She had a lovely arse, nice pair of tits, and everything, and she's walking round with all these horny blokes, psychos, the lot! Anyway that was what she wanted, and she explained to me how the thing worked. I began to get very interested. I said to her "Can anyone do this?" and she said yes, they could.

Next thing, I wrote a personal letter to the Home Secretary of the day, Roy Jenkins, to see if I could be allowed to take part in the scheme. Apparently they had been doing it at some Borstals up north. The Home Office wrote back and said they would consider it. Then another letter came to invite me to an interview at the CSV offices in Pentonville Road, London. I was given a day release pass to attend it. I met Carol and managed another quickie before going on to the CSV offices. They asked me what I'd like to do if allowed to participate in the scheme. (Thankfully it turned out that I'd at least served enough of my sentence – six months or more – to be technically eligible.) I knew that you had to 'live in' on the various schemes and, of course, that suited me down to the ground. I didn't somehow fancy working with the mentally handicapped or anything like that, so I plumped for helping dossers and tramps.

So, where did they send me? You've guessed it – to Peckham! I was actually given a posting to St Giles Crypt day centre for the homeless at Camberwell Green, and was given accommodation in the vicarage across the road which was used as accommodation and offices for all the social workers and probation officers. I was told by my PO, Mr Shellcock, that I was actually the first inmate on the CSV scheme to be allowed to work in his home area. And he told me that this new concession had been authorised at the very top and, therefore, I should do all I could not to let him down. I assured him I had no intention of doing that.

On the first night I was at St Giles I stayed at the vicarage. It was to be the first and last time because from then onwards I worked out my own little scheme for my sleeping arrangements. I would go to my room every night, stay for a while, and then ruffle up the bedclothes to make it look as though I'd slept. Then I'd creep out via the back window and go to our bed-sit, which was just up the road, and spend the night with Carol. I'd be up at five am, shoot back to the vicarage, again via the back window, and then have a short kip before getting up well in time for breakfast. It worked like a dream, sweet as a nut.

Working with the dossers, handing out clothes, serving in the soup kitchen and so on, proved quite interesting because I met some unusual and surprising characters. There were people like doctors, even war heroes, there who'd hit hard times or fallen foul of drink, drugs etc. The vicar who ran the place, a nice bloke who christened my daughter Lynsey, used to give me a crate of Mackeson once a week. He told me I was doing a good job and that he was getting good reports back about me. Something else I did to make my way of life even more acceptable was to go and sign on the dole while I was on the scheme. The dole office didn't seem to know I was actually in Borstal, and the probation people were none the wiser about me signing on because I'd make an excuse and say I'd got to go out and see the dentist, or whatever. Anyway I got away with it somehow because I know I got paid from both sources plus getting my food and lodgings free. And, of course staying with my wife every night – I really had it made.

When I finally 'got my dates' (after serving thirteen months) Mr Shellcock came down to see me. He told me my reports had been excellent. "Mack, you've really done us proud," he said. "And you haven't been home at all have you?"

"No sir," I assured him. "I haven't been home"

This was about the preceding Wednesday or Thursday to my release date. He explained to me that normally I would be released from where I was without having to return to the Borstal.

"That's great," I said, "so I won't have to go back"

"Yes, I'm afraid you will," he said. My jaw dropped about half a yard.

"Oh no, why is that?"

"Because there is a big rugger game on Sunday and the governor wants you to play in it!"

So that was how it was. I went back on the Saturday, played the game on the Sunday, and on the Monday and Tuesday was given an office in the unit so that the lads could come in and have me tell them what it was like doing the CSV scheme. I must admit to feeding them a nice line in bullshit because I wasn't about to tell them what had really happened. And that's how I finished my time at Borstal.

Chapter Four

SCRAPPING AND CABBING

After a spell of nearly sixteen months away, taking into account my time on remand plus my thirteen months in Borstal, it was back to the bed-sit with no hot water, shared toilet, and no heating. I was on license and had to report every week to the probation office. It must have taken me a month or so to adjust myself to this sort of life style again and, of course, to get used to being with Carol again – 24/7. Anyway, Carol had a job as a secretary working in a bank, and I signed on and looked after Lynsey.

I'd promised Carol that I would keep on the straight and narrow and really made a big effort to live up to this. Eventually I managed to get some building work, mostly via employment agencies. I'd phone up different agencies three and four times a day from a local phone box. I was really keen. And when I got something, usually I'd walk to the site as money was tight, do ten hours work then walk home. Often I would try and get a sub the first day but, failing this, I'd have to wait for payday before I could afford bus fares. And having my own transport was not an option; I just couldn't afford it as the agency work was a bit spasmodic. One day you're in, the next there's nothing going, a bit like the depression in the thirties.

Then the old man offered me the chance to work with him again at Vauxhalls auto manufactures in Dunstable. Again it was doing the air conditioning, steel erection, and spray booths etc for their forty-eight hour shutdowns. I've got to confess I just got bored with this after a while, possibly due to the fact that I was seeing my old mates earning well on the proceeds of crime, which unsettled me. And remember, I'd learned so many scams from other criminals in my time away that it seemed a bit of a waste somehow not to put some of them to good use. And, of course, there were the 4am starts, and then driving to work with the old man in his methodical manner, always keeping to a certain speed and the classical music on the radio.

Anyway, I went out and nicked an MGB tourer sports car, changed the number plates, forged the tax disc to match, and used that for work. I remember taking the registration number off another other white MG travelling along the Old Kent Road.

My mate from previous honest work, Mitch, came with me in the car. We'd both get up at 4am and not get home until 8pm, sometimes working seven days a week, because we'd cover the forty-eight hour shutdowns at Dunstable and Luton. We'd get twenty pounds a night lodging money but would travel home every night so we could keep it. Petrol was only about fifty pence a gallon so we were quids in. Then we finished the job there and had to go up to Scotland. I couldn't face the thought of going up there with the old man, leaving Carol and Lynsey so I stayed on doing second fix stuff. This involved replacing rivets that had come out, putting grilles on, things like that.

There had been a bit of a power struggle going on between the old man and another supervisor called Strobal. Not that Dad was especially ambitious; he was a supervisor, but didn't want to know about going on to management, as he preferred to be just one of the lads. Anyway this Strobal geezer would give him grief and when Dad went up to Glasgow, he thought he'd start giving me the same treatment, I suppose just because I was his son. One winter's morning Mitch and I broke down on the M1 motorway going to work. I couldn't stay with the vehicle because it was nicked, and had a fake tax disc etc, so we walked all the fucking way to Whipsnade exit. We only had light clothing on and were freezing our bollocks off. We managed to get picked up by a truck at the junction that led into Dunstable. I remember feeling so warm and light-headed when I got in the cab I reckon I must have been suffering from fucking hypothermia.

We got to the site about 1pm. This made us about five and half hours late which gives some idea how long we'd been walking. It was just what Strobal had been waiting for, an excuse to have a pop at me; he more or less implied I'd made the whole thing up about breaking down. I just turned on the fucker because I was in no mood to be got at and kicked him round the site from pillar to post. Then I walked, leaving him battered on the floor and Mitch quickly followed me. That was the end of that job. The only real comeback on that was that Strobal, the snaky bastard, took it out on the old man, after he got promoted and eventually he got him laid off from another site, on the south coast. At least I'm sure it was his doing because I know he had a say in the matter. To me, it was just a case of spiteful revenge.

After that Mitch and I bought a couple of vans. We started working for a few printing companies, making deliveries for them. We were well cheap, to be fair, and this printing company in Peckham used to send us up north to Manchester and Liverpool and so on. Anyway we'd use these fifteen hundredweight vans we got cheap from the auctions, no insurance, no tax, fuck all. One day Mitch broke down on the motorway and had to get someone to tow him off. He phoned me and told me what it had cost him. I can't remember the amount now, but know the poor bastard didn't have enough money to get back home. As it happened he was carrying some Prestige leather clad photo albums and luckily I knew a guy I'd met in Borstal who I thought would probably be interested in the gear. About three hours later, after I'd contacted this guy, he was unloading the stuff from Mitch's van. So Mitch was back in pocket and managed to get back home, I'd give a moody story to the printing company, explaining the van got stolen. That's what it was like. It was hand-to-mouth stuff, living day-to-day, and you couldn't run a business like that. It wasn't too long before the whole thing collapsed.

After that I went back into the scrap game. What with the bit of 'totting' I'd already done, I figured I'd stand a chance of earning better money. My partner was an old mate called Victor ('Dickie') who I'd met up with again. Dickie, by the way, ended up doing a ten stretch for a shooting at the Southwark Park Tavern, South London when a couple of geezers insulted his girlfriend. But that's another story. How the scrap business worked was like this. We got hold of some corrugated iron sheets from building sites which we used as fencing, and started to squat on this bit of waste land. That became our yard. We bought a Bedford breakdown truck (on tick), a six cylinder petrol job with a 'hook' which you could actually drop down in front of a car, then wind back up again to take the vehicle away. We would go round housing estates with this hook looking for dumped cars, then hook them up onto the truck and bring them back to our yard.

We'd get five or six cars a day like this, and I managed to borrow the old man's cutting equipment, after promising him that I would not cut open any safes with it; we used propane instead of the acetylene as it was cheaper. We'd cut the engines out and cut the axles off. That went as steel shearing, which I remember bought in at £65 a ton at the time, with light iron (car shells) fetching £13 to £14 a ton. The car shell would be taken to a firm called Thames Metal in Greenwich, put on their weighbridge, then taken by a grab and put in the crusher. We'd get paid by the tonnage. The engines and gearboxes, which went as steel shearing, would be run down to the firm about once a week and we'd get paid our £65 a ton for that lot, so money was starting to come in and it was legal.

We did get a fair bit of aggro from the council about the land we'd taken over but, providing you paid your rates on it, they would normally leave you alone. A lot of people did it. It's much like today with the pikeys (travellers) turning up on common land and taking over. It was about this time that Carol and I moved from Peckham over to Brockley, just a few miles up the road, to a two-bedroom flat. I can remember, thinking that things were looking up for us as I was really working hard and pleased to be earning an honest living. Well, honest by my standards anyway. It wasn't my fault, was it, if people did silly things like leaving their cars untaxed? All we did was pick them up and tow them away.

It was about this time that my luck was about to improve. I met a bloke called John, who was in his forties. He was the father of an old school friend of mine. John had worked as a chauffeur for rich Arabs and had good connections. He asked me to come in with him on a project he had going. The idea was to run a second-hand car parts shop, with a scrap yard at the back, selling second hand spares and the like. The owner of the premises, in Camberwell New Road, had wanted it kept as a shop but couldn't find anyone willing to cough up the rent until John came along. It had a forecourt where you could park four or five cars; it had tyre machines, racks for spares, and a cellar full of boots, bonnets, and windscreens etc. Behind this was a spray booth, and behind the spray booth was the scrap yard. John had approached me because I had my 'hook' and the knowledge; he also knew I could get the stock that was needed to maintain the business.

The deal was that we'd go fifty-fifty, with me supplying the stock and John paying the rent and working the shop. I suggested to John we use a bigger truck, we could get more stock, so we got a sixteen ton dodge with HIAB (hydraulic arm) so I could pick up five cars in one go instead of the usual one. I was now able to cut the engine and gearbox from a car in ten minutes. And I'd flog any good doors and tyres from the shop. Everything was going sweet. There we were on the main route for the A2 with a good business going. We worked seven days a week and even advertised our wares in the Exchange and Mart. An extra bonus was the three bed-sits we had above the premises which were rented out to nursing students from Kings College Hospital.

Of course you can never have too much of a good thing. I always wanted more, so we operated a couple of little schemes of our own just to help boost the profits up. There was this one-legged bloke who worked for the council putting 'abandoned' tickets on untaxed cars as the law states, 'Tax the car in seven days or the council will remove it'. Well, that was what he was paid to do anyway, but what would really happen was that he'd see a car, make the entry in his log book, but instead of actually putting the ticket on the car he'd flog the ticket to me for a fiver. I'd then wait for the due date on the ticket, then go and stick the ticket on it at the same time that I hooked it up to be brought back to our yard behind the shop. Occasionally someone would see us and complain that no ticket had been stuck on the car originally, but they didn't really have a leg to stand on as the council records showed it had been officially logged seven days earlier, so the ticket was legal and so were we. So many more cars were coming in by this method that we had our work cut out for us. We were well pleased, even pleased at what you could get out of the oldest of cars; we were on a roll!

Another little scam was put in place to help our puncture repair service; we would charge customers three pounds fifty a time for a puncture-repair with labour, a five minute job. You wouldn't call it sophisticated, but it worked a treat. I'd just chuck a few roofing tacks out into the road just before rush hour, and before long, grateful motorists were queuing-up with flat tyres after spotting our sign advertising our tyre repair service; after all they never really had a choice.

So, what with the decent, re-saleable cars I got hold of being put on the forecourt, we could now offer the public car sales, parts, scrap sales, and tyre services. Plus, of course, we were pulling in the rents from the flats above. I was driving round in a Mark II Jag and Dickie was also enjoying the rewards of our hard graft. If we needed any money it would just be taken out of the business, as John assured us we didn't need to worry about the books – that was his side of the business.

One day we got broken into and the till was ripped out of the wall. It looked like the work of kids. Either that or it was specially made to look like it had been kids. Then some more things started to go missing. Generators, then oxy-propane cutters and battery chargers. I realised someone was having a go at us, but when I took it up with Dickie he didn't really want to know because he was only on wages and not a partner. Where I was fiery he was more placid. But I wasn't having this sort of shit happening, not when I was working my bollocks off seven days a week and really putting my heart and soul into the business. I began to have my suspicions about John.

One bank holiday weekend we had some time off and I decided to take Carol down to Brighton for a bit of quality time. It couldn't have been much fun for Carol though because I couldn't stop thinking about the business all the time. I said to her that I thought John might be having me over. "What makes you think that?" she wanted to know. I explained to her that certain things had happened recently that had made me suspicious. I told her about the fact that John had got rid of his beloved 'Roller' which he'd loved to drive around and was around the business a lot more than usual. What I didn't know at the time was that the man was a compulsive gambler. It later came out that it was him who'd taken the stuff from the business because he was badly in debt. Also he hadn't been paying the agreed rent money for the flats to the owner, who was away doing a three stretch for GBH at our local hate factory.

I couldn't handle this feeling of not knowing what was going on any longer, and decided to cut short our weekend at Brighton. We came back on the Saturday afternoon. I went straight to the garage and the first thing I saw was some fucking great lorries outside being loaded up with our stock. It was clear that John the 'bastard' was clearing the place out. I'd caught him bang to rights. All the scrap yards in the surrounding area had been coming in to pick up stuff on the cheap. I just lost it, right there on the main road. I looked for something to hammer the bastard with. There were some steering wheels hanging up and I grabbed one. I started to batter John with it. I hit the cunt with such force that the wheel became wedged round his neck with his head sticking through it. I began to drag the fucker backwards and forwards, my hands holding onto the wheel. The guy from the antique shop next door had some pianos out on the forecourt. He rushed out saying, "John, John, my pianos," because they were getting knocked about. This was all happening on a very busy road but no one tried to help him. I dragged him back into the shop and told all these scrap guys to fuck off! But not before they all coughed up the money they originally owed John and squared me off instead. I managed to get about five or six hundred quid out of them, and it was clear they'd been at it since the day before.

I was now like a raging lunatic, screaming at him. Although I was still only about nineteen I was built like a brick shithouse. I locked John in the spray booth with me and made it clear I wanted compensation or I would kill him. He promised me everything. He ended up giving me a V8 Rover, the old police car-style on account and a promise of five thousand pounds. I never did get all of my five grand because he had spunked most of his dough on gambling however, I did manage to get three grand. I went to his house and demanded he pay up, but he wouldn't open the door to let me in. So I kicked his door through and slapped him around a bit but, in the end, I called it a day because I liked his son, who explained it all to me later about his dad's gambling addiction. I never saw John at all after that; he just disappeared from the face of the earth as far as I know.

One of the few things I had left from the business was my hook-truck, exactly what I started with. I was gutted really because I'd put a lot of hard work and effort into that business, and had not even seen that much of Carol and the family. She had been working and put Lynsey in with the childminder for most of the day, and it was my usual practice to shoot into the local for a couple of pints straight after work, about 7.30pm. So there had not been a lot of family one-to-one contact at the time. Still, I resigned myself to the fact that it could only end in tears if you went into partnership with a geezer as weak as John.

With the bit of money I had left from the business I bought some stuff for the home, like our first colour TV and some shag-pile carpet. After that I did a bit of ceiling fixing with a couple of lads from Peckham just to keep things ticking over, but what I really wanted was a change now. I'd always liked the idea of branching out with new ideas and showing enterprise. I knew a few geezers, most of them fences, who'd were into cockle and winkle stalls. I decided I'd like to get into the game. I went to a couple of publicans and asked if they'd mind me putting a stall outside their pub, and also whether I could store my stock in their chilled rooms, as it would only be from Friday to Sunday, I told them. Quite a few agreed. I bought some ply-wood sheets, picked up some old sideboards, put wheels on the bottoms, made them up into stalls, and painted them a nice bright white to suggest cleanliness.

Soon I had a wet fish business doing cockles, mussels, whelks, crabs, and jellied eels. I went to a place in Euston called 'Micks Eels' for my jellied eels, and also to Billingsgate Market to get my shellfish stock. I'd sell on Fridays, Saturdays, and Sundays. Traditionally many cockneys had seafood suppers on a Sunday, and things started off quite well. My first stalls were outside the Newlands Tavern in Peckham but I soon added a couple more, employing girls to run them; I trusted women more than I did men. We also had some lights put round the stalls to make them look more attractive and paid the pub owner for the use of their power. I was approached by a guy called Billy; he suggested I start selling hot food like dogs and hamburgers, things like that.

Billy came from a well-known local family, Billy being the eldest of the three brothers and Morris 'Mo' being the youngest. I got on well with these two but did not go much on the middle brother, Peter, an ex-pro boxer-cum-hard man, who I considered a flash bastard. They were a mixed race family – what we then called half-castes. Another thing about Billy was he used to go out with a gorgeous young model from New Cross. I remember once seeing them together in a pub called The Hope, in Rye Lane, Peckham, and having a long chat with this model. Not only was she gorgeous but she had a lovely, friendly, down-to-earth personality. Her name was Lorraine Chase and she later, of course, went on to make a big name for herself in the showbiz world. I believe Billy went out with her for five or six years altogether, the lucky bastard.

Anyway, I decided to accept a financial offer to go in with him on my stalls and his own; we agreed on a fifty-fifty split in profits, with us both taking a stall each, and four other stalls being operated by the girls we employed. They were paid five pounds a night – not bad money for that time. Carol was then working at the Newlands Tavern as a waitress; she was pregnant at the time with Frank, our second child. This little arrangement worked well, and went on for possibly six months before things started to go a bit pear-shaped. Where I was dead keen, Billy, on the other hand, seemed to lose a bit of interest in the business. He'd always been a bit of a Romeo and he started to take nights off to have a good time around town, without bothering to tell me he wasn't going to open up.

I put up with this a couple of times – remember we'd already bought stock, so it was wasted – and then I called a halt. I just didn't bother to open at all for a couple of weeks. Naturally the punters were a bit pissed off and so too were the landlords who asked me what the fuck was going on. I went to Billy and put it to him straight – did he want to carry on or not. He said that he didn't, but gave his blessing to me carrying on by myself with the business. After that Carol ran a stall for me, we kept the other girls on and, for a time, things started going well again. Each stall was bringing in about hundred quid a night clear profit, so we were showing a nice return. At the same time Billy was starting to have second thoughts about his decision because his money was starting to dry up. Peter, his brother, started to stir him up by telling him that, while he was struggling, I was taking the piss by raking it in – in a business that was rightfully half his – and all this sort of old bollocks.

One night I was standing in the bar of the Newlands Tavern having a break when this girl, who ran one of my stalls, came running in, in tears. She said that a flash sports car had just pulled up and a big guy had got out with a whopping great heavy duty metal chain wrapped round his hand, with the remainder dangling down like a dog lead, and started to smash up the stall and stock with the chain. When he'd finished and ruining everything, he just tipped the front of the stall right over. I asked her what the guy looked like and she described him. I went outside and inspected the mess and then went round to discover my other stalls had had the same treatment. The girls were all frightened and I just went mental. Apparently the people coming out of the pubs who witnessed the destruction had not lifted a finger to try and help, although I could understand this because Peter – who I realised, was the geezer responsible – was a well-known local hard case.

What I didn't yet realise was that he'd then gone on to my place in Brockley and got his younger brother Mo to throw a rock through my window. I got home not long after the incident to discover that the thing had just missed Carol, who was in our upstairs flat, and had showered glass which went dangerously near our new son Frank, before becoming almost embedded in the opposite wall.

In a rage, I went back to the Newlands Tavern to get some transport that would not be associated with me, because my thinking was that I was going to kidnap these cunts and bury them in the sticks and I knew there was a guy who was drinking at the pub who had a Bedford van – he used to deliver fresh trout to restaurants and carried a big tank full of the fish in the back. I more or less bullied him into borrowing this van. He could see I wasn't in the mood to be turned down, and just said for me to bring it back in one piece – as it belonged to his firm, and not him. I drove to the top of the road and parked up near Billy's house. The three brothers were all outside talking and laughing, Peter still had the chain in his hand. I stepped out into the road, so they could get a good look at me, and then shouted out to them. They got into Peter's sports car, did a U turn, and started to come after me. In the meantime I'd gone into a nearby garden, got hold of an old fencing post, and slung it into the van ready for use. When their car came round the corner into this narrow street, I drove the van at it and rammed it against some iron railings. They couldn't get out because the car, Peter's pride and joy, was mangled up and wedged between the van and railings. Next thing I was out of the van, on to their roof, smashing and stabbing away with this fence post in a total frenzy. There was screaming coming from the car and from me on top of it, street lights were coming on, then someone came out of a house and said they were going to call the police.

At this point I drove off, and their car started to chase after me. It had taken a good bashing. The windscreen had gone, both sides were dented, and the convertible roof was beaten in. The driver, Peter, had blood pouring from his ear hole and a lump on his head, and the other two had facial injuries; even the one sitting in the back had not escaped my Zulu attack. I carried on driving. As they came up behind me I kept slamming the brakes on, not realising that the trout tank in my truck did not have a lid on (or else the grill had come off). Soon there were trout sloshing around round my feet and all over the show. It would have looked hilarious if a passer-by had seen it, but no one was laughing at the time.

The car kept trying to get round the side of me but I wouldn't let it. We got to the bottom of Peckham Rye, to the one way system at the top of Rye Lane. I went round it the right way, but the car went round the wrong way to try and catch me. We were on a collision course, driving round this oblong-shaped system. As we came round I noticed this black taxi come haring round the bend. Peter, driving the car, couldn't see it properly because his windscreen was caved in and, being a tall guy, the mangled up roof was getting in the way. He hit the vehicle head on. I pulled up alongside. The taxi driver was going berserk. The passenger got out and, by sheer coincidence, it happened to be a bloke I knew. In slight shock he said, "What the fucking hell's going on here then?" I just shrugged my shoulders to deny any knowledge, said, "See you later mate," and drove off quickly.

I never re-opened the stalls, but I was expecting comebacks all the same. A couple of weeks later I went into a pub in Rye Lane called The Hope. Mo was at the bar. When he saw me he froze. I walked up to him and he said, "Sorry John. Please don't start anything." I didn't. The only thing I really had against him was throwing the rock through the window and he had felt the end of that fence post enough times to make amends, but I knew that he and Billy were both easily manipulated by Peter. In any case I'd always got on well with the pair of them. What was important as far as I was concerned was that I'd made Peter look a prick. I'd hurt him, smashed up his car – his pride and joy – and he'd failed to come back. All this enhanced my reputation further, and people began to take notice.

After this I started work as a taxi driver with a local firm. Dickie my good mate, who had been employed at the car-part shop, came in with me. We had an old Austin Cambridge, a wreck of a car with a plastic back window, dodgy gear box and fucked-up front suspension which made me feel like I was driving along on an ocean wave as I drove it. I went into a breakers yard to get a back window for it but saw this other car which was in better nick, so I swapped over and used that instead. I would drive at night and Dickie in the day time. I worked all hours often starting at 4pm and finishing at 8am.

It was the age of mini cabs; many of the cars around were old bangers. We'd get hold of an insurance cover note, use brake fluid, or tippex on it to remove the legal name, photocopy it, and put our name on it. Insurance documents would be forged using this method. We would pay the taxi company twenty to twenty-five quid a week for the use of their radio, and they would give you work via the radio.

I hadn't been there long when a punter came in, about one in the morning, and said he wanted taking to Chelsea. I ran him over there and he says to me, "I suppose I'll have to give you my name and address?" – in other words telling me he had no money to pay his fare. This was something I hadn't actually come across before so I radioed the office to find out what the score was. The bloke at the other end said, "What do you want me to fucking do?" I said I was just asking, as I'd never had to deal with it and wanted to know the rules and regulations.

He said, "It's up to you what you do mate."

This geezer was still in the car as I'd left the child locks on. I started to get a bit angry. I said to him, "Did you think if you were on a bus or a fucking train you could just leave your fucking name and address?" I dragged him out by his hair and stuck him in the boot of the car, then drove him back to the office. When I got there it was about 2am and there were some other drivers waiting around. They asked how I had got on, expecting me to grumble about having had my first 'knocker' (non payer). I informed them that I'd put the fucker in the boot. They couldn't believe it. "What do you mean, you've put him in the boot?"

I went out and brought him in, to show them. Then I said to them, "What was I supposed to do about the payment then – just swallow it, or what?" They said I'd have to swallow it anyway because I didn't really have any option if he didn't have any money.

I said, "I'll show you what I *can* do."

I made the punter strip off to his underpants and socks. Then I booted him out onto the street saying, "When you've got my money, you can come and get your fucking clothes." And out he went into the freezing cold night. I had a bit of a go at the other drivers for not wising me up about the 'knockers'. The funny thing was about half an hour later a panda car comes crawling past the office with the guy in the back, covered in a blanket. They were obviously looking for someone but didn't stop. What I reckon had happened was that, clearly, the Old Bill had picked him up, but he'd been frightened to tell them that the taxi office had been involved for fear of comebacks. He must have said that he'd got mugged, and that was why they were out and about looking for someone. I never did get paid my money. The clothes stayed in the office for months and eventually some of the drivers stuffed them with newspaper, made a guy out of them for Bonfire night and put the words 'Chelsea Knocker' on it. Again this little incident added to the reputation I was getting locally.

Another time I picked up some guys in Deptford who I could tell straight away were villains although they never said as much (I just know one when I see one). They wanted to go to Croydon. When we got there, about 4.30pm, I dropped them off and they said, "We'll be back." I told them I didn't give a monkey's what they were up to, but all I was interested in was getting my money, Now! They asked me if I'd wait for them, and I said I'd wait twenty minutes, and no longer, but insisted on getting my money there and then – which I did. I waited the twenty minutes but they never did return. I later found out that they had done a payroll snatch.

Some of the work was quite eye opening – I'd run call-girls up west to wealthy Arabs in the big hotels, stuff like that. But I wasn't doing any real crime at this time; I was still trying my best to stay clean. I started accumulating Austin Cambridge and Morris Oxford type cars – they were 'plodders' and good for cabbing. I got a second job as a controller, earning one hundred and eighty quid a week, with 'free rent' i.e. no radio charge. I could do my own driving in my 'spare' time, and not have to pay out anything to anyone. I had four cars which were paying *me* twenty-five pounds a week per driver plus my own earnings of about a monkey (five hundred) a week, not bad for the late seventies.

However I worked such long hours that I started taking amphetamines to keep me going. This was an idea that I believe started in America, where the truckers would use them. We called them 'blues'. They almost gave me a heart attack. I was taken into Lewisham Hospital with pains down my arm one time and I remember them pointing out to me the damage these things could do to your body.

One night I was on controls in the cab office. It was a busy set-up there with twenty-four telephones in a row, no switchboard, and you might have up to forty drivers on at one time, so you'd always have to work your arse off. These three black guys came in and asked for a cab. I had to blank them because I knew one of them as a known troublemaker. I said to him, "You caused trouble here a few weeks ago and you know the score – no cabs for you." They then gave me a lot of grief, verbally. Soon more of them turned up. There were five – then seven, until there was a crowd and I really thought it was going to kick off big time. They're talking to me in West Indian dialect and I'm getting called all sorts. In the end I hit the button – there were twenty odd drivers on the road at that time – and it was a case of "'Mayday Mayday', all drivers back to the office." I said to one of the guys speaking through the grille of the glass partition (my only defence), "You'd better fuck off mate, twenty-five drivers will be back here soon and they ain't going to be happy."

In the event just one turned up. I couldn't believe it. This guy was an Irishman known by the drivers as 'Irish John'. He parked his car just round the corner and came into the office via the drivers' side door. I told him that we needed to get rid of the mouthy guy as he was stirring up the others, and they were likely soon to put the windows through. We always kept tools in the office like baseball bats and lumps of wood. It was a dodgy area which saw a fair bit of racial trouble and this night there was a definite tension in the air. These guys had been in a local pub used by black men and were pissed as well as stoned. Worse still, they knew there were only two of us in the office as they could see us through the glass. Irish John pulled me out of the front office and into the driver's side office. He said that he agreed we had to get the lippy one, but I said it was impossible to go out and have a straightener with him without the others becoming involved. He said, "No, what we've got to do is get him in here."

We had to think quickly. We turned out the light in the drivers' side office so that we couldn't be seen. This mouthy prick knew I must be somewhere in this side office, which had a door and window at the side of the building, while the main office, which I had been in before, looked out onto the pavement and was obviously empty. He came round to the side door and I opened it inwards. Irish John was behind it holding a four inch diameter copper pipe, about three feet long. I goaded the black guy to come in. "Come on you cunt, let's have it! Just me and you in here. What's the matter, no bottle then? You fucking wanker, you're fucking yellow. You haven't got the fucking balls have you?"

His mates were shouting, "Go on, get in there man, fucking whip his backside."

I said, "Don't worry about them. This is just between you and me."

As he put his head in the door, John came down with this length of copper pipe right across his fucking skull. Whack! Down he went like a sack of shit. The other guys were going berserk outside, shouting the odds, but we threatened them that if they tried to come in we'd kill the cunt by cutting him up into pieces. Soon the Old Bill turned up. After all, we were right opposite Brockley railway station and passengers getting on and of the trains couldn't help but notice these black guys milling around and shouting. Fortunately the guy on the deck was still conscious, although he was in a bad way with his head split open. We managed to talk him into getting out of the office and fucking off before anyone actually got nicked.

There was a bit of comeback to this shortly afterwards. A cousin of mine had a mate who'd just left the merchant navy and was looking for a job, so I agreed I'd let him have one of my cars to do a bit of cabbing. He was to be charged twenty-five quid a week and I said that I'd teach him the ropes. We agreed to go and have a pint and talk things over in this pub near the office, just over the railway bridge. Crossing the bridge on the way back, I noticed two black guys with a young white girl about fourteen. They had an Alsatian with them. The dog looked like a bitch I'd used for mating purposes with my long haired German shepherd. Curious, I said to the young girl, "Is that dog called Lady?" The two black guys butted in and started having a go at me. "You're the one who caused the trouble the other night." They began to get threatening. Obviously they'd been part of the crowd that night.

I knew I had to act quickly. The biggest of the two had most of the lip. I let fly a right hander which caught him right on the chin and he hit the deck. I ran after the other guy who, I always remember, had this white mac on. As I grabbed hold of him he stopped and I pulled the mac up over his head so he couldn't see. While he was blinded I rammed his head into the wall and kept on doing it. I left him screaming out and just kept on walking after that. All the time this young girl, who was a white cockney girl, was shouting out in West Indian which I couldn't fathom at all, but I guess maybe she'd been brought up with West Indians.

There was no sign at all of the bloke I'd taken to the pub; I learned later that he'd been so scared he'd pissed off and decided cabbing was not for him. I never saw him again after that. When I got back to the office I could hear the guy in the white mac outside shouting, "Knife, knife, knife." I thought 'Yeah right! If you didn't have the fucking sense to come up behind me and use the knife when I was walking away, it's obvious you haven't got one at all'.

I'd like to say that that was the end of this aggro but there was another incident shortly after when these black guys came to the office with a bit of wood and started smashing the windows. The bloke who owned the company was in there at the time and said, "I've got to get the Old Bill." Before long there were about twenty of these black guys aiming missiles at the windows; there was glass coming in all over the show. Then the Old Bill turned up in the form of the Special Patrol Group (SPG). They just piled out of their vans and started hitting everyone over the head with their truncheons, and dragging them out of the way. That's how they operated then.

I finished that job when I fell out with Brian, the guy who owned the business. Brian was a big guy who liked to throw his weight around, a fucking bully. He'd been a driver for years in the business, and it was somehow handed down to him; he never really paid for it. A new driver from a rival cab firm started work for us. This guy was a harmless, family sort of bloke who couldn't have weighed more than eleven stone. One morning he turned up ten minutes late for work – I was just leaving after doing my night shift on controls. Brian wanted to humiliate the new guy, possibly because he'd come from a rival firm, although of course he had been well aware of this in the first place, when he took him on. Anyway he just knocked the poor little bastard spark out. I wasn't having this at any price, so I got a baseball bat from the drivers' room and proceeded to knock the shit out of Brian. Fortunately for him he was a motorbike rider and just happened to have his helmet on at the time, otherwise he could well have been killed. I was so wound up and angry, after a hard night's work that I also smashed up all the office, phones and so on for good measure.

You could say this incident was another example of why my reputation was spreading. Although it wasn't a reputation that everyone would want, it would often prove useful to me in the years to come.

Chapter Five

KING OF THE ROAD

After finishing at Speedy Cars, which, by the way, is still there today, but under different management, I went to Peckham and worked for a firm called Royal Cars. It was while I was there that I did what must have been the quickest bit of business I ever did in my life. I'd just dropped off a customer when I bumped into a geezer called Black Lenny, a criminal acquaintance – more of him later – who asked me if I wanted to do a bit of work that he'd been given. It involved giving a smack to this big Indian geezer who'd conned a rich, older relative (who by the way was paying for the job) out of an off-licence the older guy had owned (along with quite a few other properties). After ripping him off, this younger relative now ran this certain off-licence himself, and was apparently doing very nicely thank you, at the older geezer's expense.

Although quite a cultured sort of guy it didn't mean that the older man was above looking for a little bit of 'revenge' as far as his relative went. I asked Lenny to be a bit more specific about how far we had to go with this retribution. He said, in so many words, that he just wanted the geezer chinned, in the shop so that he would lose face, preferably in front of a lot of customers. It didn't sound too difficult for me and the money, as ever, would come in useful.

I parked up near the shop in question, walked casually into the place and straight up to the counter. The big Indian guy said "What can I do for you?" I pointed at some stock which was positioned at a lower level at the front of the counter, so he'd need to bend forward to get it. "I'd like to look at those," I said. Sure enough he bent forward, and straight into a powerful right uppercut which knocked him spark out, and he went sprawling backwards into some other stock which crashed to the floor. In a flash I was back into the cab and had soon picked up my next fare – eight hundred quid richer for about a minute's work.

Although I'd been largely staying away from crime while doing the cabbing, I have to admit that I did use the work as a front and I did relapse on a couple of other occasions as well. It was around this time that I met a respected villain called Harry, known as 'H'. Harry was a well-known and a respected face with previous links back to the Krays. He looked the typical sixties type villain, with the suits, shirts, ties and greased back hair. He was not tall but was stocky, although this could have been mainly down to the booze. He owned a pub in Deptford.

H was a lovely bloke – if you were on the right side of him, which fortunately I was. If you were on the wrong side – God help you! I met him through a barmaid at a pub called the Thomas a Beckett in the Old Kent Road. How this happened was that one day, finding myself in need of a bit of extra cash, I got into a scam involving getting a job as a delivery driver using a false name, and a moody driving licence. After three days at this firm I arranged for the lorry I was driving to be boarded by an accomplice, and we drove to my flat, where we unloaded all the goods. And, believe it or not, the haul, which nearly filled this flat and actually snapped the rafters in the kitchen, was caviar. Yes, caviar! What I'd call top notch, I mean you wouldn't normally see this in your local supermarket. It was fancy stuff in decorative tins, jars and china pots, which would set you back about sixty to ninety quid an item. I became desperate to move the stuff after being let down by a fence, a real waster, and was reduced to knocking the pots out at a fiver and tenner a time on the street because the floor in the flat was about to collapse. Anyway, in the end I went to this woman at the Thomas a Beckett, which was the famous boxing pub. She arranged a meeting and introduced me to Harry but, as it happened, H wasn't interested in the stuff himself because of the unusual nature of the haul, but put me in touch with a geezer who was into restaurants and club diners. However, we did hit it off very well right from the start, and a friendship developed.

I think, at that time, Harry had just finished a ten-year stretch. To me, he was a complete gentleman. He'd phone up the cab firm sometimes and say, "It's Harry here from the pub – we want ten steak dinners delivered." It was nearly always me who did the job, so I'd go down to the kebab house in Peckham, which had a steak house next door, order ten steak dinners, with chips, peas, mushrooms etc, wait for them, then take them over to Harry's pub. This would usually be about three in the morning. The card tables would be out and the place full of villains and gangsters, most of them pissed.

Harry would greet me. "There you are, come in boy, have a drink." Sometimes I'd have one with him but my main concern was getting paid, after all I was well out of pocket, having paid for the dinners. Paying me was always the last thing on Harry's mind, he just wanted everyone to be enjoying themselves. Not that he would ever screw me – he was always straight as a die and I knew that I'd get paid, often with a very generous tip. In the end though I'd make a point of going straight to him and asking for it. "Alright, alright son," he'd go. Then he'd say, "Which hand is it in?" or something playful like that, but I always got it. It wasn't the same for some of the other drivers though. Occasionally they'd do the job, spend out say fifty or sixty quid of their own money, and someone or other in the pub would just say "Thanks, see you then," and close the door on them. When you were dealing with that sort of company you had to be careful how you asked for your dough – the last thing you wanted to do was upset anyone.

But, as I say, Harry was a thorough gentleman to me and treated me right, but you had to let him know that you knew the score and if I'd forked out say fifty quid for the meals, he'd often slip me twenty-five quid, or even fifty. Mind you, I met a lot of useful contacts through Harry which proved very helpful to me later on when my criminal career took off big time.

After I finished altogether with the cabbing, my mate Dickie went his own way. He wasn't really part of the criminal element, he was just a likeable geezer, but he got involved with a dodgy little crew I knew. One of them was an evil bastard called John Richards, a real psycho who was definitely not right in the head. He would shoot you as soon as look at you and I swore that I would never work with him because he was a mug – he was a loose cannon. He actually stabbed me right through the neck with a metal comb, one of those with a wire handle where you could just pull off the plastic. How it happened was like this. One day I was in this Indian restaurant having a ruby, when Dickie came in with a bag of 'tom' (jewellery). He'd done a jewellers in north London with Richards (they wanted me to come in on it, but I turned the job down because Richards was on it) and he started to flash the tom about and even showed the owner of the restaurant; the snaky bastard then phoned the Old Bill. Anyway, next thing the Old Bill are swarming all over the place, and I got a tug as well. The bastards kept me in Holloway police station (a place I got to know very well – more of this later) for five days without a brief or any communication with Carol. I could prove I'd been working as a driver (legally) at the time of the blag (robbery), and one morning they just opened the door and told me to fuck off.

Dickie and John Richards both went down for the job; I used to visit Dickie inside because he was still a good mate but lost touch after a while. Then one Saturday morning, after they both got out, I was walking down the road in Deptford and I bumped into the pair of them. Dickie wasn't too friendly and I assumed that Richards had probably been putting the poison in about me, perhaps he even tried to tell Dickie I'd grassed them up – something I'd never do, but as I said before, Richards was a shilling short of a pound. We were in this cul-de-sac with a high rise estate at the back. Richards made a remark to me and I told him to shut his fucking mouth. Next thing I knew I felt this blow to the neck which I thought was a punch but what he'd really done was stab me through the side of the neck with this comb – the handle snapped off and went right in, almost coming out the other side, I had this bulge at the other side where it nearly broke the skin and came right through the whole of my neck. Without realising what had happened, because I thought that I had been punched, needless to say I just lost it. But there was no kicking, biting or anything like that. I just punched the nutty bastard to his knees, gave him a right hammering. In the end he was sitting on his arse on the pavement, totally fucked, as I finished him off; I really felt satisfaction. He was a big fella, well over six feet, but he was more used to using axes, knives and other tools than to fist fighting. I heard later that he told someone it was the worst beating he'd ever had.

There was another guy that I fell out with around this time. His name was Danny Roth. He wasn't what you'd call a villain; he worked as a scaffolder, but he mixed in the same company as us and drank at my local, the Marlborough Head, in Peckham. He'd come in with his mates on a Friday afternoon and they'd buy a bit of 'charlie' off us and we'd all have a drink together. He was about six feet tall, had short dark hair, and was quite a fit looking, handsome sort of geezer. To be honest I quite liked the fella when he was just a scaffolder looking for a bit of fun. But then I used to start hearing reports about him acting a bit flash and upsetting some pretty tasty people – people he should have known better than to fuck with.

I did take the trouble to mention this to him, acting a bit like an older brother I suppose you could say, but he failed to heed the warnings. Anyway there was an incident in the pub one Sunday afternoon, long after closing time (lock in), when this bird started getting verbally abused by Roth and his mates who were all well tanked up. They were touching her up and everything and she didn't want to know and was scared. I pulled her over out of the way to stand by me and Roth came out with this remark challenging me to make something of it. At this time all my mates had gone, and as I fronted Roth up, his mates all got up to front me as well. I wasn't one to run from trouble but I was completely outnumbered here and had to use my loaf. Roth gave me a lot of verbal abuse and I had to swallow it, although I was fuming. I got a cab for the girl and then I fucked off, while these guys jeered at me.

Needless to say I wanted revenge. I talked it over with my boss, Del French (more of him soon), and we agreed I had to get the bastard on his own. It wasn't long before I spotted him, one lunchtime, going into the Marlborough Head, followed him in and clumped him good and clean, knocking him over the pool table. I would have left him there but John, the landlord, made me drag him outside. Del told me I'd have to watch out for comebacks from his mates but it wasn't as though I didn't know a few pretty heavy people myself – and that included some of Del's contacts.

I never heard from Roth again, he stayed out of the way. And there were no comebacks. Well, I did hear later that he had changed from a free spending scaffolder into a not very good armed robber, because he got caught and drew a thirteen stretch, I believe it was. Then he escaped and landed in Spain. Then a while later I picked up a newspaper and read that he had murdered great train robber Charlie Wilson: arriving at Wilson's villa in Spain on a mountain bike he entered the grounds and gunned him down in cold blood. Charlie (more of him later), was a well-loved and respected guy in the criminal fraternity, and it was pretty clear to me and others in the know that Roth had made a big mistake and gone too far this time. And, sure enough, he didn't live long to enjoy his notoriety because before long he too was gunned down – victim of a gangland hit.

I decided, finally, to get my driving licence as I wanted to drive lorries legally. I booked on a course in Nottingham with the Wallace School of Transport. I remember getting a hundred and eleven quid together and taking my provisional and provisional HGV licences up with me. I booked into a B&B for a couple of nights and then had three hours training in the cab and two hours on test. I failed. I remember the instructor had been a bit worried beforehand as I only had a provisional ordinary licence. I can still hear him complaining, in his northern accent, "How the fuck are you going to get through this lot when you haven't even got an ordinary licence?" much to the amusement of the other instructors. He also had to go out and get two extra sets of L plates for me – one as an ordinary car learner and the other one for my HGV. It turned out that I'd only failed on coming up to a roundabout too fast, that was all. Anyway, I sold our first colour TV and new washing machine to get the money to re-take it a month later. This time there were no mistakes and I got through.

I now had an HGV Class 1 license and went straight onto agency work. I enjoyed the work, even though it meant early starts, sleeping in your cab and so on. And the merchandise I carried was worth a lot of money. But, after about eighteen months, I had a bit of aggro with one particular firm in Greenwich that I'd been doing runs for. This firm would get me to pick up from Silvertown Way in East London on the Monday, deliver to Ellesmere Port in Merseyside, pick up a load of paper rolls used for the printing of tabloid newspapers, bring it back to London, get back onto the office and then they'd send you back, to pick up another load; you were out on the road continually and I would take pills to keep me going. I used to carry three log books in the cab so that if I got a tug from the Old Bill or the ministry and I'd been on the road say sixteen hours, I'd just give them one that had two hours, or whatever, logged. And the firm would be making money out of me because it saved them employing two or even three drivers in my place. They'd pay me one hundred and eighty quid in my hand plus twenty-five per cent of the cost of moving the freight.

One time after I'd been away all week working my bollocks off I got told abruptly that I was not getting my extra twenty-five per cent because it was not 'my turn that week' it was the other driver's turn. I was fuming. But rather than do my nut and turn violent, this time I decided I'd box clever and get my own back in a different way. I'd use the job to my advantage, I thought. It happened that soon after I was put on a job picking up trailers from Felixstowe and Harwich with video players from the continent. With a bit of help from my friends in the criminal fraternity, I got hold of some security seals. These I would use to replace the ones I broke when I unloaded some of the merchandise.

This is how the scam operated. I'd pick up a trailer, set out to drive a hundred miles down the road to a drop-off point where another driver would take over the load (trunking). Only half way along the route I'd park up somewhere secluded and open the fucker up and help myself to say twenty or thirty videos, for which I could get two hundred and fifty quid each (mostly the old Ferguson lever button type, which cost nearly four hundred when they first came out). I'd then put bricks back in the boxes, put on the new seal I'd got hold of, and, as far as anyone else was concerned, the boxes hadn't been touched since they left Belgium, or wherever. At the height of the scam there was a suggestion made that I take a knock on the head when on duty, so that the whole load could disappear. But I said that, somehow, I just didn't think the Old Bill would wear that one. With somebody else, maybe – but with me, definitely not!

Carol knew nothing about this racket. She knew, of course, that I would work a fiddle if I could, but I made sure not to have any of these dodgy videos around the house. I was dealing with people who respected my ability to keep schtum – if you didn't, of course, you were in serious trouble. Anyway, this particular company I milked well. They eventually lost this main contract because of theft, and the insurance companies were going ape-shit, which meant the firm had to lay off people big time. The only way out was to start with new hauliers. So, as far as I was concerned, the bastards didn't get anywhere by ripping me off.

The next job I took resulted in me getting nicked. It was a crap job really – driving round to slaughterhouses to pick up lungs, and pigs heads which went to dog food factories in Melton Mowbray, who made dog food, biscuits, and the like out of it. It really was the most smelly, disgusting job you could wish for. I was always making promises to Carol about going straight but it was very difficult. You see I was earning about eighty quid a week for sitting in this stinking lorry all day, whereas when I took the opportunity of a few 'extras', that figure could shoot up to be nearer five hundred a week.

A particular slaughterhouse that I went into was a processing company also, and when the animals had been bolted, stunned or whatever, they were cut up into joints, ready for the shops. I had people inside the place that would get, for example, a whole leg of pork, or half a leg of beef, and stick it into big sealable plastic bags, then drop it into the bottom of a big drum for me. The drum would then be covered completely by all the lights, lungs etc that I had to deliver to the dog food companies. No one was likely to want to paw around through that lot looking for a leg of pork. And so, of course, I'd sell these joints off to butchers when I was out delivering. I'd flog off say a quarter ton of meat at a time like this, and this was what brought my eighty quid a week to up between four and five hundred, and no one was any the wiser.

One particular place I picked up from was Bury St Edmunds bacon factory. One day I had a little chat with some of the guys there which put an idea in my mind for getting an extra few quid on top. Their cold store room, which was massive, had fluorescent tubes and there were very strict rules governing contamination of the frozen meat, which was all on pallets, wrapped in plastic, ready to be taken away to supermarkets etc. When I was loading up my lights and lungs one day which were kept in the chilled room, somehow a fluorescent tube got broken. I won't say how it got broken – I'll leave that to your imagination – and the whole cold store was condemned. As I had to take the lights away anyway, I was given instructions to take away the whole fucking lot in my wagon. What I didn't do though was to let my boss know about this arrangement when it came to putting the paperwork through.

I spent the best part of an afternoon loading up this sixteen ton lorry with great lumps of this condemned pork, bacon, sausages etc. I took the meat to a guy in Thetford – an illegal horsemeat exporter and trader. I thought my boss would never find out as I'd cleared the lot in one hit, but somehow he did find out, and the Old Bill was called in. I got hauled off to Bury St Edmunds nick but I wasn't saying a word. Carol knew nothing about all this and when, after five days away, the Old Bill finally brought me back home, I found my bags had been packed. Not only that but it was my birthday and my card had been ripped up. I said to these two Old Bill, "Why didn't you even let her know?" but they were more interested in the meat than in my strained relationship with Carol. They said, in so many words, "Look, this meat is contaminated. What if a kid, or a young baby, had got hold of it?" Anyway, after them fucking me about for five days, when they were only supposed to keep you for forty-eight hours, and now what with all this aggro with Carol, I guess I had just about had enough of it all and, in the end I put my hands up to doing the job. And, to be honest, I really did start thinking about the possible consequences of the scam. Fair enough, I knew the meat was wrapped, but what if a young child *had* eaten it? You never really knew for sure what might have happened…

Obviously I lost my job as a result of all this. I started drinking in a local in Peckham and I met up with another family of villains called the Frenchs who were based in Deptford. I was always friendly with Del and had done some work for him in the past. Del offered me a job, and I started working for him when he started up a new transport company. When I told him about the meat job I'd been nicked for, and told him it looked like I'd be going down for it, he sent one of his cronies to the court. This guy, who described himself as assistant managing director of this transport company, gave me a glowing reference in court, saying how reliable, hardworking and genuine I was, and how the crime had been totally out of character – just a silly, one-off, mistake that wouldn't be repeated. In the end I got a three hundred quid fine and suspended sentence. But I knew for a fact that they'd been really looking to send me to crown court for sentence, and to have me put away, rather than having me dealt with like this by a magistrate's court. So began my relationship with the Frenchs, and now my criminal career started to take off big time.

Chapter Six

THE SPIELLER

After the court case at Bury St Edmunds I carried on working for Del French. He had a couple of contracts, one with the London Brick Company in Surrey and the Portland Cement Company in Kent and delivered forty ton of bricks or dust a day, which was fucking hard graft because it was all unloaded by hand. We had this six-wheeler lorry, twenty-six ton gross, me and Del's son, also called Derek, would deliver all over the south east area and down as far as the coast. The money was good for the time, about one hundred and fifty a week cash in hand. I really liked Del's son, he was a great geezer, but he was never really into crime. And although he was a big fellow he wasn't really much like his old man at all, because Del senior, all six feet four of him, with his big gut and wavy gingery hair, braces and trader boots, always put me in mind of a pikey. Although most of Del's family, especially his younger relations, were out-and-out villains, Del wasn't all that much into it, he was just a bit dodgy. At least our relationship was always based on the business rather than any villainy. I worked hard for him and he looked after me.

Del had a silent partner in the business who was a 'face' and silent is how I'm going to keep about him. Let's just say that there was a lot of money around that had to be quickly put into something legal, laundered if you like, and that was how the business got started up. Del had always done the deliveries himself but it became too much for him, especially where he liked a drink. At the time I knew him, he'd start off drinking in the pub at lunchtime every day and that was it; he'd come out at fuck knows what time. But he never got falling-over pissed and he never got loud. I genuinely liked and respected the guy, he was a great character. People would say to me that I needed to watch myself working for him, that he was slippery. Well I already knew that. In any case you just had to look at him – he looked like he'd just got off the horse and cart! But he was a good looking guy in his own way though, with a friendly face and these broad shoulders, and he had a lovely wife and family. You would never confuse him with some of the other Frenchs, who looked every bit the hardened villains that they were.

Gradually the work started to peter out a bit, probably because Del was spending too much time and money in the pub. He wasn't paying the VAT man anyway, that was for sure. When things got slack, I'd do a bit of mini-cabbing just to make ends meet. One night, when I had just finished a few hours cabbing, I went into a club in Catford called J. Arthur's. The club was a well-known haunt and attracted quite a few villains. I was with a friend of mine, a guy called Terry Fitzpatrick. After a drink and a chat I went out to the toilet; as I opened the door leading into it, I noticed that the lights were off in the toilet at the end. As I went in, I saw a geezer standing taking a piss just behind the door; he was wearing a leather coat, as I was. He was about the same build as me but I didn't get a clear look at his face. I went past him into the room and, after the door had slowly closed behind me, I stood there in the dark, at the urinal, having a piss, and wondering what the geezer was up to because I could not hear any splashes. There was no doubt he was still in the room, behind the door – it was as though he was trying to hide from someone. Suddenly, out of the blue, there was a flash of light as the door opened, and three or four people rushed in. Next thing, I felt this liquid sprayed into my face, which I didn't realise at the time was ammonia, then I felt thuds against my body as I came under attack. These thuds were not just punches, as I found out pretty quickly, but were stabbings from several knives. I fought back as best I could in the darkness, as well as trying to put my cock away, lashing out with my fists, then feeling a terrible sensation that my face was on fire. Then I felt something sharp across my face, followed by what seemed like a warm liquid flowing down my face, as though the ceiling was dripping. I grabbed at someone's hair and then started punching the face underneath it and heard him moan in pain. In a matter of seconds it seemed it was all over and the attackers had fled. As I wiped what I now realised was blood out of my eye, I could see a bit, because the blood had washed the ammonia away. I saw the guy in the leather coat leave. My attackers had completely missed him.

When I got into the corridor I noticed that the smart white, hand-made, Italian shirt that I had on was now red with blood. And the blood from the head wound was pumping out in tune with my heart beat, going over the walls and everywhere. I'd realised then that I had been slashed across the main artery. I was starting to worry about all the blood I was losing when these two bouncers noticed me and came over and just got hold of me and dragged me downstairs, then slung me out of the back door. There was no "can we help you mate" they just chucked me straight out into the street, the fuckers! I staggered round to the front of the club where there was a kebab shop next door. It was now a good five minutes since I'd been stabbed and the claret was flowing big time with me getting weaker and weaker. And it was just my luck that at this time there was an ambulance work to rule over pay. Anyway the geezer in the kebab shop had obviously phoned the emergency services when he saw me, and two coppers turned up in a car. By that time I felt faint and totally fucked. A copper stuck his knees into my knees to keep me upright against the shop window. I could just see out of my left eye but it was very blurred because the blood kept flowing into it. Next thing I knew there was this woman asking the Old Bill if they had a cigarette. They said to her, "couldn't she see they were busy," but she told them she was an off-duty nurse and needed a cigarette to help me. Somebody produced one. It was lit up, and then she put the lighted end straight onto the severed artery over my eye. I'd never felt so much pain –it seemed to shoot right through my head. What she had done was to cauterize the wound. It didn't stop the bleeding completely but it stopped the worst of it.

The Old Bill wouldn't take me in their car although Lewisham hospital was only about five hundred yards down the road. They said this was because of their insurance! Eventually an ambulance did arrive though, and I was taken off and whipped into intensive care. I remember lying there, drops in my eyes, head covered in bandages, and listening to these Old Bill keeping on at me, "Who did it, who did it?" I was on this portable X-ray unit and people were pulling me around.

I said to this evil bastard of a copper, "You've got to let my wife know."

He said, "We've already told her and she doesn't want to know."

What a thing to say! That's how the bastards were; all they were interested in was who had done it. It turned out though that they had been half expecting things to kick off in the club that night, and that was why they were so intent on getting information. So I suppose, in a way, I can understand their keenness. But more of this later.

When my X-rays came through it turned out I'd got a punctured lung, other damage to the lung area, a damaged kidney and the knife wound above my left eye which I still bear the scar of. I'll always be grateful to this Chinese plastic surgeon that happened to be on a six week visit to the country and working at this hospital and at Kings College at the time. He made a great job of stitching me up. By the time Carol and my brother-in-law turned up to visit me in intensive care I could see a bit better, but I must have been pretty light-headed because the first thing I said when Carol asked how I felt, was, "Okay, did you bring any apple pie?"

"What are you going on about- apple pie?" she said, and my brother-in-law burst out laughing. But it seemed the most natural thing to me to ask because I felt so fucking hungry and that was just what I fancied, whether I was in intensive care or not.

My brother-in-law said, "You don't realise how badly hurt you are do you?"

And the truth was I didn't. Fortunately I had no bad internal bleeding because the knife had sliced straight in and out of my lung without tearing it, although the lung did have to be drained out the following day. It was very lucky I had fought back like I did, because there was no doubt that whoever carried out the attack didn't intend that I should survive it. They'd used a stiletto knife and had really meant business – if I hadn't punched one of the bastards like I did then I'm sure I would have been a goner. I've got to admit though that the incident really put me off knives for a good time afterwards.

I was only in the intensive care ward for forty-eight hours, and then put out into the main ward. I had this catheter put in me which I didn't enjoy a lot, especially as there wasn't too much privacy. It seemed like there were doctors, nurses, Old Bill and every other fucker milling around all over the show. Anyway I reckoned that the off-duty nurse with the cigarette was the one I owed my life to most of all. I never found out who she was although I did do some checking around later. Maybe she was a nurse from another hospital; I guess I'll never know now.

I discharged myself from the hospital a few days later. I wasn't fit to go back to work and Del French came round to see me. He gave Carol some money to keep us going, and then we had a little chat. He told me that the attack had definitely not been meant for me. I said, "I know that Del, because I haven't upset anyone that badly, and I certainly wouldn't have walked straight into something like that if I'd expected it in any way." He said to leave the matter with him and he would sort it. It turned out that it was one of his relatives who had put out a contract on someone and it was just my bad luck to be in the wrong place at the wrong time. And wearing the wrong sort of coat, and having the wrong sort of build! On a proper identification parade, the guy in the toilet and me would never have been mistaken for each other, but in a darkened room that's what happened.

I soon started to get a bit pissed off and angry about the whole thing; maybe it was the shock coming out. Del said to me, "Look John, I'll get you some compensation."

"The only compensation I wanted was their fucking heads." I said.

But he explained to me that there was no going back for revenge, what had happened had happened, and those responsible were sorry for what was a genuine mistake. Out of respect for Del I reluctantly accepted this. And he was as good as his word and got me three grand in compensation, a lot of money in those days. Although Del's days of serious villainy were mostly behind him, he still had quite a bit of influence when it mattered. His trouble was that he was starting to hit the booze a bit heavy.

I was still doing the odd bit of work for him when he phoned me and he said that he had this load to deliver, and would I do it for him. The next morning I went round to the yard, went to open up the corrugated iron gates, and there stood the lorry with no fucking wheels on it. He'd jacked up the whole thing and gone and sold the wheels and tyres. I went round to his place and he was pissed. That was how he had started to decline. Reading between the lines I think he'd fallen out with his silent partner, and was losing interest in the business. In this instance someone had offered him a good price for the wheels, so he'd taken it and just said 'fuck the load' – which was still on the lorry when I saw it in the yard. I couldn't believe it!

He seemed to just lose his grip on things, and soon after, he suffered a heart attack. I never saw much of him after that but I believe his son, Derek, got another job somewhere. Derek was a lovely bloke as I've said, not what you'd call a villain at all compared to the rest of his family, but a guy with enough about him to get by okay in the straight world.

With my three grand I bought another motor and went mini-cabbing again. Not full time, but I knew I could always pick up fifty or sixty quid for a night's work, and I tried my best to keep on the straight and narrow after the stabbing. But with wages low and unemployment high, there always seemed to be the temptation of easy pickings elsewhere and I didn't have too far to look when it came to finding these because of the people I knew. At about this time we had a letter come through from the council housing department as we'd been on the waiting list for five years. We were given a new place at Wentworth Crescent, right next to North Peckham Estate. It was a brand new, three-bedroom, and centrally heated house with balcony at the front. I couldn't get over the rent, which was £58 a week – at a time when the average wage for a skilled person was about £75-£100 a week. We were one of the first families in, but were later joined by quite a lot of West Indian, African and Irish families. There were the odd problems at first but soon we all got to know each other better and the atmosphere improved.

Once we were settled in I liked the place a lot but as always I was looking for 'business opportunities', and after talking to a good friend of mine Eugene Carter, who at the time had a 'spieller' (unlicensed drinking club), at Dog Kennel Hill, and it was him that explained to me the potential of running one of these clubs as they were very popular at the time. Eugene also explained to me that this sort of enterprise could be used as a front for cocaine dealing, which was now getting very common on the club scene. Eugene went on to be the biggest cocaine baron in the UK and was dealing with the Colombian cartels; he raked in millions, but unfortunately for Eugene he was found hanging from the rafters of his mansion in Kent in February 2001. No one knows for sure if it was suicide, still, it was Eugene who put the idea into my head. I made up my mind I'd have one of my own. The building was suitable because we had an upstairs front room, bedrooms and bathroom – and downstairs was the passage and kitchen only. You overlooked the estate from the kitchen side of the balcony, and when you went in and upstairs you could go out of the other side of the building from the living room side. So the two fire escapes came in handy when it came to avoiding the Old Bill – you could go in and then into next door, and no one would know you were there.

So, I started ripping all the walls out. I had no money, just the earnings from the cabbing. But it was a good time to start renovations because, with the new buildings still going up on the estate, there were plenty of building materials lying around. And it was nice and handy to help myself to bricks, floor tiles, and the rest. Anyway I built a beautiful L-shaped bar out of brick, which was long enough for about eight people to stand at, the top made from a lovely bit of oak timber. Some of the local lads burgled the tenants' association club, nicked the chillers and pumps, and promptly sold them to me. We had draught beer, spirits, and the lot.

I used to go to a bar in Forest Hill called Close Encounters, run by a couple of faces. I announced that I would be opening up my spieller on Friday and Saturday nights plus Sunday afternoons, and the guys from this club started to come to my place, which I would open up at 1am. I had a couple of barmaids working behind the jump (bar) and a big Scottish geezer as a doorman. He'd charge everyone a quid to get in and that would be his wages, plus he had free drinks.

After about a month I found that I had to start turning people away because it got so popular. Of course it was not ideal on a council estate, what with all the noise at night, but we managed to get round the worst of that problem. There was a bird called Lynn who lived bang opposite. Big fat girl she was, but she had a heart of gold. And, very conveniently, she happened to work at the council complaints department, which meant she could make sure that any complaints were intercepted before they got to the people who mattered. Lynn had a shy sort of manner, but underneath it all she was a raving nymphomaniac and we were able to make sure that she was kept well sweet by letting her come in the club, where there was never a shortage of horny guys more than willing to oblige her. So it was a nice little set up for her and for us.

Once in a while the Old Bill might turn up and ask if we were taking any money for drinks and, of course, we'd just say no, we were having a private party. Another thing was they were quite happy for me to operate, because as they put it, 'All the rotten eggs were in one basket'. In other words, if there was any trouble they'd knew where to come to first! So we made sure we never had any trouble.

One thing I'd always do was take the furniture out and leave it in the bedrooms before opening up. I didn't want to take any chances especially after the trouble I'd taken to make things look nice. I'd knocked one of the bedrooms into the living room, which was then used as a dance area with flock wallpaper, raised tongue and groove flooring, with soundproofing underneath it, a dropped tongue and groove ceiling, sunken lights, and leather sofas round the outside wall. It all looked really smart. Carol helped behind the bar for a time but got fed up with the late hours (1am until 8am which was understandable). Sunday lunchtimes I would get two 'anything goes' strippers in, and paid them £70 each a session. We'd sell entrance tickets for £16 apiece, and this included a basket meal of chicken and chips. There were free drinks at the bar while the strippers were doing their act, but you had to pay for drinks when the strippers were not performing. Not many guys came to the bar when the strippers were on; most of them were trying to get up to the front to get a blow job!

Micky McAvoy, (who later got twenty-five years for the Brinks Matt robbery) would often visit the club along with his brothers Johnny and Ploddy. Micky, with his longish hair and short beard growth was a guy who kept himself to himself and gave nothing away. He wasn't loud or offensive at all, a real gentleman, not like some of the other geezers. Johnny McAvoy on the other hand was very likeable, the geezer always had a smile on his face and two or more birds on his arm, and they were always real lookers. Johnny could really put the booze away when he was at my club; in fact he was my best customer. To his credit, he was a shrewd guy and a marvellous fence, always ready to shift whatever dodgy gear you had on offer. Ploddy was the quietest one of the three. He ended up going down on a drugs deal (heroin) and firearms charges and I can remember being quite surprised when I heard about it. It was a case of 'not *Ploddy* surely – you mean someone else, don't you?' Anyway, I was well pleased to have them in the club because they spent a hell of a lot of money between them.

It wasn't often that things kicked off because many of the guys wanted to keep a low profile from the Old Bill and didn't want to draw attention to them. They treated the place like a sanctuary. The only real bit of bother we had, was when a bloke accused his missus of shagging someone else. The owner of the Close Encounters club at Forest Hill, a geezer called George, was a regular; it was him that helped me at the beginning by sending his punters down to my club. He used to open his club during the weekdays and weekends he would close at 1am, so our interests never clashed at all. Carol didn't mind the fact that most of the girls in the club were on the game – she knew that it was strictly business with me. The Sunday afternoon sessions would normally last a couple of hours. I'd pay off the strippers then they'd often take blokes home with them so they could earn a bonus on top.

Occasionally a Sunday afternoon session would develop into an evening one, just depending how busy we were. It was around this time that the Brinks Matt job (the country's biggest ever haul) went off, but Micky McAvoy would come in and act as normal, obviously keeping a low profile. No one knew who'd done the job and Micky would just turn up with his brother Johnny, who later died of a heart attack, and Ploddy, who ran a newsagent shop and later went on to do twelve years for the drugs and firearms offences I mentioned before.

I remember one particular Sunday night when they were all in, and the two barmaids on duty at the time kept phoning me at the nearby pub, where I'd often slip out to for an hour or so just for a change of atmosphere. They kept on about that we were running low on vodka, (normally I'd use the cash and carry). Anyway I asked John, the publican at the pub, The Marlborough Head, but he said "Sorry mate, I'm low on stock myself." So I came back to the club, where everyone was well oiled; I got the empties, went into the bathroom and filled them with water, then added a drop of tonic. I brought the bottles out, put them in the optics, and started serving Micky and the others. They didn't really know what the fuck they were drinking by now, because fortunately for me they were all pissed, so there were no complaints.

Sometimes I'd have to dilute the whiskey down with cold tea. It wasn't uncommon for us to run out of some booze or other, it just depended how busy we would get. And, of course, the barmaids would help themselves to a few, but that was understandable – you had to allow for that. But the point was if I'd kept on running out of booze and not done anything to keep the customers sweet, they'd have soon started going elsewhere, and I'd have lost out on a nice few quid. Not only that, I had the advantages that comes with running the club and was mixing regularly with real villains who would always put a bit of work my way when I needed it.

I also found that having the club seemed to make me a bit of a babe-magnet. Don't ask me why, but there always seemed to be some bird or other hanging about at the end of a session more or less asking for it – just because I was the guv'nor of the place. But I can truthfully say I wasn't interested – I had my Carol. Sometimes women would say to her, "How come your old man is such a saint when mine will shag anything that moves?" But that was just how it was. Some of the blokes I knew would tell their wives they were going to go out in my company for the evening because they knew their old women trusted me. But some would say that they'd been with me even if they hadn't, and it could drop me in the shit if they'd been out shagging somewhere.

One Sunday I was in the spieller and a geezer called Johnny called in – he was an associate of the George who owned the Forest Hill club I mentioned. Johnny was a nice fellow and he told me he'd been asked to store some hooky antique gear for a couple of faces, and they were using his garage as a 'slaughter.' He explained that these faces had fucked him over a few years ago and he wanted compensation. He asked if I was interested in removing the gear and said he'd go fifty-fifty with me. What he meant was for me to nick the stuff, then to split the proceeds between us. All he had to do then was to apologise to the guys who'd left it with him, saying that he couldn't help it but, unfortunately, someone had come along and nicked it. These guys could do fuck all about it as the last thing they wanted to do was draw attention to themselves when it was them who'd nicked the stuff in the first place.

Anyway, me and a geezer called Eddie Mitchell (who later got fifteen years for chopping a bloke's toe off and shoving it in his mouth) went down there in a van and cleared this garage out. There was some really tasty stuff there – Queen Anne furniture, paintings, you name it. Anyway we came back to the club and I gave Johnny back the key he had given me. So then it was left to me and Eddie to sell the stuff, which we arranged to do a few days later. Unfortunately, before we had the chance, Eddie went out and got pissed one night and his old woman wouldn't let him back in the house, so he put his fist through the window and cut all his tendons, ending up in hospital.

So now it was down to me to shift the gear. I went round in this Luton van that we had it stashed in and called on various people I'd been directed to, specialists in antiques. If it had been videos, or gold, I'd have been more confident, but I'd never dealt with anyone in the antiques game before and you needed to know what you were doing. I had read up a bit about it in this big Gibson book of furniture and I had to rely on that knowledge to see me through with these guys. Well, that and a bit of bullshit. I think I did quite well, considering, and we all ended up with a couple of grand apiece. I heard later from Johnny that when his guys came to him for their gear, he gave them the key and told them to get it. When they came back disappointed and complaining, he just denied all knowledge of its whereabouts, saying how the fuck did he know who had nicked it. So, he earned his cut by taking the flack from these guys. And, to be fair, I made sure Eddie got his whack also when he came out of hospital.

A lot of jobs were planned in that club. People like Eddie Mitchell, George Bradford, Johnny Bradford (known as 'John Boy'), and others would sit there and talk over different bits of work that came in on the grapevine. I suppose you could say it was like a villain's jobcentre.

Guys would turn up and say, "What's on offer then, anything new?"

Then they'd say. "Yeah, that sounds alright, I'll have some of that," or "No, that's a bit heavy for me," just as though they were talking about painting and decorating jobs, or whatever.

Payroll snatches would often come up: there was always someone on 'obbo' watching the goings-on at banks and other places. Who went in and out, and when. I always picked my jobs carefully. Sometimes I'd 'sub' the work out to someone else, and then they'd give me a drink out of the proceeds.

The club must have gone on for a couple of years; it amazes me, now I look back, how we got away with it for that long. There was never any 'skag' in the club, at least as far as I know, but people would do the odd line of cocaine. I'd do a bit of 'charlie' myself when I got too pissed and needed livening up a bit. Although I wasn't a great drinker when I started the club, I did tend to start hammering the booze at that time. But there again, I was pretty fit because I kept up the boxing training and went to the Fisher club, and also took the kids up to the Thomas a Becket, in the Old Kent Road, where I'd train religiously.

Mind you, we did have to shut down the club for a short spell when I got nicked and ended up in Brixton on a serious charge. This was at the time I'd started working with this little team that included a geezer called Arif, Billy, Eddie Mitchell and John Boy. We'd go out and do a significant job say every three or four weeks and that would keep me going, what with my earnings from the club. Mind you, at that time, I was getting through a hundred quid a day and not even noticing it. I'd convinced Carol that this was the best way of going on and she stood for it, although I can't say that she was completely happy about the villainy involved. But I just treated it like a job – if you wanted money then you went out and did some work.

We'd do little jobs where there would be little or no comeback. That is, if we heard about someone doing a robbery for instance, then we'd steam in and rob the robbers. Of course this meant knowing about the job beforehand and sometimes even watching it get done, before we charged in and grabbed the haul for ourselves. Obviously the geezers we'd taken the stuff off couldn't then scream about it, could they.

Another activity I got into was known as 'creeping'. I'd start off early in the morning and go up into the City of London, usually posing as a cleaner; I'd get into offices and rob them. I enjoyed this because I'd be finished my work by 7am and have the rest of the day to myself. I usually worked the city area and did newspaper offices, solicitors, and what have you. In my brown overall I'd just walk into these places at about 5am – it wasn't like today with the CCTV. There would just be an attendant who'd open up the door for you. It was surprising what you would find in the offices. If you could get into the mailroom of a big company you could pull several thousand pounds in cash out of them, which they'd carry as a float. And there'd be books of stamps as well. It could be a good earner if you were lucky but, of course, things didn't always work out.

Sometimes I'd find a company cheque book but I would never take the book, just the last cheque. There'd be a company stamp, and I'd stamp the cheque and open up a moody bank account for say a couple of grand which, again, was much easier at that time. Then I'd cash the cheque when it had cleared and then leave that account well alone. I always used a different identity of course, and it was surprisingly easy then to go round and open up different accounts. Anyway, the companies I'd robbed wouldn't smell a rat until they did their accounts and the cheque had come back through the sorting house. Signatures didn't seem to be checked properly either. Still, that's all going back to the time before computers and high-tec took over.

Anyway, back to how I got myself banged up in Brixton. In one of the offices I did over, I came across what I think must have been a diplomatic bag of some sort. It had all these different IDs inside – passports, credit cards, and the like. There was some cash as well which, naturally, came in handy. It was a beautiful pigskin case which must have been worth a few hundred quid itself. I didn't get it open myself as it had a combination lock which I didn't want to fuck up, so I took it round to a mate who opened it up for me. On my way back to the estate I thought I'd just call in for a quick drink, as the pub had just opened at 11am, and I took the case in with me.

Soon my quiet pint was interrupted by this little Scotch prick, a mechanic who lived on the estate. He started giving me grief about some money I owed him. He used to do little jobs for me on the cars I had, and about a week earlier he'd repaired one for me which I hadn't yet paid him for. I remember it was fifteen quid for something he'd done to the exhaust, nothing major at all. Anyway he was half pissed and, instead of going about things the right way and showing some respect, he started slagging me off and giving me abuse in front of everyone. Where I had this bag with me I didn't want things to get out of hand, so I just told him to shut up. When he carried on I walked out of the pub and he started to follow me back to the estate still running off at the mouth. I got indoors to what was the club, and my missus was in the kitchen. I threw the bag down, took my jacket off, and picked up this brick hammer. I was ranting on about this little Scotch bastard disrespecting me in the pub and Carol didn't even know what I was on about because I steamed straight back out of the club again.

I went round to where I knew the cunt lived on the estate, and it just happened that by now he'd got back and had his head under the bonnet of a car he was working on outside his house. I came up behind him and smashed him across the back with the broad side of the hammer and he collapsed into the engine. Then I slammed the bonnet down on his head. This, remember, is on a crowded estate with a tower block next to me and he's screaming his fucking head off. Next, I dragged him out from under the bonnet and smashed him across the shoulder blades, arm, and legs, then finished by cracking him over the head and fracturing his skull. I just lost it. I remember it was a Lotus-Cortina he was working on, I didn't know whether it was his or a customer's, but I just smashed all the fucking windows and bodywork in. Then I threw the hammer through the window of his place before I scarpered, leaving him in a pool of blood.

He was later taken off to intensive care with a fractured skull, broken collar bone, and other injuries. I heard nothing for a full week, and then the Old Bill came round and nicked me. The geezer had obviously grassed me up, which a real villain would not have done, but there again he wasn't a real villain -- just a mouthy Scots fucker off the estate. I denied the charge; there were no independent witnesses out of all the people on the estate who must have seen something. They were talking of charging me with attempted murder but settled for GBH with intent, which was still quite a naughty charge and carried the same sentence. I knew the jock had pulled a knife from his bag at one stage and, as my hands had been cut when I smashed the car windows, I said that he'd attacked me with this knife. That was my defence, which I hoped would get me bail to give me time to take care of a few things.

After two weeks in Brixton I eventually got bail and I went back and opened up the club again. That was when another piece of work came up, and I copped for another very serious charge as a result of it. It concerned armed robbery from a financial institution, and the case against me was that I and two accomplices had had someone working on the inside. My two alleged accomplices were Nigel and Billy. Nigel, at the time, was a good friend but turned out to be a wrong'un, as far as I was concerned, because he shat on me big time later on. He had this short, curly, blondish hair and he looked like Roger Daltrey, only taller. I always thought that, underneath the entire swagger, he was not as hard as he liked to make out. And he treated women like shit. He went on, by the way, to try and tunnel out of Parkhurst prison by breaking through three cell walls, but ended up getting caught in the exercise yard. Then, when he was being shipped out to Winchester for his trouble, he and another geezer did a runner from the back of the van. They were on the trot for six hours, running round chained together. He was doing seventeen years for armed robbery at the time and he got another five on top for that.

The other guy, Billy, was a wild man who could intimidate even people he was working with on a job, let alone any poor bastard he was robbing. He was a tubby, stubble chinned psychopath, not all that big but he would face down anyone. When the six feet four nutter John Richards (mentioned earlier) held a gun to his head after they fell out over the money from a bank raid, he stood his ground and got what he'd been demanding – it amounted to about twelve and a half grand I remember, and Richards had to cough up.

Anyway, a lot of money, nearly thirty grand, was involved in this particular blag so I found myself, in a short space of time, in the frame for two very heavy charges. The difference with this latest one was that I knew exactly when my visit from the Old Bill was coming because I realised I was on 'obbo'. I'd met Nigel in a pub in the Old Kent Road and I noticed he was being followed when he came in. And the geezers doing the following stuck out like sore thumbs to me as Old Bill. When they did come round for me early the next morning I was expecting them. Just as well, because they piled into my place armed to the teeth with Heckler and Kochs and Smith and Wesson 45s.

I was taken away and interviewed by the Det. Chief Inspector in charge of the case. Later on I was put on an ID parade but was not positively identified. Or at least, one witness failed to identify me but the other one did, and that was enough for me to be charged. There was nothing to connect me with the case, such as any trace of the cash, the guns used, or clothing etc. They did say though that they were awaiting tests on some forensic. I decided to take advantage of the rule at the time which gave me the right to appear at a magistrate's court every week to have my bail application reviewed. This went on for about nine or ten weeks. Nigel had fucked off to Spain and Billy went low. Carol would turn up every day at Brixton to see me except for Sundays, when she'd leave a meal at the gate.

Chapter Seven

BRIXTON

I was allocated to C wing at Brixton prison on the 'threes', or third floor, out of four. There were so many prisoners in at that time that each cell would be 'three'd' or 'four'd' up when they were really only designed to hold one man. There were no toilets, sinks or anything like that – just buckets. I was given a job as a 'number one', which meant I was in charge of the cleaners on the landing, and my cell, which was close to the stairwell and the screws' office, was allowed to be left open all day. As far as being able to earn myself a bit on the side went, I landed on my feet quite well. Apart from having Carol able to open up the club again, I was well into the fiddles which were available on the inside.

I was very lucky to get the number one job because most of the cons were on twenty-three hour bang-up, and were only allowed out to get their grub, which they had to eat in their cells, and to exercise. And there was me with my door open all day! I was banged-up with a geezer called Byron. He was a very unusual geezer, not like your average con. I can only describe him as white, about forty, with a tense, hunched-up sort of body, messed-up hair all over the show, and he spoke in a deep voice, which was a bit more refined than you'd normally expect to hear inside. To me he was like a Chelsea hippy. He was also a well-off, successful heroin dealer who supplied people like pop stars. One of these was Jimmy Page of Led Zeppelin, and another was the group's drummer, John Bonham. He'd also been out with Marianne Faithfull and was well-known in the pop world.

My other cell mate was a black cocaine dealer. I found him a bit of a poser because he'd speak cockney when he was with us, then he'd go off and play backgammon with his West Indian pals and he'd change his dialect. He was always trying to impress and saw himself as a bit more than he really was. Anyway, these two dealers would get drugs smuggled in for themselves when they had visits, and I started to get cannabis smuggled in as a 'calmer' to get over my quick temper, which could often lead to me flying off the handle and punching someone's lights out. This block cannabis, which we used to call 'squidgy', would be rolled up by a friend and sewn into the outside seams of my own jeans, which I was allowed to wear as a remand prisoner. The squidgy would be the whole length of the jeans, so I would have thirty two inches of cannabis handed to me unknowingly by the screws every time someone made a visit.

I'd use some of it myself but mainly I'd give it to other cons in exchange for things like diamond studs, gold necklaces, watches and the like. You were allowed to wear this stuff with your civvies. Another privilege was you were allowed to drink beer, a can and a half a day. Carol would bring me in Special Brew because it was strong, which I would then transfer into plastic milk bottles (which we bought our powdered milk in) and store it on the window sill of the cell (so it would be chilled) to be traded, with the cannabis, to other cons.

I didn't just get jewellery for me to wear. Often there was more valuable stuff that I needed to get out of the prison so it could be sold to help Carol get by. Sometimes I'd get this stuff out via a visitor and sometimes, especially for the more precious stuff, it would be smuggled out for me by a friend's solicitor, who was very much one of the lads. So I had things organised pretty well, but one thing I couldn't get round was that I had to take a risk every week when I renewed my bail application, because I could never be sure I'd come back to the prison.

The background behind this was that it was the eighties and Margaret Thatcher's government had a policy of banging up everyone regardless of whether there was room in the prisons not. This often meant using police stations as prisons, and you could never be sure that you wouldn't suddenly be carted off to one even though you weren't supposed to be held there for long periods without proper facilities. But it happened, and most times a prisoner's family didn't even know his whereabouts. I know this because it was what happened to me. But more of this soon.

Every week I'd put in my bail application at Tower Bridge Magistrates Court, which I considered was the most corrupt court in the UK. It was known to us as a 'police court' and if you went there, and didn't admit to the offence, you knew fucking well that you'd end up in custody whether you were guilty or innocent. And it would be twelve, sometimes eighteen, months before you even got to Crown Court. Funnily enough I'd spent some of my childhood playing snooker at Tower Bridge police station, next to the court, because my Mum had worked at the court as a cleaner.

Anyway, every week I'd cause a bit of uproar in court when I appeared. The way I saw it, I was probably looking at ten years anyway, because I didn't know if Nigel had fingered me for this blag, and he was sunning himself in Spain, so I began to feel I didn't have much to lose. Two or three times I was literally carried out of the court horizontal, shouting my case. "I'm an innocent man, you've got no fucking right to hold me. You've got no evidence, there's no fucking forensic evidence..." I'd yell. I really felt strongly that the whole justice system stank and that the police and courts were the real criminals. And I'd seen quite few innocent men get sent down in that place. In particular I hated the magistrate, a shit bag called Cook, who I considered was a total pig and when he died, I've got to be honest, I laughed with joy. He was the most evil, corrupt magistrate I had ever come across, and I believe he deserved to have been a victim of the inquisition.

On one occasion I was in the holding cell at the court with the police. My Dad had attended the bail application and had put up forty grand, which he had got by putting up his house as a bond. The idea was for me to live not in Peckham, but on the south coast where he had recently moved to. When we got upstairs the police said they opposed bail because there was a chance I'd abscond, all the usual crap that they always came out with. We had a stipendiary magistrate this time, and he refused the application, so they had to drag me, horizontal, out of the court shouting my fucking head off. People in the gallery were shouting as well – not that they knew me, but they were friends and relatives of other cases, taking any chance to have a go at the police and the court. When I got outside I calmed down and told the officers to put me down, then went to the holding cell quietly. A little while later one of the Old Bill, a detective sergeant, came to see me and told me that if I told them where the other two, Billy and Nigel were, then they wouldn't oppose bail the following week. I told him to fuck off.

About half an hour later my brief came to the cell and said that the court wanted me back upstairs because they had only dealt with my application for one of the cases, and there was still the GBH with intent to be heard.

I said to him, "Does it mean I'll get out of here?"

"No, it didn't," he said.

"Well, tell the magistrate to go and fuck himself," I said.

My brief tried to reason with me but I really went into one. I was storming round the cell shouting the odds and I was told later, because of the acoustics in the place, that they could hear me upstairs in the court. The fucking cheek of the bastards I was thinking, refuse me bail when they've got no evidence, my old man comes all the way from the south coast and puts his house up, and then he gets blanked, now they expect me to co-operate with them just so they can put their paperwork straight. Fuck them! I threatened that if anyone tried to physically take me out of the cell they would have their fucking nose bitten off.

My brief went back up to the stipendiary magistrate and told him I wouldn't co-operate, which probably came as no surprise anyway from all the effing and blinding that could be heard coming from downstairs. He said "How dare he?" and the next thing was he'd sent these prison officers to get me. When I threatened them with biting their noses and ears off if they came near me the gaoler went upstairs and told the magistrate in effect sorry, but his job wasn't worth it to take that sort of risk. So they had to swallow it and sort out their fucking paperwork as best they could.

But back to my story about cons being put in police stations. And this is where the bastards got their own back on me. After our bail applications it was normal to make us go back to this sorting house in Lambeth. The place was used for all the courts in South London and it had massive cells which were all underground. So, after court, you'd get in your 'sweat box', which was the van used to transport cons (where you could hardly move and you virtually sat underneath the bloke in front of you) and you'd be dropped off at this place. When the place was full up they'd start calling out your names so you could be allocated. If you'd pleaded guilty and were, basically, a convicted remand prisoner, then you'd go off to Wandsworth prison. If you'd pleaded not guilty you'd go off to Brixton.

So, this particular time after I'd kicked off in court, my name got called, and off I went in the sweatbox. But, instead of going to Brixton, the driver turned off the other way over Lambeth Bridge and we ended up, me and eleven other cons, at Holloway police station. What I noticed was different about this system though, and you had to watch everything like a hawk, was that when your name got called out at the sorting house, you'd have your picture taken with a Polaroid, then it would be stuck inside this temporary file that was used instead of your usual one. It was all disposable so it could be chucked away afterwards because it was illegal; you were supposed to have certain privileges as a remand prisoner, and this whole thing was well out of order.

We were taken downstairs at the police station. There were no screws about, just uniformed old bill. Then we were two'd up in these one man holding cells. There was a police rubber mattress on the seat and one on the floor. The toilet was a hole in a wooden bench which you could only flush from outside. We found out from the old bill that we were there for a week until we were due in court again.

Somebody asked, "What about exercise?"

No exercise!

Then someone said, "What about our fucking food then?"

"And what about visits?"

We were told no visits and we'd eat the canteen food like everyone else. After a couple of days of this regime I got well pissed off and angry. None of our friends and families knew where we were, it was really taking the piss. I decided to go on hunger strike. As my food was brought to me I'd just chuck it back. This didn't go down too well and the Old Bill soon got pissed off with me.

"Look, I want a visit; I want my missus up here," I said.

Three or four of the other blokes joined me in the hunger strike; they were right behind my cause.

Anyway, to keep me quiet they allowed Carol over to see me. When she came in the station she had to talk to me through this cage I'd been put in. She brought some Kentucky Fried Chicken in but I had to tell her I couldn't have it, even though I was well hungry. It was the principle as far as I was concerned and there was no way I was about to give up the protest. Carol told me she'd been trying to contact me via Brixton but had got nowhere. She'd begun to think something had happened to me because of my performance in the court. I told her that what they were doing was illegal, and that was why I was on hunger strike, which of course she had known nothing about. I told her to go to the Press, and we actually got a small write up in the Sunday People.

The following week, after my hunger strike finished, I went to court again and got the same treatment from the magistrate. I kicked off again and shouted the odds, and again had to be carried out. When I got back down to the cell, the gaolers actually brought me some beer and food to keep me quiet. And a friend of mine brought me a change of clothes, complete with cannabis in the seams of the jeans. But I knew the score now, so when I got taken to Lambeth sorting house I waited to see if this thin yellow folder – the temporary one – would come out again when my name was called. So there we were, about a hundred of us cons, waiting there for our names to come up, and when mine was called I just ignored it. Not much notice was taken at first, more names were called out, and gradually the group got smaller and smaller until I was the only geezer left. This big sergeant came over to me. He said, "I suppose you're name's Mack?" I said it was. He said, "Come on then, you're going."

"No I'm fucking not. The only place I'm going to is Brixton," I said.

"But you're *going* to Brixton," he said.

"No I'm not. Not with that piece of fucking paper in your hand, I know I'm not. You want me to go to the police station then you fucking carry me there," I said.

I jumped up onto this bench, really angry now, and I saw some other Old Bill getting ready to come and physically restrain me. I was marching up and down on the bench, which was about three feet wide, ranting at them. Then I heard one of them say, "Just get this fucking geezer to Brixton." So that's what happened.

As I was going out of the cell looking for signs of a trap they were trying to pacify me, saying, "Alright, it's alright." They put me in a taxi with two blokes who I was pleased to see were screws, not coppers. I knew one of them anyway and he confirmed that I was going to Brixton. So, as far as I was concerned I'd won that little battle.

When I got back to the prison they let me have a shower (which I'd not had for a week, so I stank). The police station had only had two wash basins between twenty four of us. I also changed, which was handy because I had the puff in my jeans. I saw Byron and, after bang up about 8pm, we had our usual evening session. Like me he had his daily visits, and he'd produce this foil from a cavity he had in his tooth. I'd unpick my jeans and get out my puff. The other guy would take 'charlie' out of his nostrils and ears. Byron would 'chase the dragon' by unfolding his foil and putting a match under it. I'd just have a puff on a joint.

We talked things over and Byron told me that people had been coming in for me, and he'd had some orders for my puff. But the week at Holloway had taken quite a bit out of me mentally and physically, probably more than I realised at the time, because this was when I made a bad mistake. I was more or less convinced by now that I was probably looking at a fifteen year sentence, and I decided I'd like to join Byron in chasing the dragon as I needed to mellow out. He refused, nice bloke that he was, saying it would do me no good and to steer clear of it. But I insisted, and in the end he gave in. So that was how I got started on heroin. That first time, I was physically sick. But it was, stupid as it may sound, a nice sort of sickness, and all my problems just seemed to drift into thin air.

Byron reluctantly kept me supplied. I think, underneath it all, he was a bit wary of me. And also he was beholden to me because I did him a big favour – more of this later. We were to become friends on the outside and he introduced me to some of his showbiz friends. It's just a shame that our relationship eventually turned sour due to the very thing that had started it – drugs. Anyway I carried on taking the heroin for the rest of my time in Brixton and beyond.

My cases were by now coming up to the committal stage whereby I'd soon be committed to the crown court. Once committed, it could take twelve or even eighteen months to get to Crown Court, and I didn't want to have to wait that long. There was just one witness against me in the armed robbery case and no forensic evidence. My solicitor told me we should go for what was, I believe, called a section seven, and this was an old style committal (mini-trial) at Tower Bridge Magistrate's Court, where the magistrate would have to weigh up the pros and cons to see if there was enough evidence to actually send me to a Crown Court. So without this one ID witness against me, I'd have a chance. I received a visit from someone I knew and this person knew the score, that I was being fitted up, and I asked that person to help me out. As far as this witness was concerned I'll say no more than that.

And funnily enough, I also got the opportunity to put a bit of pressure on the main witness in my other case – the GBH one. This was because the Scottish geezer I'd bashed up had now, himself, been charged with manslaughter for an unrelated incident, and he was now actually in Brixton prison with me. He had stabbed his neighbour fifty-one times with a bread knife, the mad bastard. How it happened was, he'd been at his neighbour's house at a New Year's party, got pissed and staggered home in the early hours, gone to sleep with a lighted cigarette and caught his mattress alight. As some other people were leaving the party a bit later they noticed smoke coming from his bedroom window. One of the geezers decided to go in and help. He tried to wake up the Scottish geezer, and when he finally succeeded the prick was so pissed he didn't recognise the bloke trying to rescue him, what with the smoke and everything, and started to have a go at him. It ended in a brawl with the Jock stabbing the poor bastard fifty-one times with this serrated bread knife which, instead of a proper point, had one of those ones at a 45 degree angle.

But it wasn't actually the stabbing that killed the geezer. It was a combination of having to try and fight off the Jock (who was on top of him), the shock of the attack, and the smoke he breathed in, which had all brought on a heart attack – and that was the cause of the guy's death. As a result of this the Scottish geezer was charged with manslaughter, and not murder. So here he was at Brixton, in the hospital wing, on remand. Luckily I knew the hospital orderlies and every day for three weeks he got a pasting and had his tea pissed in and suffered bits of aggravation like that, after all he was a grass. But more of him later.

Getting back to the 'old style' committal we planned for the Magistrates Court: when the case came up, the hostile witness failed to turn up. And the police had to admit that, after all, they did *not* have any forensic evidence, something they'd claimed all along that they would produce. The judge gave them one more week to come up with some, saying he'd have to release me if they didn't. I went back to Brixton for this week before being released.

I told Byron there was every chance I'd be out soon and he asked me to do him a favour. This involved somebody having a quiet word with a witness due to give evidence in his case. Byron's so-called witness was a fellow drug dealer who wanted him out of the way so as to poach all his customers and take over his patch, so it was a case of dog eat dog.

I was still using his heroin and paying him for it. He said to me that when I did get out there was a good chance that I'd be feeling pretty rough without the drug. He said if this happened to contact his French wife, Nicky, and she would sort me out. I think he realised it was a big advantage for him to have this hold over me because it ensured that I'd sort his bit of business with the witness for him when I got out, and not just forget him. But on the other hand I had to admit that he did go out of his way to warn me against starting on the 'smack' in the first place so I couldn't really criticise him.

It worked out that someone did do the favour for Byron – and it led to his acquittal. And I did have to go to see his wife Nicky at their home in Streatham to get sorted out with some powder. And, when Byron got out of prison, he came and thanked me for my help. After that they'd both come and visit me and I'd also go to their place.

They were very good company and I'd like to have met them before they got on the gear. Byron more or less lived in the bedroom at his home in Streatham. Everything was around his bed – video, TV, music system, his drugs, all within arm's reach. He'd eat stuff like tiger prawns and lobster, and he'd have his sweet stuff, chocolate etc which smack makes you crave for. He'd tell me about the rock stars and groups he supplied.

Another guy I had the pleasure of meeting in Brixton was great train robber Charlie Wilson. I remember that me, another face we'll just call Jack, and Wilson were all in this room one day waiting for solicitor's visits. Jack, who appears later in the book when he helped me with some property deals, introduced me to Wilson. Charlie was a tall, well-built guy with fairish hair that he wore a bit longer and combed back in the area just behind his ears. And even in Brixton – where he was given a Cat A purely because of his record – he wore this smart silver-grey suit. We got talking and I asked him what he was in for. He just shrugged his shoulders and said, "Oh nothing really, just a bit of VAT fraud." I had to laugh later when I found out from Jack that it was about two and a half million quids worth he was talking about – him and this little team had been bringing Krugerrands in, smelting them down and re-selling the gold and claiming back the VAT. Anyway, he got off with it, bless him. For me, Charlie was a complete gentleman: 'Ah, nothing, just a bit of VAT' – that seemed to sum up his whole attitude.

As mentioned earlier my old acquaintance, Danny Roth, signed his own death warrant the day he blew Wilson away in Spain, because Charlie was a very respected and popular face.

I had to go to the Old Bailey for my GBH trial. It lasted four days. I had a great counsel, he was a QC. And, by the way, the Scotsman had actually been convicted by this time, but was given only three years for manslaughter – a right result as far as he was concerned. I had to give evidence in the witness box for a day and a half. I still had the scars on my hands from where I'd smashed up his car windows and I made a big play of this to the jury who, in any case, seemed to like me. In fact it wouldn't be overstating it to say I had them eating out of my hands. They really took to the way I acted, and to the way I put things. I would crack jokes, I complimented one on the hat she was wearing, saying my Mum used to have one like it, and they would piss themselves laughing. I would never look at the prosecuting counsel; I just concentrated on the judge and on entertaining the jury. And remember at this time I had been released and was travelling daily to the Old Bailey. So occasionally I'd bump into one of the jurors when it was time to go home and always gave them a smile and a cheery greeting. It shouldn't have happened, but it did.

And once, when I was trying to explain to the jury how my fingers got cut, I was pointing to my scars and then said, "Oh, you can't see that properly can you?" and suddenly jumped out of the witness box and ran over to show them, with the judge looking at me as if to say 'What the fuck *is* he doing?' They were all leaning over and looking as I showed them my scars, but the judge never spoke and just let me go back to the box when I'd finished, commenting, " Have you finished now, Mr Mack?"

Then came the moment when the Scotsman was called to give evidence. Remember, he was the only witness against me, in spite of all the people on the North Peckham estate that day who must have seen what happened. I remember well that the first thing my counsel asked him was where he lived. Of course he reeled off his address in Peckham but my counsel said, "No, I want to know where you are living now."

The Jock said, "Well, er… Wandsworth Prison."

"Ah, Wandsworth Prison." Can you tell me; is it true that you are serving time there for manslaughter?"

"Yes."

"And is it correct that you stabbed your neighbour fifty-one times but, because he died from a heart attack, you were charged, and subsequently convicted, for manslaughter only?"

"Yes."

"And is it true that when the Scottish police arrested you, after you had fled the country, that they found a tool box containing a knife similar to the one my client states you used on him?"

"Yes."

"And is it true that you have previously served six months in prison for indecent assault?"

I was watching the juror's faces as this was going on and you could tell that they weren't too impressed with the witness, to say the least.

And, of course, the defence had a hand in selecting these people by using our right to object to any we didn't like the look of. I remember one black guy who reminded me of Huggy Bear from *Starsky and Hutch*. He had all the 'bling', and he had the 'attitude'.

When the Judge summed up he told the jury they had to consider the 'intent' – was there 'intent' to batter the victim? I had to smile to myself when I thought about how I'd deliberately gone home and picked up the hammer. How much more intent could there be? I went downstairs to the cells for the jury's decision. I just had time to eat my dinner and was about to get myself some of this tasty mousse they had for afters when the call came. I remember asking if I could take my mousse upstairs with me and they said no! I could not. Anyway, when I got back in the dock, the verdict was unanimous – not guilty!

As the jury were discharged they had to pass by me, and they were winking, and saying "Best of luck" and "See you" and everything, just as though they were my mates. It was incredible. Not how you would normally think of an Old Bailey trial.

We had a great party at the club that night. No one paid for any drinks and it must have finished about eight the next morning. This was now two serious charges I'd beaten. Carol was delighted of course, but told me I'd really have to try hard from now on to keep out of trouble. I can only say that I did try but somehow things never seemed to work out that way.

Chapter Eight

JUMP UPS, DEATH THREATS AND SHOWBIZ

It was about now that Nigel decided to come back from Spain, and also Billy came out of hiding. Billy apologised for all the shit I'd been through and put it down to wrong place, wrong time that got me implicated in the armed robbery case. Nigel approached me through his old man at first, because he knew I was pissed off. I had good reason to be, I had just been banged up for something I had nothing to do with, and it was his fault that I'd been nicked in the first place. I told his old man I'd see him and Nigel turned up in this Daimler Sovereign Jaguar, full of apologies and "Sorry mate" this, and "Sorry mate" that. I liked the geezer really, and his family and I didn't want to hurt him. I agreed that we'd call it quits but decided that it was only fair for me to have his Daimler Sovereign as compensation for all the aggravation I'd had to put up with. Nigel agreed reluctantly that this was a fair settlement.

Another geezer turned up on my doorstep as well, a bloke called Alf, a taxi driver who I had thought was my mate. I'd done a bit of business whilst inside at Brixton getting him sorted with some weed (cannabis) which his girlfriend, a black bird who was into prostitution, would sell for him. Alf agreed to give money to my Carol out of this, to keep her going, but all he'd done was give her excuses. I'd thought the geezer was too wary of me to try and have me over, but I was wrong. The prick owed me more than five grand but this black bird kept telling him that I was certain to get ten to fifteen years, so why worry about it? I even had him come into Brixton on a visit to see me and believed the bullshit he came out with. Anyway, when he turned up at my place I was so angry that I smashed a china plate in his face, and also sliced his arm open where he was trying to defend himself.

Byron started to come into the club but the other guys didn't really accept him, he wasn't their sort. Not a villain's villain. He had this precise way of talking, with his deep voice, but he was a very shrewd geezer with degrees coming out of his arse. Also, if I remember rightly, he had once been selected for the British Olympic team for diving, but that was before he started on the drugs. He also went out with Marianne Faithfull at one stage. I remember many a time when I was in his place at Streatham, a member of Led Zeppelin would phone up for some gear, and Byron would drive out to his place in Windsor with maybe an ounce of heroin. I would wait with Byron's wife Nicky, and we'd sit there just getting coked up for two or three hours until Byron returned. He'd say "That's it – I've got him out of the way, he's all tucked up." It was business pure and simple to the guy. His bread and butter. Then the member of the band might phone up again. "Byron, I've lost it, I can't find the stuff, and it's gone missing." Byron would say, "I've just given it to you." But it was no good; he'd have to go out there again with some more. Poor bloke must have been in a bad way, but I know now, for a fact, that he's clean. The group's drummer, John Bonham, wasn't so lucky because I believe he died from a drug overdose.

The club was going along quite well at this time. I spent a lot of time with the McAvoy brothers – not so much Micky, who'd just done the Brinks Matt job – but his brothers, Johnny and Ploddy. Johnny was a great fence and he would sell off for me a lot of the goods I brought to him through the club. He was always surrounded by young girls, gorgeous young birds of sixteen or seventeen. They seemed to flock round him three or four at a time at his home above his shop in Westmoreland Road, off the Walworth road. How he did it, I don't know. It could have been the money, but he was certainly a character. I loved the guy and it was really sad when he died at a young age; he could only have been about thirty-eight. This was after Micky got banged up for Brinks Matt.

The other brother, Ploddy, had a confectioner/newsagent shop in Peckham, just off Marlborough Road. He later got involved in supplying heroin and got caught with a shipment. I believe he ended up getting twelve years for drugs and firearms offences after Micky went down. And, of course, Micky himself got ripped off big time after Brinks Matt, which, by the way, was a much luckier job than people realised because there was no way that they were expecting to get that amount of gold when they went in. Anyway, I felt sorry for the family. Their mum was a lovely lady, and so too was their sister, who I knew quite well from her visits to the club.

When people used my place they knew they were safe and didn't have to worry. For instance if the Old Bill turned up – and you always knew it was them because they'd ask for half a lager or something silly when everyone else was on gin and tonics, vodka or whatever – I'd change the music from, say, George Benson or the Supremes to this loud, fuck-off reggae music just to piss them off. And I'd double charge – anything to discourage them – but I never let on that I knew who they were. I would even sneak out and take the hub caps off of their Hillman Hunters just for a laugh as I was told that they had to pay for them!

Around now was the time that I realised that drugs were beginning to dominate the crime scene because the profits were so high. Villains were coming to the conclusion that it was easier than going out to work on the pavement (blagging). I'd been one of the old school in believing that drugs were not a good earner, especially after my experience of getting ripped off by Alf. And of course Byron had told me how cut-throat the game was, and that you couldn't trust anyone and had to keep your friends very close. But there were still other jobs around that I could earn from and I found that they came in useful to supplement the nice business that the club was doing, for instance, hi-jackings.

There was a particular bit of work where a team from North London had came onto our patch (very naughty) and had hi-jacked a load of electrical appliances and stored it for a few days at a slaughter (till things cooled down) which was owned by a good pal of mine. He explained to us that the load was being moved soon and would we be interested having the lot away, because there would only be the driver picking up the gear. This sounded sweet to us and we were given all the info as to when the load was to be moved. On the morning it was happening, we lay in wait, and true to my pal's word, the driver turned up bang on time. He picked up the truck and started his journey; we started to follow him in our Transit van at a safe distance. He drove down to Woolwich, parked up the lorry, and then got out. We were expecting the load to go to north of the river and would you believe it, he went into the local dole office to sign on. We sat and waited for him to return to the truck, we were fucking pissing ourselves with laughter, thinking, the cheeky cunt. So, now he starts heading for the south circular, with us following up his arse and, sure enough, he's back on track; we wanted to grab the load this side of the river and decided to do it at the next opportunity just in case he decided to stop and do some shopping or something.

We followed him over Blackheath. We didn't want to follow him too far because we had this 'slaughter' nearby where we were going to store the goods. So, when we approached some traffic lights I said to one of the lads, "Right, we'll have him here."

The lights were on red and we jumped out. I went to the cab, opened the door, and said, "Right, you're fucking nicked. Move over." At the same time my mate gets in through the passenger door and pushes the driver to the floor. The lights turn to green and we drive off towards our slaughter, job done! with the rest of our firm following in the transit. We put the driver's coat over his head, took his driving licence, to check his name, then realised he was an 'agency driver' not one of the gang that originally had the load away. The slippery bastards had hired a straight driver from an employment agency to pick up the load and deliver it north of the river for them. Talk about take no chances, this driver thought it was all above board, just another day's work for him. We said to him, "Right George (or whatever his name was), we know who you are, and we've got your address," and I always remember the geezer's reaction.

He said in a surprised sort of voice, "Hang on… so you're not the Old Bill then?"

It broke the tension and gave us a fucking good laugh.

We said, "Well, you're right there son."

He said, "Oh fuck me, I thought I was nicked for signing on – you're not going to hurt me are you?"

I said, "You won't get hurt; you just sit there and keep your fucking mouth shut, and do as you're told."

We got to the slaughter and I backed the lorry in. The lads from the transit got out; there were six of us altogether. We had these little trolley lifts to take the gear in, they were all motorised – similar to a forklift but not as big. Once we'd got the stuff inside we decided that it was too risky to get rid of the truck that day. So a couple of the lads stayed with the driver overnight and we left the truck parked up out of the way. I went home and came back the next morning early. The driver got bunged into the boot of a car and taken out to the sticks. He was told he could expect some money in the post, and it was later sent – as promised. It was agreed he'd tell his employers (the agency) that he'd been robbed by six black geezers (which none of us were). So he did alright, we never told him that the load he had been driving had already been nicked, so he would react normally, as he was none the wiser.

When we drove the lorry away to get rid of it, me and two other guys got about half a mile from the slaughter when this car came by us and slowed right down, and I could tell straight away that these four burly geezers inside were either plain clothes Old Bill or the North London firm looking for their load. They came past us, then put their brakes on and began to reverse up. Fuck it, I thought. As I drove off they did a U turn, came up behind, then pulled in front of us to block us in. I was turning over the options quickly in my mind. I didn't fancy legging it on foot and the chances of talking our way out were slim. I said to the others, "Fuck it, I'm going for it." I shunted their car out of the way, and put my foot down, through the South London back streets with these fuckers behind me.

The two guys with me were Eddie and his pal, a bloke who was really only there to help us get rid of some stuff that was in the lorry i.e. the stuff that we didn't want. (The stuff that we did want was already in the slaughter of course). Anyway this geezer started to panic. "We'll all get nicked," he was going, and Eddie had to slap him about a bit to keep him calm. I was thinking, 'Oh no, that's all we need. If they are Old Bill and get hold of him, we're finished'.

I turned into this housing estate and, not wanting to hit the parked cars in the narrow road, took out about fifteen small trees as I went over an embankment. When I got to the end of the road the turning was too sharp to get round, so I stopped and then reversed straight at their car. They tried to reverse their car (which was already smashed up) out of danger, and hit another car. At this point I told the other two guys they were on their own, and we all got out of the cab, split up, and legged it.

I looked back and I saw these big geezers getting out of their car which had its bumper hanging off and was in a right state and started to give chase. We still didn't know if they were Old Bill or the firm. I wasn't hanging around to find out either so I leaped over this hedge, and as I came over into the garden I landed at the feet of a bloke who was sitting in his deckchair. It was one of the luckiest moments of my life. As I lifted my head up and looked at his face I recognised him as a geezer that I used to do cabbing with. All I could say was, "Fuck me!"

"Nice to see you John." he says.

"Quick mate, get me in the house," I said.

His name was Les. Almost nothing was mentioned about my predicament – it didn't take too much to work out that I needed a bolt hole.

"Come with me," he said quickly, and he took me in his house, and that was where I stayed for the next four hours or so.

I didn't tell Les the SP about the job but he knew he was onto a drink for his help. He offered to drive me home after things had died down a bit. That's when the next major coincidence occurred. We were driving over Catford Bridge just by the dog track, in slow moving traffic, when I looked to the left and saw this pair of hands coming over the wall next to the bridge, followed by a blonde head and a flat boxer's nose – and it's Eddie. "I can't fucking believe it!" I'm going, "what a fucking result." The other guy was with him, they both got into the back of the car and Les drove us all the way home. It turned out that when we had split up they'd gone down to the railway line, laid low for a few hours, and then legged it. I'd been a bit worried about the other guy getting nicked although we still never knew if they were Old Bill, as I knew Eddie was staunch. So, if that wasn't a lucky day, then I've never had one.

Eddie was another one though who, unfortunately, got into drugs later. It changed the geezer completely. He ended up doing a newsagent in Peckham Park Road, adjoining the Old Kent Road, for drug money. He and two other geezers heard the owner and his wife, who lived over the shop, kept a lot of money on the premises. But Eddie was totally off his head that night on drink and drugs, and he actually caved the front window of the place in to get upstairs – remember he'd lived in this area all his life. Then the three of them hammered and tortured the shop owner to find out where the dough was. They ended up cutting off his big toe and sticking it in his mouth. But not before Eddie had taken the geezer's wife, who was in her fifties, into the other room and buggered her. Now a lot of things were acceptable in our code, but that was definitely well out of order. It went right against the grain for anyone who liked to think of himself as a true villain. Anyway, the three of them got nothing from the raid because the owner wouldn't spill the beans about the dough, but the Old Bill were everywhere looking for Eddie. They got him a few days later after he jumped about forty feet out of his back window in a tenement block in Peckham Hill Street, where he lived, onto some shop roofs below. He ended up getting fifteen years and I never saw him again – I didn't want to know him. As I've said, some things you don't do.

Getting back to the hi-jack, we kept the electrical goods in the slaughter for quite a long time after the raid, before successfully getting rid of them to a guy who was a big villain. We did this with the help of Johnny McAvoy. The villain's name was Bill, and he was a swarthy, stocky looking fella with a moustache – you'd take him for a Turk but he was an out-and-out cockney. Bill was definitely a face, and I first met him at his place near Deptford. He had a retail shop which his missus used to run and which he used as a front for his other activities. Funnily enough, I was to run into him some time later in Winchester prison when he was in for smuggling Krugerrands into the UK via the Channel Islands, and we discussed our little bit of business there. He owned a transport company and a storage depot in East India dock, so he had been well able to store our electrical goods. And looking back, we all had a nice little touch out of the job.

There was one job though where Bill let me down. It was when I took charge of a big load of expensive hardwoods, teak, and mahogany etc., on a trailer to an arranged place in North London so it could be collected by Bill. I waited for three hours and the bugger didn't turn up, so in the end I just dumped the trailer outside his work place. Next time I saw him was in Winchester Prison and I reminded him that he owed me for this one. Funnily enough I was in the church, where I'd go to watch these national geographical films on Friday nights, just to get out of the cell for a couple of hours, when in he comes and sits right in front of me. I tapped him on the shoulder and he didn't recognise me straight away. Anyway I found out where his cell was and paid him a visit the next day – being prison barber I was allowed the run of the wings. Although he was a respected villain on the outside, he was forced to swallow a bit of verbal aggro from me in there because he had just come in from Guernsey and had fuck all now, no back-up or anything. But I've got to admit that I liked the geezer really. And when I eventually got out, which was after him, he came across with a few hundred quid for me, which was very welcome, plus a car – a nice Volkswagen.

Another hi-jacking we did well on was when we nicked some power devices. Again we had the information come in through the club. The geezers who gave it to us were not part of the job – they just got their drink out of it after it was done. Anyway, I had looked at the set up when it was touted, and fancied it for myself. A mate, who was with me at the time in the club, agreed, and said it, was surprising how much these small devices were worth. The job went off as sweet as a nut, and the driver was totally compliant after having the shit scared out of him. Unbelievably, an hour after the job went off, I was sitting there with fifteen grand in my pocket. It was as easy as that. The gear, of course, had been sold off before we actually went in and got it from the lorry, which the driver had been unloading at the time. (He just carried on doing it – only this time for US – after we persuaded him!) We did give the poor bastard a drink out of it later on though, and eventually he came out with the usual rubbish to the Old Bill about being attacked by a group of black guys just to put them on the wrong track.

One guy I got to know was a geezer called 'Mad Frank' (nothing to do with Frankie Fraser). He was a total head-case who had been in Rampton but, amazingly, had this gorgeous bird he lived with. It couldn't have been his looks that she went for because the fucker really did always remind me of Frankenstein's monster; that's the only way I can describe him. He used to come into the club and people would use him if they needed anyone bashed up or frightened. His favourite tools were a machete and a club hammer. He'd already done time for cutting a geezer's hand off with a machete and I believe he also murdered someone by smashing their head in with a hammer. He was forever being seen by psychiatrists and was definitely not the full shilling.

He came over to me at the club on this occasion and said he had some stolen film equipment which he wanted to get rid of. When he mentioned he had video cameras I told him I was definitely interested – remember videos hadn't been around that long at the time, never mind video cameras. Later, I went up to his council flat near Brockley to take a look at the gear. The flat was on the third floor of one of this old-type, pre-war tenement blocks, right at the end of the landing. And outside the flat – not inside, but *outside* the door – was a big canvas sheet which was covering the gear. It was all film crew stuff. What had happened was that this film crew had been out in Thailand for a year or so filming wildlife for a TV company and, on their return, they'd parked their van in the Old Kent Road where they'd gone into, I believe, the Green Man, to watch a strip show? Unfortunately for them, Mad Frank was in there at the time, chatted to them and, later, while they were lining themselves up for blow jobs off the strippers, had sneaked out and driven their van away. Anyway, all this stuff he'd got was 35mm and the like, and I couldn't really do anything with it. I said, "Frank, I thought you told me it was cameras."

"Well, it is cameras," He said.

"Look Frank, I don't know *anyone* who would want this stuff, apart from someone in the BBC. It's no good to me," I said.

I left it at that and thought no more about it. A few days later I got a phone call. It was Frank. He said, "I'm going to fucking kill you."

"What are you on about Frank?"

"You've had all my stuff," he said.

"What stuff Frank?" He accused me of taking his film gear. Now when you were threatened by Frank, if you didn't take it very seriously then you were dafter than he was. If he said it, he meant it. At the time of the call I was in company – Billy was there, one of the Arifs, and a guy called Chris. They were the team I normally worked with and we were actually at Chris's place in Bermondsey. I told them what Mad Frank had said. We talked it over and, in the end, I said there was only one way to deal with Frank.

"What's that?" they said.

"I've got to fucking shoot him," I said.

We had this arsenal, with several guns from automatics to revolvers, and pump action shotguns. There was a strict rule that no one could take a weapon out without first asking permission from the others. Remember, this was their bread and butter for people like Billy, who were hardened armed robbers as opposed to 'jump up' hi jackers and 'creepers' like me and some of the others, who preferred not to have to hurt people if possible. They allocated me a beautiful antique Churchill shotgun. It was cut down, not completely, but three quarters. I asked if anyone would drive for me. Billy wasn't really much of a driver, Chris was having some emotional problems at the time, but Arif said he'd come with me.

I collected the gun and some shells. Arif went out and nicked a car, and we went looking for Mad Frank, knowing where his haunts were. I was sitting in the back of the car, and we went to a couple of clubs in Forest Hill, another drinking club in New Cross and one in Catford, but no sign of him.

I said to Arif, "He must know we're coming for him, we'd better leave it."

Arif said, "We've got to find him John. If we don't, he'll end up coming through your door doing you, doing your missus and doing your kids. If he really thinks you've got his stuff, he'll do it."

I'd have to say that, out of all the blokes I've met in or out of the criminal fraternity, Arif was the most loyal and sound. If I was in a war he'd be the first bloke I'd want to have with me. It was a great pity that we fell out in the end over a silly thing – a job I did with Billy that Arif didn't go on because he didn't like working with Billy, and he expected me to pull out of it due to the loyalty factor. I tried to make it up with him after and give him a cut from the proceeds but he wasn't having it. A great shame, because the guy was a diamond.

We went over to Mad Frank's tenement block near Brockley and I noticed his car, a beautiful 3.5 coupe Rover, parked up. There were no lights on at his place and I said to Arif, "He's gone to ground; he knows we're looking for him." We talked it over and I said that if I couldn't shoot him then at least he should be given a warning which, hopefully, would make him see some sense. After all I certainly hadn't nicked his gear; it was no good to me. And anyway, only a mug would have left it all outside like that in the first place.

I went over to the back of his car with this double-barrelled shotgun with twelve-gauge cartridges in it. I fired the first one through the back window, blowing all the backs of the seats, windscreen and dashboard to pieces with the heavy duty thick lead ball shotgun shells. Then I walked round to the front of the car, used the other barrel, and did the reverse, which took everything out, leaving just a mass of feathers and stuffing from the upholstery. This was at maybe one or two in the morning but only a couple of lights came on in the flats nearby. And remember, the report from this sort of weapon could have been heard in the East End. No one came out. We thought we noticed a curtain twitch in Frank's flat but, other than that, no reaction. Arif took me home and dropped the gun off at our safe hiding place.

My club was like Fort Knox, even the Old Bill couldn't get in there. I had steel doors with big four-by-four drop bars on the back of them, there was a double door, and bank-type bolts that went through the floor and ceiling. They were sunk in the floor about six to eight inches and you couldn't have kicked that door down with an army. So I went to sleep safe in the knowledge that Mad Frank knew the score, and now it was all-out fucking war. Carol didn't know what had happened but later in the night she woke me up saying there was a phone call for me. I asked who it was and she said it was Frank. I went to the bar where the phone was, taking my time, and said, "Hello."

A voice said, "It's Frank."

"Oh, hello Frank."

"Listen mate, I think I made a mistake," he said.

"Yeah, absolutely. Did you find the gear then?" I said.

"Well, no… but I know it wasn't you who nicked it."

"Oh. So does that mean you're not going to kill me now then?" I replied.

"I'm sorry," he said.

No mention of his car, no mention of the threat. I said "So is that the end of it Frank, you're going to behave yourself now?"

"Yeah, yeah, I'm sorry."

"You sure?"

"Yeah, I'm sure."

And that was the end of it, and I didn't see him any more after that.

I kept up my friendship with Byron and by this time he had started to give me some ideas about honest work. After all, it was work that didn't involve going out with a shotgun. He suggested some bodyguard work and I told him I was interested. He arranged the job through a company called Artiste Services, and they employed me and a mate of mine called Johnny Lockly, who I'd known most of my life, as our parents had been friends. Our first job was on crowd control at an open-air gig at Crystal Palace Park in South London, where they had Madness, Hazel O'Connor and Ultravox performing. Tickets were about sixteen quid apiece. It was an all ticket show and they had these booths with turnstiles where a girl would take the punters' tickets as they entered, tear off the stub, and return it to the punter. There was temporary fencing all the way round the park – it was a huge concert, one of the first after the big Hyde Park one.

The money was crap to me – thirty-five quid a day – although you did get free fish and chips and you got to see all the bands. But, in wages terms, for the average guy the money was good and I didn't have to steam in with a shooter. Also there was an extra large bonus to be had if you had your head screwed on right, and we both copped for it big time. This is how it worked. There were masses of people outside the turnstiles with no tickets who wanted to get in. After having a quick word with my mate Johnny, who was inside the turnstiles with me, I approached this particular bird who was working on a turnstile. I told her when she took the tickets *not* to give the stub back as she had been doing, and I would make it worth her while. I said to her, "Keep the *whole* tickets, and when you've got a nice pile, tip me the wink and you can just pass them out of the back door to me."

Meanwhile Johnny had gone outside to where all the punters were waiting to get in, many of them without tickets, and found a couple of touts who agreed to buy the tickets we'd be getting, for eight quid apiece. So that was what happened. The only snag was, that being summertime we only had light clothing, we didn't have enough pockets to keep all the dough in. People were coming in droves, leaving their tickets with this bird, she'd pass them out to me, I'd give them to Johnny, he'd let the touts have them, then bring back the money.

In the end we had to go over to the wooded areas in the park and just bury the cash as a temporary measure. This went on all day until we were totally knackered – the park was teeming with people. At the end of the day we were offered a lift home by one of the bosses of the company, there had been a little bit of trouble with some punters earlier in the day which we'd sorted out quickly and this geezer was quite pleased with us, offering us a full-time job with the company. We were far more interested in getting our cash home than getting a lift or a full-time job, so I said to the guy to contact us later about it. Some of the other security blokes thought we were barmy not to grab his offer straight away, but he did phone us later anyway. Meantime we went and bought a big holdall, dug up our money and put it all in. Much of it was in change but, by the time we'd got back to my club, Carol asked me, "How did you get on?" I had it all laid out, and it came to about three grand each. Not bad for a day's work.

As mentioned, I did receive a call from the guy from Artiste Services offering us more work. We went to Earls Court Olympia for a Bob Dylan concert for about three days. We were on crowd control but I couldn't stand the hassle of all these stupid fucking girls climbing all over me. It wasn't me at all and I said to the geezer in charge, "Can't you put me on something else? I've got more to offer than this." So he offered me stage security. This involved going to pick up the artistes from their hotels, taking them to the venue and staying with them. When they were on stage, it meant standing in the wings. You worked in pairs, so one could stand each side of the stage keeping an eye on them. Then, when they'd done their performance, it was back to the dressing rooms with them, and on to their hotel, where you'd stay for the party that they'd usually have. It was regarded by the other guys as a dream job.

The next gig Johnny and I did, was for the Rolling Stones, but unfortunately there weren't any parties. Then it was UB40 at the Apollo theatre in Victoria. I found the band really nice, ordinary guys and we went back to their hotel where they had all their families with them, and we had a great time. There were no hard drugs, just plenty of whacky baccy. They were just pleasant, down to earth, genuine sort of people and we went on tour with them to Birmingham, Manchester, Newcastle, and Scotland.

After I'd flown back from the tour I got a call from the bloke who owned Artiste Services about stage security for a Marvin Gaye gig. I was well up for this and agreed. This, again, was at the Victoria Apollo. Marvin was staying at a posh hotel in Park Lane. A lot of the American stars would bring their own minders over but they weren't allowed to be tooled up and, for insurance reasons, they had to use Artiste Services staff.

We collected Marvin at the hotel, took him over to the Apollo in the limo, and downstairs to his dressing room. He looked much as I expected him to with the little beard and everything, but I was surprised how lean he was and how much he sweated. Well, surprised until I found out how much cocaine the guy got through. I asked him if he'd stay put there while I grabbed myself a bite to eat and, when I went back, I opened the dressing room door and there was Marvin with this fucking great line of 'charlie' in front of him snorting away. He had this little moustache at the time and it looked like it had gone grey; the stuff was all up the side of his face, everywhere, and his eyes were like saucers.

"You alright there Marvin?" I said.

"Yeah, yeah I'm alright."

I was surprised the geezer could fucking walk, the amount of charlie he'd shoved up his nose. He asked me if I wanted some and I said yes I'd have a bit, just to be sociable!

As we were going up to the stage he asked me to pick him out a pretty black girl from the audience and ask her if she'd be willing to dance with him on stage to promote his song *Sexual Healing*. I spotted this gorgeous girl and went up to her. I had my suit and my badge on and asked her would she be willing to go up on stage with Marvin?

"Oh, can I?" she said.

"Yes, you can-I'll give you the nod when it's time, then you come over to me," I said.

I went back behind the curtain and told Marvin. He wanted to take a look at the girl and was trying to pick her out through a gap in the curtains. I had to more or less pull him back because he still had all this charlie down his sideburns and face. I was saying "Look Marvin, you need to clean it off." I couldn't believe that I had to play nursemaid to a superstar like that.

Anyway, when he got on stage and the curtains went back he did his introduction, then gave the nod to us in the wings for this girl to be brought up to him. After he had danced with her she was invited back to the hotel as Marvin's guest, along with some other girls and record company bosses for some partying. By this time Marvin would be totally out of his box. But I didn't stay on late at his hotel with him, because I could be earning more money at my club. So I just told him that I'd got to go and then I left. I did work for him for the three nights he was booked though, and on the last night I did stay behind and there was a great party. Although I've always been a bit of a seafood fanatic, and everything was on the house, I did waste some great lobster and shrimps that night because of the amount of charlie I did; coke does tend to deaden your appetite. Marvin was going back to the States, and he gave me and Johnny five hundred quid each as a parting gift.

After this I worked with The Jam at North London. Paul Weller I found a decent sort of geezer, but some of the young guys around him had let the success go to their heads, I thought. They seemed to think they could talk to people how they liked because they'd made it big. Then we did one night with Frank Sinatra, who had his own minders. All we had to do was driving, so we had very little to do with him. His friend Sammy Davis Jr was a bit too much to handle though, and it led to my downfall. This is how it happened.

I was in the club one night with no plans to work when I got a phone call. I was asked to go to the Victoria Apollo but I told them I was busy and didn't want to go out – I had strippers in and needed to get them organised. I suppose I was getting a bit greedy because I liked to pick and choose the gigs I worked at, and only take those that really made it worth my while. And also, to be honest, where I was still on the skag that Byron was supplying me with, I could get wound up quite easily.

It was a Sammy Davis show I was wanted for as someone had let Artiste Services down at the last minute, and the insurance stated that someone from the company had to be there or the show could not go on. It went through my mind that I'd seen something in the papers about Davis's bodyguards being tooled up when he flew over from the States, and Pan Am had kicked up a fuss.

Anyway the company offered me well over the odds, and Johnny, who was helping in the club at the time, said he'd look after things for me back home. So I went to the theatre and when I got downstairs there was Davis with his two bodyguards. He was wearing this silk shirt which had this kind of two tone effect, like mohair – as he moved it would sometimes look maroon, sometimes mauve. And there was a lot of gold chain around his neck, crucifixes, and a Star of David. I was introduced to him by one of the guys in charge. I wasn't expecting what came next.

"Fucking Limeys –who needs 'em," he said, and started raving on about having to employ us, which made me feel a complete prick. I started to mutter things like, "I don't need this," and he said, "Who the fuck do you think you're talking to?" His bodyguards stepped forward and another one of ours came up behind me to show solidarity.

There was a really bad atmosphere and I was getting more and more pissed off. I said, "Look, I've been called out at the last minute; I can earn more money than this in a better club, listening to better music than yours. I don't even like you. The only reason I'm here is that these people wanted me, because these two wankers here aren't insured to look after you." All this was going on in the corridor outside his dressing room. The effing and blinding went on a bit longer and the theatre guys were trying to make it clear to Davis that he couldn't use his own bodyguards instead of us, or else there could be no show.

Davis insulted me again and I actually tried to go for him, but got pulled back by the security guy who was working with me. But I did still manage to get my finger pointed right at him between his two security men who were shielding him. I said, "Fuck you! I asked my colleague if he was staying and he said, "No, bollocks to it." And that was it, we both just walked; and I think the show had to be cancelled. Of course that was the end of my employment with Artiste Services.

We had a laugh about things when I got back to the club. It could have gone a lot worse though because I'd had my telescopic cosh with me at the time, and if I'd hit the geezer with it, I would have probably signed my own death warrant, considering Davis's alleged links to American organised crime. I don't think I would have gone as berserk as I did though, if it hadn't been for my drug habit. The truth was I was beginning to feel pretty rough each day now until I took my skag, to get myself straight. Then I'd need some coke to liven myself up for whatever I needed to do, because of my hectic lifestyle.

Byron was now getting into the coke scene and we would take what we called 'snowballs.' We'd mix a piece of skag and a rock of coke, the coke would be 'washed' in ammonia or bicarbonate of soda to produce crack. Then we'd put the heroin and crack into a little glass pipe, fire it up with a little blowtorch – like thing and get the hit off that. The smack would get you feeling well and the crack would give you the 'rush' so that you had plenty of energy to get things done. But of course this only lasted for so long and then you were back to square one again. But, although I didn't realise it at the time, much worse was to come.

Chapter Nine

DRUG DEALS, RACE RIOTS & THE YARDIES

For a time the club continued to be a centre of villainy. Dodgy gear would be put on offer and different jobs would come in, some that interested me and some that didn't. Mostly they would be the result of guys keeping their eyes peeled for any signs of weakness, when it came to protecting, storing, or transporting valuables. But things gradually began to change as narcotics took over as the main money earner for villains, especially as many operators tended to be users as well. And if you were a user then there was no question of you living by the rules of trust, which the older generation of villains had built up. Skag-heads could not be trusted because they were a potential threat to those they worked with. If they got nicked, it stood to reason, that they'd grass up their mates – or do literally anything – just to get a fix.

I kept my own habit a strict secret from most of the geezers I associated with. And, to be fair, the more I used drugs the more I started to rely on them as an earner as well, tending to turn my back on going out with a shooter and stuff like that. Charlie was regularly used at the club now so it wasn't *that*. I had to keep quiet about; it was the skag that Byron supplied me with. Skag was about fifteen hundred quid per ounce at that time; it was high grade, mainly Persian gear. After cutting it with glucose, it could be doubled in weight. I began learning the ways of drug dealing, something I now deeply regret, but I had no choice, thinking about it, because I had become one of them, an addicted scum-bag with no morals or self-respect. I had now entered the short-lived world of doom. We started selling; at first we sold in ten quid wraps on the Albany Estate, off the Walworth Road. The estate was very similar to the North Peckham estate, a maze of tunnels, bridges, and walkways.

How it would operate was, we'd find a couple of skag-heads, and give them ten of these ten quid wraps. They'd disappear into the estate and when they'd sold nine wraps, they'd come back with the ninety quid and we'd let them keep the other wrap. Punters would come to the estate from north and west London as well as south, and we'd always be busy. Byron of course had the main source of supply for the stuff and we did good business. What with that income, the income from the club and the odd jobs I did on what I called the 'straight' side (any villainy *not* involving drugs), I got by okay. But the straight jobs were becoming less and less because I was being as careful as I could not to let on to my old mates about my skag habit. Even Carol didn't know I was a user, not yet anyway. Luckily she was quite naïve about the drugs scene.

Skag-heads were used on the Albany estate to sell for us and they could not be trusted of course. So we'd use them for about a week, promise them the earth and then fuck them off and use somebody new. It was better to use people who had just got into the drug, because they were in it just to feed their habit and they didn't get too ambitious. I'd work mainly on cutting the drug and I would get someone to make up my wraps for me (one ounce of skag wrapped in magazine paper) so my prints were not on it. This guy, the 'runner', would then meet a pusher on the estate and give him his ten wraps so he, the pusher, could go round the tunnels and walkways to find his clients. Meantime the runner would go and sit in a local pub and wait for a phone call from the pusher telling him he'd sold out and to meet him again to collect another ten wraps. The publicans knew the runners well enough not to pry too much and, in any case, they were good customers for him.

We took a calculated risk by giving the pushers ten wraps only at a time; if they didn't come back with the ninety quid we'd lost very little, and also they knew they'd have a job getting any further supplies. We'd get rid of anything from sixty to a hundred wraps a day per pusher so we did quite nicely out of it. And we only worked the estate for about four hours a day between about 11am and 3pm. Not that the Old Bill were that much of a problem, they seemed to be shit-scared of going on the estate. Remember this was before CCTV and the estate was a lawless one, almost impossible to police properly. It was literally a drug haven and, once on the estate, you could get from the Elephant & Castle to Peckham without even touching a street or pavement.

At this time I was only doing about half a gram a day of heroin and I could or thought I could, still think properly and do what

I had to do. But I didn't have the enthusiasm for straight jobs that I used to have because the gear was taking over. Byron was beginning to get more into the coke scene now because coke users were inclined to be better-off people on the whole, than skag users and he found it more profitable. And he was in a position to get hold of some really excellent gear. With cocaine, you would never get a hundred per cent pure, the best available would be about ninety per cent – and the stuff Byron got was eighty-seven per cent. It was known as Peruvian flake. When you smoked it as crack it gave you this tremendous rush and feel-good sensation, and people were beginning to do this more and more, as opposed to just snorting it. Byron discussed with me how we could best move the gear. I agreed to manufacture the coke into crack in my kitchen, and when that was done I'd give it to a couple of black guys who lived on the estate to sell for us – their community would go crazy for the stuff. They called it rock. To us it was just 'freebasing' because that was what it really amounted to.

This proved profitable because at that time we could get an ounce (28 grams) of charlie for about seven hundred quid. If we sold it in powder form we'd get sixty quid a gram, but if we sold it as crack it would be nearer one hundred and twenty a gram, so you could double your money by getting rid of all the impurities in the drug. The two black guys couldn't get enough of it and kept coming back for more. I said to Byron that we should make the crack our priority. It made more sense than selling powder, which I had done in the club as there were always blokes keen to have a toot to liven themselves up after a day's drinking, especially if they had a bird on their arm.

One day the two black guys came to me and said that they had some people who wanted to do business. These people had an untold supply of cocaine and an untold supply of money. This was the Jamaican 'yardies'. I did not have any fear of them because, at that time, their reputation was nothing like what it is today. They were certainly known, and you wouldn't mess around with them, but the name didn't carry the same weight back then. I agreed to talk to them and that's when I first met Leroy, a big black guy with a face lined like a jigsaw puzzle from where he'd been chivved up so much. And I swear that when they'd sewn his ear back on, after it had got chopped off, they hadn't lined it up properly because one ear seemed to be higher than the other. It happened that a friend of mine had been inside with Leroy and when I asked if he was okay, my friend confirmed that he was sound. When Leroy came to see me he brought another black guy with him called Winston, and what they wanted me to do was to wash their coke for them, to turn it into crack.

They asked how much I could produce per night and what I would charge. Up until then I'd only really washed coke by the ounce, which was quite difficult, and unless you were a fairly good chemist you could easily cause an explosion and fuck up all your gear, especially if you were using bicarb and a microwave oven, though ammonia wasn't so bad. I asked how much they needed me to do, and we agreed I'd start with half a kilo. They brought this round and it took me all night to wash it. I was reminded of the uncut diamonds I'd got involved with a few years back, because to look at, they were very similar to a piece of crack cocaine. When Winston and Leroy came back the next day to pick up the gear I made sure not to keep any back, just in case there were any problems later. One thing I'd learned is that the worst thing a villain can do is nick off another villain. Anyway, for my night's work – and remember *they'd* paid for the charlie, not me – they gave me a grand. When I told Byron about this he said, "You've got to be careful John, you can't mess with these people."

"I'm not messing with them, it's all Kosher. They've got shitloads of gear; this is something that *we* should get into," I said.

And I was one of the first, if not the first, to introduce the smoking of crack into the club circuit of south London spiellers. I had a glass table downstairs in my kitchen which I would bring my customers downstairs to, say half a dozen at a time, leaving barmaids upstairs to look after the bar. These guys would then chip in ten quid each. The first one would then take a 'rock' from the pile that I'd put on the table, stick it in the pipe, which he'd then light up, and take a 'hit'. As soon as he'd done that he would be as high as a kite, love everyone, and want to kiss them all. Then it was the next geezer's turn and so on, and that rock would last long enough to be passed round to all six blokes. Within five minutes the pipe would have gone round again and by now another sixty quid would be in the kitty, making a hundred and twenty.

When you worked it out, one rock would cost say twenty quid on the street then, but would only cost me about four quid to produce. So, in five minutes I'd have used two rocks at a cost of eight quid, and have a hundred and twenty quid in cash waiting for me on my glass table. Not a bad return by any standard. And this would go on all night. We had a rule of no credit or, as we used to say, 'no bail'. Now and then geezers who'd run out of cash and wanted more rocks would take their coats off – leather Gucci's and stuff like that, not rubbish, and nice watches and so on – and ask if they could leave them, in return for a pipe; usually I'd agree. Remember, they were people I knew, not your ten-a-penny skag-heads, who I wouldn't have in the house, which now made me a hypocrite.

With all this activity, it was a case of reviving the club and working there seven nights a week instead of three like we did before. I found it began to get too much for me; I was working all hours, out of my head a lot of the time and Carol was beginning to get pissed off with me. If I wasn't working in the club I was organising the skag pushers on the Albany estate. If I wasn't washing coke for the yardies I was doing my own crack circuit on the table in the club. I don't know how Carol put up with it all.

By now the yardies would come and see me about once a week and I'd do their freebasing for them. They paid me good money and it was all clean notes, not the 'drug money' that we sometimes saw which was stained and screwed up where it had just been shoved up someone's nose. They treated me with respect. And this was at a time when Peckham High Street was known as the 'front line' because of the recent race riots. Whites would not venture out in the area, especially at night, which was fast becoming as infamous as Brixton's Ralton Road. But I'd go there with no problem, and even walk into the Caribbean Club and totally enjoy myself.

I got on well with yardies, Winston and Leroy, and they would sometimes ask me if I could get hold of a gun for them. A lot of guns came in through the club circuit at the time and I could get say £250 to £300 for a shotgun or say £400 for a revolver, if it was a 45. It was the ammo that was hardest to get hold of. Anyway I sold Winston and Leroy several guns from a little arsenal I had of my own. Most of these came in via this burglar, who lived close by, who'd raid country mansions in Surrey and Sussex, where he'd often come across gun cabinets, because many of the mansion owners were keen members of the shooting fraternity.

One day a yardie guy called Dante came into the club. He was a fella who stuttered badly and I'd come across him several times before. He was after a gun, and it happened that I'd just got hold of this piece which resembled a flare gun, about fourteen inches long, a beautiful tool that had apparently been made for an army officer in the First World War. It fired a twelve-gauge shotgun cartridge, but the barrel was very thick in gauge and it could really take the power, although it didn't have a great kick on it. You could fire it with one hand, so maybe this officer could jump in a trench with this in one hand and a Webley in the other and, for all I know, a whistle up his arse. Anyway, I sold the piece to Dante, and gave him about a dozen shells. He went out to a place called Abbey Wood, near Eltham, to practise with it – after I'd made a point of telling him how it was really a close quarter piece.

So away he goes to Abbey Wood and he's back that same day to see me. "J-J-J- John," he goes, "This f-f-fucking gun, it w-w-won't w-work".

"What's the matter then Dante, doesn't it go bang?" I said.

"Yep. B-b-but it don't h-hit anything"

When I got to the bottom of what he was trying to say, I realised that he'd been using this close quarter weapon, designed to fire from just a few feet away, and had been blasting at a tree about thirty feet away and then he wondered why the fucking pellets had sprayed out and probably hit all the other trees either side of it – and probably killed half the rabbits in the wood. I tried to tell him where he was going wrong, gave him some more shells and off he went. Instead of going back to the woods though, unbeknown to me, he went out and tried to shoot a geezer that he had the hump with and, luckily for this geezer, Dante missed him. Back he came to me, saying the piece was no good and asking for his money back. This time he was quite aggressive, and me, not knowing the full SP about what had happened, told him he'd bought the gun fair and square, that he was wasting his time and to fuck off.

That night me and Carol were asleep in bed when Bullseye, our Staffordshire bull terrier who was a brilliant guard dog, heard someone trying to get in. I went downstairs, leaving Carol and the kids in bed, and where I had left the door flap up – something I would never have done before the drugs started to affect me – I saw this big black hand coming through. It could have reached this clasp I had, which unlocked all three locks on the door, so I had fucked up badly by forgetting the flap. I had this meat cleaver with me and Bullseye followed me down the stairs, keeping quiet like the obedient dog he was. I undid the lock silently, grabbed hold of the hand, opened the door and it was Dante. With one hand I kept hold of his arm which, remember, was stuck through the door flap, and I bent it backwards while, at the same time, my other hand came round the front of the door with this big, sharp, fuck-off meat cleaver which I held against his throat. The bastard was screaming out in agony, and I could see the claret starting to drip down his throat where I'd accidentally cut him because of his struggling. Then I got him on the deck, put the boot into his head a few times and cut his cheek with the knife so he'd carry the sign of disrespect.

By this time he'd had enough and had fucked off, Carol came downstairs, a bit alarmed at seeing all the blood, but I managed to pacify her, telling her it was nothing to be bothered about because I didn't want her worried.

This incident made me think, and I knew I'd have to do something about the guns I'd got stashed away at home because I was staring at a lot of bird in the face if I should ever get nicked on firearms offences. I had this Lee Enfield 303 rifle with a bayonet, and a German Mauser sniper rifle from World War II, which were both antiques without firing pins and I classed them as ornaments. Also there were three or four hand guns, plus ammo. The hand guns would all have to go. Well, not all, because I'd always keep a reserve one buried *outside* the house. (I did, for a while, keep it *in* the house, but gave up doing this when one morning my son Frankie, who had just started to walk, was seen strolling round the front room with a loaded revolver in a holster hanging round his waist. Carol went ape-shit when she saw it). So that was how I came to get rid of my private arsenal – and it was a weight off my mind I can tell you.

One night around this time Carol and I were indoors with the kids. She was pregnant with our son Danny and, though she had been spending a lot of time round her Mum's place where the club had been so busy, this particular night we were together. I'd just settled down to watch a bit of telly and Carol had brought me up some dinner when there was a knock on the door. Carol answered it and I could hear this deep voice rabbiting on and on in West Indian dialect. She came back looking frightened and told me that this big, black geezer in a leather coat had been ranting on at her and, being very wary, she'd shut the door in his face. He looked like the singer Barry White, she said, but she couldn't understand properly what he was trying to say.

About five minutes later there's another knock on the door. I was still eating my dinner so Carol went down and answered it, only this time she shouted back up for me to come down. Down I went and the big black geezer's standing there. "Yeah, what do you want?" I asked him. Out he came with this Jamaican talk which I couldn't understand. I quickly became pissed off because I was trying to eat my dinner, I was tired, and, where there were loads of newly arrived black people living near, I felt sure he'd made the usual mistake of knocking on the wrong door, which happened a lot. I lost patience and shut the door in his face.

Next time there was a gap of about ten minutes before he knocked again. Carol, bless her, went down again, and I followed behind, with the right hump by now. I stepped outside into the passage, ready to tell this fella he had the wrong door and to fuck off, when he says, "One of us has gotta die." As he said this he opened his leather coat and pulled out this enormous knife with a razor sharp point on it. I couldn't believe it – there I was in this closed corridor about a hundred yards long with an armed Barry White look-alike, and not a tool in sight to defend myself.

Carol, who was pregnant, remember, got so frightened she shut the door. I was now on my own with him in this corridor which must have been only about six feet wide. I knew that even if he knifed me to death no one would open their door or try and help me. I began to back pedal, at first slowly and then quicker as he quickened his step to come at me. He lunged with the knife a few times and I managed to grab it with one hand and, at the same time, grab his collar with the other. Somehow, instinctively remembering an old judo move I'd learned years before, I fell backwards holding him like that and brought the soles of my feet up into his stomach as we hit the floor. At that point I pushed hard with my feet so that he was thrown straight over the top of my head and onto the deck. This was called the monkey throw, and was all done in one smooth movement. I was astonished that it all came back to me, because I hadn't done it for years. The knife went flying and I heard the wind come out of him as he hit the deck. But it wasn't over.

He was up like a shot and he managed to pick the knife up. Now I had to move backwards in the opposite direction (towards my place) while he came at me again with the knife. I realised now that I'd have to get back indoors – there was no way I'd get away with another monkey throw, and if I didn't move quickly I knew that fucking blade would be shoved right through me. I turned and legged it back as quickly as I could and banged on the door for Carol to open it. She was still in a panic and tried to shut the door back on me when the geezer caught me up. I managed to push back inside and I grabbed the antique Lee Enfield with the bayonet off of the wall. The guy thought I'd bottled it when I went indoors, and was just turning to go off back down the corridor when I came outside again with the rifle.

He saw me and, I've got to give him his due, instead of legging it as soon as he saw the gun (which he didn't know was unloaded) he turned round and came right at me again with his knife. It must have looked like a scene from the film *Zulu* – me trying to bayonet the fucker and him dancing around trying to stab me. I lunged at him and the bayonet missed his neck by inches and went straight through the collar of his leather coat, almost pinning him to the wall. He must have thought that this was a bit too close for comfort because that's when he decided to fuck off! And he ran off down the stairs. But by now I'd lost it and really wanted to kill the bastard.

I found it quicker to go back through my house, through the kitchen doors which led out on to the front balcony, and from here I leaned over and watched the guy come back out of the end of the flats.

He was trying to get into the house underneath me. As he came below me I got the bayonet off of the rifle and launched it at his head, which was about sixteen feet below me. It missed and hit the metal framed door he was just opening. I was totally off my head with temper and frothing at the mouth by now. After the bayonet came more missiles. I slung tins of dog food then I slung the fucking hoover. Then, believe it or not, I launched myself- I leaped straight over the balcony, landed and picked up the hoover and the bayonet. I slung the hoover straight through the window into the kitchen area of the place, and followed behind it with the bayonet in my hand looking for the fucker.

He didn't want to know now. He and some others were holding the kitchen door shut to stop me getting through; they were trying to protect him and themselves. The next thing I knew the Old Bill had turned up. They got hold of me and dragged me outside and pinned me to the pavement, where they cut off my air supply by putting me in an arm lock to quieten me down. Then I was slung into the riot van and taken to the nick. Remember, this was at a time when the big race riots in south London, and the smaller ones that followed, were still fresh in everyone's minds and the Old Bill were very sensitive about it.

I thought I'd be charged with having an offensive weapon – the bayonet – and I later learned they'd also found the Lee Enfield and had sent it off for examination to a laboratory. (Surprisingly it wasn't a .303 as I'd thought, but had been converted into a kind of semi-automatic shotgun. Apparently a lot of soldiers from the Second World War would do this – take a .303 and bore it out into a .410 shotgun.) So there I was, down at the nick, having a right go at the old bill for pulling me in when it had been the other geezer who'd started it all.

While this was going on I didn't realise that my dog had run over to the local pub where my mates were drinking and, a bit like Lassie, had alerted them to the fact that something was wrong. Several of them then came over to Carol to ask if she was okay, and ask where I was. This, in turn, resulted in several black people congregating outside my house. At first just a few, then more and more turned up until Carol got frightened by the large numbers of them – maybe a couple of hundred – and phoned the police. The next thing the Old Bill are asking me to speak to Carol on the phone to calm her down.

When I got to the phone she was panic stricken, like most people would be, let alone a pregnant woman. "We're surrounded," she said. "There are hundreds of them." Apparently they were chucking things up at the windows and shouting. Luckily they couldn't get in downstairs, which was like Fort Knox. And at least Carol wasn't alone, my mates being with her – they were looking for weapons to retaliate, but Carol didn't want any of that.

I said to the Old Bill, "Look, what the fuck are you doing about this? My wife is surrounded by this crowd and she's in serious trouble." They had the bullshit excuse to try and tell me that I didn't understand the politics of it. I told them what I did understand was that if my wife got killed or injured, then it was down to them. The next thing I realised was that in the office next to where I was using the phone, they had the Barry White look-alike yardie standing there talking to another Old Bill. The cozzer I was with said, "We're going to have to get this sorted right now." Remember, I'd been caught with a firearm, I'd put the windows through, I'd tried to take the geezer's head off with a bayonet, I'd chucked the hoover, the tins, I'd gone through his relations' or friends' window, or whoever they were, intending to do him, nearly caused a riot etc, and they were preaching politics at me!

What it boiled down to was that the Barry White geezer was a community leader for the West Indian community, although he was also a yardie. And the reason he'd come to my door was over the Dante escapade. What I hadn't realised was that he was the guy who Dante had shot at and missed.

Anyway, next thing is the Old Bill are letting me and the yardie geezer go without charge. The yardie nodded to me as I passed him and I nodded back. As far as the Old Bill was concerned he'd done nothing wrong anyway, because I didn't really grass him up like I could have done. Still, I asked the Old Bill what the fuck was going on, and they said to me that they had such a situation back at my house that the yardie was the *only* person who could put things straight, because it was only him that the crowd would listen to. So he was taken out first to my place to talk to them and, by the time I got home, they had all disappeared.

When I thought about it all later, it became clear to me that this geezer must have found out from someone that I'd sold Dante the gun that was meant to kill him. That was why he'd had the right hump with me. Anyway, by the time the Old Bill brought me home that night it must have been about one or two in the morning. It was pitch black on the estate and I didn't know whether anyone was waiting for me round the corner as I went to my place. I did have a tool outside but couldn't use it because the Old Bill was watching me go in.

When I did get in Carol told me how bad it had been, with hundreds of the fuckers outside throwing things up at the windows and everything. My mates had been in there with her with knives, and keen to have a go, but there had just been too many of them to do anything. Carol thought they were all going to get petrol bombed. When the yardie geezer turned up though, the crowd had all gone quiet – she was surprised at the authority and influence he'd had over them.

The next morning I got up and went down to the 'front line', as Peckham High Street was known. I wanted to find out more about the yardie geezer and also to speak to Leroy. It took a bit of front to do it, but I walked into the Caribbean Club. And the amazing thing was everyone kept coming up to me saying, "Respect, respect," and patting me on the back, or trying to stick a spliff in my mouth. Leroy was there and confirmed what I'd suspected – that the Dante business had been behind the aggro. Where Dante had used my club a lot and people associated him with me, this yardie fella thought it was me who was after him. His mates must have told him, "Yeah, that Johnny Mack who washes our coke, he is out to get you, man. He wants to take over, man."

Anyway Leroy told me that he'd put the geezer straight now about what really happened, so everything was okay – and I was a bit of a hero for standing my ground and not getting walked over. I'm sure that if I had run away, and lost face, it would have just invited them all to take the piss as much as they liked and I would have had no peace from them. They would probably have wrecked all my cars that I used to park outside – whereas, as it was, the black people around me always made a point of reserving me a space, and would tell their friends to keep clear of it.

I found the friendship of the black community well worth having because, believe me, their attitude could be every bit as aggressive towards whites as the other way round. The blokes I'd gone to school with, who spoke cockney and everything, they were one thing. But the newly arrived ones from Jamaica would look down on them for mixing with whites. So the original immigrants would be faced with a problem: do I stay as I am and act 'white', or do I join the newly arrived blacks, talk West Indian and live by their code? I realise this is a touchy subject with the politicians and the police and so on, but I am just describing things as I saw them. And remember, South London has had its fair share of race problems.

When the Indians and Pakistanis came onto the scene, for example, they were regarded as just corner shop owners, there to be mugged and robbed. Me, and mates of mine, were often asked to provide protection for them and we would stick a geezer on the door of their shops. Now, of course, all that has changed and they look after themselves.

One day I got pulled in off the street by this CID geezer. He told me how lucky I'd been in the incident with the yardie, and explained to me all about their set up. I already knew this, and was just waiting for him to mention the gun (thinking I was about to get done for using it). He said, "You know that gun is actually a shotgun don't you?"

I said "No, I didn't know," and he explained about it being bored out to fire .410 shotgun cartridges. I asked if he was going to nick me for it and he said no, but they would just leave it on file. I never heard about it anymore and I think the reason was that the Old Bill didn't want the embarrassment of people knowing about a near riot, and them having left a pregnant woman on her own in the house to deal with it as best she could.

Chapter Ten

A FIGHT WITH THE TOUGH-GUY ACTOR JOHN BINDON

After the yardie boss incident I stopped doing the coke washing and shut the club down for a while. I had to really, as the baby was now almost due and I needed to have more time to devote to the family. And I also found that my skag addiction was beginning to take over and make me more secretive. I didn't want to mix with my old mates so much, and my relationship with Byron started to go downhill a bit as well. How Carol put up with it all I don't know. People would ask where I was and she'd tell them I was ill with jaundice, because my skin had started to go yellow.

Two mates I did mix with now, because they were well into the skag, were John Boy, who was Georgie Bradford's nephew, and a ferret-faced geezer called Ray Lake, who was okay as a look-out but useless when it came to having a row. In fact I can remember Ray once going in on a snatch and, instead of sorting the geezer out double quick and coming away with the goods, he started to argue with the fella. I then had to dive in a bit sharpish, sort the fella out, get the goods, and, when that was all done, give Ray a right bollocking for holding us up and nearly fucking up the whole getaway.

Because I wasn't really up for going out doing jump-ups etc, we would all do a bit of creeping together. This particular day we went to Chelsea, just off the Kings Road. John Boy had had a nice little touch earlier in the day with two Lowry originals and had scarpered, well pleased with himself. I'd hung on with Ray. I noticed an open door at the top of the stairs by the side of this fabric shop. Ray stayed downstairs to keep an eye out, and I climbed the stairs to where this glass door was ajar, and saw that there was no one inside the office. It was a hot day and, as I crept inside, I saw a chair with a geezer's clothes chucked on it – trousers, jacket, shirt, socks etc. At the back were some French doors leading out to a balcony and, as I moved further into the office, I saw a pair of bare feet, sticking out where someone was lying on a sun-bed, no doubt enjoying a sunbathe during his lunch hour. Next to the sun-bed was a briefcase which was half open. I managed to slip it away unnoticed. In it I found some travellers cheques, a passport and some notes which I thought were German marks.

What these notes turned out to be though were the new British fifty pound notes. And when I'd crept out with the haul, without this fella knowing a thing about it, I was gob-smacked to find out that they added up to thirteen grand. I couldn't believe my luck. I gave Ray half, because he'd been with me. So, as it turned out eventually, we both did a lot better than John Boy, who had to hang onto his paintings for ages because, like I'd already told him, they would be a bastard to get rid of. And in the end he got nicked and copped four years for the job. Anyway, after this great touch, Ray and I went back to his place in Kensington. At the time Carol had gone to stay with her sister in Buckingham for a short break, so I shot over there for a couple of days with her, then came back to stay with Ray again as it suited me nicely for the creeping game.

One evening we went to this wine bar in the Kings Road and I met a couple of geezers who I knew from my club. There were a couple of birds in the place, quite yuppie types, who looked like they were after a bit of rough, and we all started drinking together as a group. It ended up with us all going back to one of the birds' places for a bit of a party. The two blokes I knew from the club ended up shagging them. What we didn't realise at the time was that these women were actually call girls who were into actors and the showbiz scene. They never charged the two fellas I knew because they must have just fancied a bit of rough, but they *were* into charging actors and showbiz types for sex. Where they came unstuck though was by trusting the two guys from the club, because they ended up robbing the girls. I didn't know the men well, they were just customers at the club, but they were obviously ruthless bastards and they fucked off with all the money these girls had earned that was left in the flat.

The following afternoon I couldn't find my car keys. I told Ray that I may have left them at the girls' place, so he said he'd come with me to get them. We went over to Chelsea again, to their place, which was actually a basement flat right on the Chelsea embankment.

When this bird opened the door she said to me, "You've got some fucking nerve, coming back here." I asked her why (because I hadn't shagged her and it wasn't me who'd nicked the money either). I told her I just wanted my car keys, and she let us come in.

There was a geezer sitting on the sofa in her front room who nodded and said hello to us. The girl then explained how she and her mate had been turned over for a few hundred quid the previous night, but I think she must have realised in the end that I'd had nothing to do with it. The next thing that happens is that the bedroom door opens and there's this burly geezer with a scarred body standing there in his trousers but nothing else. I immediately recognised him as someone I'd seen on television. Anyway he starts giving us the mouth about nicking the girls' money, and what the fuck did we think we were doing here and all that. I couldn't put a name to the face but I knew I'd seen him in films and TV series like *The Sweeney*. Then I realised he was John Bindon and, it turned out, the guy sitting on the sofa, I think, was actually his brother or friend. Where Bindon had no shirt on (showing off these big scars that he'd got from the famous knife fight when he killed gangster John Darke), he was waiting for me to recognise him.

For those who don't know the facts, Bindon, a tough-guy actor, who also mixed with real life villains, killed a South London villain called Johnny Darke in a knife fight in a riverside yachting club, fled to Dublin with his page three model girlfriend Vicki Hodge, very seriously injured, but was then persuaded by his mates to give himself up. He was eventually acquitted of the killing – after a few showbiz pals spoke up for him in court – pleading self defence. Bindon was a party animal who enjoyed living the highlife with his showbiz pals and his aristocratic girlfriend, even joining Princess Margaret and her friends on her holiday island of Mustique. Apart from his hard-man reputation, he was also a sexual legend, due to the size of his todger which he would proudly flash at parties. His favourite trick was to hang several of the old type pint beer mugs on it by the handles. He died, still a comparatively young man, of AIDS in 1993 which he caught from a young girl called Clemy, who was infected by her then boyfriend, Nicky Bell, who had been in the States filming blue movies. It was said that he was never the same man again after the murder case because he was always looking over his shoulder for some comeback. A lot of his showbiz friends deserted him in his later years, but his old friends, the Krays, would write to him from inside.

Anyway, I tried to explain to him that I wasn't interested in robbing these women for a few hundred quid, but he kept on being leery and, in the end, I just steamed into him. His friend tried to interfere so I chinned him as well, but eventually John Bindon managed to get hold of me from behind and the three of us were grappling on the sofa. Trying to handle the pair of them, I looked over to see what Ray was doing; the girl had fled into the bedroom. Ray then came towards us – as I thought to help me out – but he just climbed over us as we struggled and he made for the fucking door, managing to accidentally kick me in the head in the process. I couldn't believe it. I thought to myself it's now or never and I really went for it, nutting Bindon, biting, and the lot. And I also started with the verbals because I knew his situation, and that he was shit-scared of revenge from south of the river.

I was saying things like, "Johnny Darke's mates will know where you are now, you cunt. You're a dead man," and stuff like that. His friend, who wasn't a big guy, was beginning to take a hiding, and then Bindon started to shout out, "Stop, stop!" I stood back, making sure to grab hold of this big wine glass on the side which I broke ready for use if there was any further action. But Bindon's manner had changed completely. He said, "Look, I've thought about this and if you did steal the money you definitely wouldn't have come back to the flat."

I said "Fucking right I wouldn't!" I was still a bit steamed up and reminded him that if certain people knew he was here giving it the big one he'd be in serious trouble. I knew what these people were like from my days at Harry's place in Deptford. I'd known Johnny Darke from seeing him in the spiellers, not well, but enough to know that he was a fucking animal and you wouldn't have wanted to cross him.

I said to Bindon that these people would fucking kill him. But he wanted to be nice to me now, and we spoke for about half an hour about his situation. In the end he said, "Look, why don't we all get cleaned up and you can come and have a drink with us at this local I use."

"I've got a bit of business to take care of first, but tell me where it is and I'll see you there," I said.

He was still a bit wary of my intentions and said, "You won't be bringing your mates with you will you?"

"Look, I'll be on my own. It's not my intention to drop you in the shit or stir up trouble. *I know* a lot of guys from south of the river, but I don't want to get involved at all in your problems, they're for you to sort out," I said.

He seemed happier at this. And he and his friend (who knew about electrics) actually helped me get my car going without my key (which I never found).

I drove back to Kensington to see Ray, who I wasn't too pleased with – I still had the imprint of his foot on the side of my head where he'd dug it in so he could spring over the bodies on the settee to get to the door and leg it. When I got to his flat I could smell the stink before he opened the door. And when he did open it, it made me want to puke up. He said, "I'm sorry mate, but when it kicked off I just couldn't handle it, I really couldn't. Look what happened." And the bastard had shit himself big time – his trousers full of it. Ray wasn't made for this type of life. He wasn't really a villain, just a geezer who needed money to feed his drug habit. And the fight *had* been vicious while it lasted. With three blokes in a small room (and, for all I knew, Bindon could have had a knife and stabbed me like he did 'Darkie'), you don't play by the Queensberry Rules – so the violence had definitely unnerved Ray. But I couldn't let him get away scot-free with running out on me and I gave him a couple of smacks. I also took back from him what he had left of the six and a half grand I'd given him, and I said, "Don't ever come across south of the river again because you're not fucking welcome: I'll let people know what you're really like."

Anyway, I decided I did want to go and have a drink with John Bindon, so later on I turned up at this pub in Chelsea. His friend was with him, but the other people there were not villains but actor friends and showbiz types. I felt totally out of place with them really, but then they started pulling coke out of their pockets, and that was what I needed to relax. Bindon's friend left but I carried on drinking with John because I wanted to know what he was really like, him being a bit of a celebrity and everything. And I wanted to know what really happened that day when he killed Johnny Darke. He told me that Darkie cut him to pieces and made a complete mess of him but, instead of finishing him off like he could have done, he took his time, taking pleasure in trying to kill him slowly. That was what you could expect from Darkie if you upset him. Anyway, this taking it slowly really scared the shit out of Bindon, and this was what made him lash out in desperation. And he just got lucky with a wild swipe.

I never saw him again after that night. Looking back, I wouldn't class him as one of the strongest guys I've mixed it with, remember, I wasn't at my strongest at the time due to the skag. And he definitely lost heart when I was giving him the verbals about his enemies from south of the river. But at least he was honest, honest enough to admit that it was only sheer panic and a lucky blow that resulted in him getting the better of Darke.

Another TV star I met was Nicholas Ball, who played 'Hazell' in the popular TV series. I saw him in the Marlborough Head in Goldsmith Road in Peckham one night playing pool, and I recognised him straight away. To me he looked no different to how he looked on the telly, with jeans, leather coat, and plimsolls etc. This was early evening, about five or five thirty and he asked me if I wanted a game of pool with him. I said yes, and we played together. The following week I went in the pub early again, and there he was, and we played another game. This went on for about three or four weeks and we'd look out for each other. He'd just say, "All right John? Pool?" and I'd say, "Yeah, sure Nick." We'd have a couple of quid on it and have a nice knock around.

Then one night I played with him, but this particular time I was carrying a weapon that someone had given me. It was an old Webley 45 and it was in a specially adapted holster which I was wearing under my bomber jacket. I unzipped the jacket a bit and when I bent down to take my shot, then realised Nick may have noticed the gun. After the shot I excused myself, telling him I needed a piss. I took the gun off in the cubicle and put it in the cistern, thinking I'd collect it after our game, but when I went back Nick had left the pub. About a week or so later John, the pub landlord, said to me he'd been trying to get that type of customer in the pub for years, and what the fuck had I done to him? "He plays pool with you," he said, "and then he's not seen again." Naturally, I said nothing about the gun and just pleaded ignorance. And I never saw Nicholas Ball again.

Chapter Eleven

COUNTERFEIT TWENTIES

As I began to get deeper and deeper into drugs and the addiction took hold of me, one of the worst things I had to handle was lying to my old mates. I'd tell them that I couldn't go and have a drink with them as I wasn't feeling well and stuff like that, because I daren't let them know about the skag addiction – all the respect I'd built up over the years as a sound geezer would have been blown away. Johnny Mack would have been just another shit-head you couldn't trust. Not that I'd felt much like drinking anyway. Instead of bars I tended to spend my evenings now in some dingy old kitchen or other waiting for someone to deliver my gear.

Byron was still on the scene but he would distance himself from me, because he could see my addiction was getting worse, with my mood changes and everything. I still got by with doing the odd bit of dealing but certainly wasn't up to continuing my old lifestyle. One thing I did do though was to nip into my local pub, the Marlborough Head, every so often just to show face and see if there was any work about. One day I was in there and I bumped into a geezer I hadn't seen since we were at school together. His name was Dave. He wasn't a 'face' or anything, just a guy from way back who was a bit dodgy but a sound geezer. He recognised me and came over and introduced himself. We got talking about work and so on and my ears pricked up when he told me that he was on to a good little earner. I could see that he'd had a couple of drinks in him and was in a relaxed mood, so I asked for more details.

He took me over to the other side of the bar, where the pool tables were, because it was nice and quiet there. Then he produced two one hundred dollar bills. He said to me, "Now, tell me which one is the snide." I put them up to the light, looked at the watermarks and everything, but couldn't tell the difference. He pointed out the genuine one but I was none the wiser. Then he explained that he was in with this little firm who were knocking out this counterfeit money. It wasn't done by laser copier or anything, these notes were properly printed with plates, and they were the business. He didn't go into too many details at the time, but he and I exchanged phone numbers after I told him I'd be able to get rid of quite a lot of the stuff for him. He gave me the hundred dollar bill samples and I said I'd call him back in a few days.

I went straight to Johnny McAvoy, brother of Brinks Matt robber Micky, and showed him the samples. He couldn't tell the difference visually but tested them with this blotting paper and pad. He asked how many I could get and I told him as many as he wanted. So I did some business with Johnny – it was only about 10,000 dollars worth – but it put me on a good footing with Dave and we all earned out of it. Anyway, a couple of weeks later Dave came to me with some good news. Although I'd got one or two other people who were interested in the Yankee dollars, it wasn't the same as having English currency – now Dave told me he could get twenty pound notes (we called them 'Shakespeares' because he appeared on the back of them at the time). The notes turned out to be shit hot. The paper they'd got hold of, which I believe was transported from Ellesmere Port down to the Bank of England, was the real McCoy. You just couldn't tell the difference and when I saw them I was really excited. I knew I had to have some of this!

As a 'tester', just to see how they went, I bought a few grand's worth which I got at a knockdown rate, about one pound fifty each for them. Then I took a trip down to Cornwall, with Nigel and a driver, making sure I'd got enough skag and coke to last me for a while. The way I decided to operate to get rid of the snide money wasn't the best way, but I did it anyway. I'd go into a shop, bar or whatever, buy a packet of Benson and Hedges for eighty pence, offer my snide twenty and collect nineteen pounds twenty pence in change. Of course you could do that fifty times with no trouble at all, with the fifty first, then something could go wrong or someone would smell a rat, probably because the serial numbers were not consistent and eventually a check would be carried out – and if you got caught, you'd get done for the lot. It was like credit card fraud – you could go and do twenty quid at a time, but if you got done for one, you'd get done for the lot. If I'd given it more thought at the time, I'd have realised that I'd be reducing the odds against getting caught by going for one big hit rather than lots of small ones. But, straight thinking and heroin addiction don't go together.

Still, we got rid of about ten grand of forged notes in two days. It was so easy that I went back to Dave and, with the money I'd made, I bought another big parcel of the Shakespeares. Dave told me he was having trouble shifting all the American dollars he'd got, so I bought the five hundred of them that he had on him at the time, just as a tester. I gave them to Nigel to take to a Bureau de Change up west. I was really putting Nigel on the line of course, but I hadn't forgotten how he'd put me in the shit before, so I reckoned that he owed me. Anyway, he took the dollars in, and it worked – they changed them into sterling! This made me realise how good they really were, just as Dave had been telling me.

After this, I found some other people willing to buy both the twenties and the dollars and I started to make a nice few quid for myself. I found a Dutch guy who bought the dollars and he did a couple of trips away to get rid of them. Then he came to me and said he had a great outlet for the twenties. He wanted £250,000 worth. I couldn't afford to pay for this amount, so I went to Dave and asked him if he could help me out. So, firstly, it was agreed that the deal was to be split into two separate transactions of £125,000 each. Then I suggested that we could split the profits three ways between Dave, me and the suppliers (which would mean they'd get their money back, plus a profit). Dave said that he'd put this to the suppliers and, later on, he told me they were happy with the deal.

Dave gave me a parcel with £125,000 worth of the counterfeit twenties. I took it up to Harwich and booked in at a hotel for the night. It was all done like a proper business meeting, and when the Dutch guy turned up for me he enquired at reception, where I'd booked in under a moody name, and he was shown to this nice, private spot with a table for our meeting. I gave him the twenties and he paid me, and off he went to catch the next boat back. I went back to London and divvied out the money as arranged.

For the second instalment of the deal, a couple of weeks later, we decided to change locations and use Southampton instead of Harwich. So down I went to the south coast with my parcel of snide twenties and booked into a hotel. (I'd always use coke alongside the skag at times like this to liven me up and keep me alert, otherwise I'd have been totally out of it, and would have fucked up big time). Anyway, the same arrangements were made as last time with me staying the night and waiting next day for him to turn up. He didn't. I couldn't phone him because, for all I knew, he might have already been nicked and the Old Bill would trace the call back to me. I waited another day. Again nothing, so I phoned Dave to let him know what was going on – I didn't want him thinking that I'd had it away on my toes with the money. Dave said to stay one more day to see if the geezer made any contact. I did this – luckily I had enough gear on me to get by – but again, nothing.

I phoned Dave but now found that I couldn't get hold of him either. Eventually I got hold of his missus on the phone and she told me that Dave, and his supplier friends, had all been nicked. I couldn't believe it. Dave's missus knew a bit about the racket, although not the full SP. So I then phoned Dave's brother, who knew the score, and I asked him what I was supposed to do with the £125,000 worth of twenties. He managed to get in touch with Dave, who was on remand in Brixton prison, and the order came back not to bring the money back, but to 'spend, spend, spend'. Apparently what had happened was that Interpol had already been alerted about these twenties going out of the country and had had this little team who were supplying Dave on 'obbo' for some time. When they were pulled in they were driving around in a limo, with the boot full of snide notes – about six million quids worth!

I phoned up Nigel and told him to get his arse down to Southampton because we were going shopping. He didn't waste any time getting to me and was down within two or three hours. I opened up the hotel mini bar and showed Nigel the parcel with the £125,000. "Fucking hell!" he said, well impressed. I brought him up to date with what had happened. "So how do we go on now?" he wanted to know.

I told him we'd knock them out singly, like we did in Cornwall. "But it'll take for ever," he said.

"This is going to be in the papers remember, it won't be safe trying to pass too many off at once," I said.

What I really should have done was to sit on them for a while until things quietened down.

So, we started on the spending spree. We drove down south, and then we came back on ourselves hitting all the south coast seaside towns. Garages were a favourite, but we'd do amusement arcades, shops, pubs, anything. Out would come the twenty for our Benson and Hedges, and back to us would come the fags with nineteen pounds odd change. The car I had was a ringer – it had been nicked but the number plates had been swapped with a legitimate car – and we had the right log book, MOT, etc, so everything was as it should be – except the serial number. I always kept a supply of log books and dodgy driving licences. And passports, of course, because you never knew when you might need them.

After a couple of days the car was full up with Benson & Hedges, drinks, Kit-Kats etc; it was stupid. All the loose change we put in a sack. Anyway, when we got as far as Portsmouth I mentioned to Nigel that my Mum and Dad had just moved down this way, just a few miles down the road, and suggested we pop over there to see them. When we got to the area we just turned up unannounced on the doorstep. Mum just stood there looking at me suspiciously, but what hit her first of all was how much weight I'd lost. She wanted to know what had brought me and Nigel down here. I tried to flannel her about just coming down to see how she was getting on, but she wasn't stupid and I could tell she didn't believe a word, although she didn't say as much. Anyway we were not turned away.

Nigel and I went out the first night and tested the notes around the main streets in town, hitting pubs mainly. It went okay and we must have made the best part of a grand. The next day we worked our way around Hayling Island and started going into the holiday camps there. We found most of the bars had half a dozen barmen on, so the pair of us would work them all in a short space of time. It was like shelling peas. Then we went into a camp near the harbour which more or less completed our little round trip. I did a couple of notes on a half of lager and some more fags, Nigel did a few, and we decided that that was enough for the Island, and we went back to Mum's place.

We'd made about seventeen grand altogether on Hayling Island and were pretty pleased with ourselves. I told Mum we'd be going back the next day and she looked quite relieved. I know Dad was – he couldn't wait to see the back end of me. That night we went back to the holiday camp at Hayling Island. We went upstairs to the Disco-bar they had there, and I was drinking Pernod and orange, which was sweet and suited my taste at the time I was taking smack. Nigel, by the way, had seen me do a bit of cocaine, but didn't know I was injecting heroin. We were starting to get quite pissed in celebration of all the good work we'd done and the fact we'd had a right result. Downstairs was a burger bar and Nigel asked if I fancied a cheeseburger. I said yes, and off he went, but I had a nasty feeling somehow that he was going to do something stupid – we'd already agreed that we wouldn't pass off any more dodgy notes here as it was too risky where we'd done the place earlier on. I should have shouted out to him as he walked down the stairs to warn him, but I didn't.

The next thing I know Nigel is walking back up the stairs with these two cheeseburgers (paid for with a snide twenty) followed by two fellas who, even in my state, I could tell were plain clothes Old Bill. I tried to signal to Nigel (by holding out my hand below the level of the bar to avoid attention) to tell him. 'No, no, for fucks sake don't come back here – look behind you!' I was trying to say with my body language. I might as well not have bothered. As he neared me I tried to turn away, but it was no good; up he came. I said, "You wanker!"

"What? What?" he went, completely oblivious to what he'd done.

Anyway these two Old Bill, both detective constables, go through the routine of telling us about reports they've had of counterfeit twenties, and let us know they've just seen Nigel pass one, and they've seen we are obviously together etc etc and now they want to talk to us outside.

I told them that I didn't know Nigel at all, that we'd only met that evening, and that I was staying on the island with my family. I took one of the Old Bill over to the balcony, looked down over to where crowds of people were sitting at the tables downstairs, and started waving and calling out to one group "All right then?" I was shouting away and, even though they didn't know me from Adam, they started waving back up at me. I almost got away with it but what really gave the game away was my accent. They had a description of us both that the staff at this place had given them. So, in the end, we had to go outside with them as they wanted. They didn't have any radios on them and I guessed it was done so they could contact their HQ or whatever for assistance.

I was still protesting my innocence though as we went outside, and we got near to where the swimming pool was. We stood there while they talked a lot of bollocks -- just to try and pacify us and keep us quiet for a while. Then they called over this guy who was a security guard at the camp and asked him to contact the local nick for assistance. I knew then that we'd have to do something. I looked at Nigel, gave him the nod, then whacked this Old Bill a couple of times and he ended up in the pool. The other one – they were both only young – just stood there looking shocked. I asked him if he wanted some and he just backed off. Then I legged it as fast as I could back into the dining room area (as it was late at night there were no diners), jumped over the tables to an emergency exit at the back, went through that, through a hedge, and ended up by the beach. I didn't have a clue where I was. I saw boats in the distance and noticed the tide was right out. By now I could hear dogs barking and sirens wailing.

I jumped from the sea wall on to the beach and made for the direction of the boats, over to my left. I had this lovely smart suit on, Italian shoes, and Italian shirt (if it was Italian I'd buy it in those days) and there I was, racing along the beach listening to the sound of the Old Bill back in the distance. I also had quite a lot of genuine money on me, plus the dodgy twenties. Where it was dark, and where I was a bit pissed and disorientated, I couldn't remember which pocket each was in. I went right out to the edge of the sea, turned my back to the shore, and lit a fag. Then I read the serial numbers on the notes by the cigarette light – what I didn't want to do was get caught with the dodgy ones on me, so I needed to know which lot was which. I couldn't bury them because I didn't have a clue where I was and I'd never have found them again.

I must have waited out there a good couple of hours watching the lights on the shoreline come and go and listening to the dogs. Eventually it seemed to quieten down a bit and I walked back to a part of the shore where there was a wooded area. I made my way through the trees and came back out by the back of a school. I went through the grounds to the front and recognised the road as being one that was close to where my Mum and Dad lived. I waited until I thought the road was clear, and then made to cross it. Just at that moment this police dog van came along. The copper got out and started to walk towards me. I thought to myself: 'What the fuck do I do now?' I decided to try and play it out. He came up and said, "We're looking for someone in connection with an assault on a police officer, etc." I answered with a fake Bristol accent I'd picked up from a geezer I knew inside. I was rolling my R's the best I could and he said, "Oh, you're not from London then?" I said

"No, I bloody ain't," I said, and started to slag off London and Londoners. He fell for it completely.

"No, we're looking for two Londoners," he said and off I went, thinking how stupid the Old Bill could be at times. I knew that on the way back to my parents' place there was another busy road and I didn't want to push my luck, so I took off my nice jacket, which contained all the money, and I shoved it in a motorbike sidecar parked outside a house. Then I continued on back in my shirtsleeves.

Nigel wasn't at the house but Mum wanted to know why I'd come back without my jacket. I told her there was nothing to worry about and went to bed. Next morning I came downstairs and I told my old man what had happened. He wasn't silly and I didn't intend to take the piss out of him, which was what it would have boiled down to by keeping schtum. He said to me that I'd have to get away double quick, which I fully realised. I didn't know what had happened to Nigel (I later found out he *hadn't* legged it, even though he'd had the opportunity to). I knew the Old Bill was still looking for me and that the island was not an easy place to escape from, with the only road off being watched.

In the end I phoned up Byron. I told him I'd got a car, so asked if he could come down to the island by public transport or get someone to drop him off at Portsmouth, then take a cab over so he could take me back. I offered him money for his help, although he'd probably have done it without. Meantime my Dad put some cases in the back of the car and made a little compartment underneath, so I had a place to hide up. All traffic leaving the island would be searched, remember. So, once Byron had arrived and I'd recovered my jacket with the money in from the motorcycle sidecar, I got into my hiding place with Byron driving and me in the back. Fortunately luck was on my side though: the police were there at the roadblock, but we weren't pulled over and allowed through.

Byron bought some drinks, brought them back to the car, and passed one through a hole in the armrest in the middle of the back seat, to where I was hidden, then let me out to take over the wheel at an arranged point along the M3. When we got to the outskirts of London where Byron's car was, we swapped over cars and I set fire to the one we'd been in. I also burned all the dodgy money I had on me.

When I got back home I told Carol what had happened and said I thought Nigel must have been picked up, although I wasn't sure. She said she felt uneasy about things, but I told her not to worry because Nigel was sound and wouldn't drop me in the shit. I was so confident about this that I didn't bother to go into hiding for a spell, which was what you'd normally do. Anyway, about three days later, I remember it was on a Sunday afternoon when you'd least expect it and I was in bed, I suddenly noticed a shadow coming from the direction of my fire escape at the back. I was a bit out of my head and had about a gramme of charlie on the side. Not thinking straight I just jumped up and made for the door, and suddenly found a Smith and Wesson stuck in my face. The Old Bill were coming through the front *and* the back. It was the 'Sweeney' and they told me I was being arrested for robbery. Even though I was not feeling too clever, this didn't seem right to me. Dealing in counterfeit money, yes. But robbery?

They turned the place over and actually went to a secret hiding place that only Nigel and I knew about. It was a false wall-cum-cupboard that I'd installed, and they tried to make it look as though they'd discovered it accidentally – but this was something you'd have to *know* was there to find it. Anyway, they seemed surprised that there was nothing inside, not knowing that I'd moved my firearms out of there already. They carted me off to Peckham police station and slung me straight in a cell at the back; there was none of this taking you to reception and booking you in. At that time it was a disgusting place where the stinking blankets stood up on their own. After a couple of hours the Sweeney came back, about half a dozen of them – four in the cell and two outside – and started to try and wind me up as I lay there on the bunk. They never talked to you like ordinary police officers would, more like another villain who was trying to intimidate or annoy you. It was 'fuck this' and 'fuck that' with them – none of your 'Can I help you sir?' I decided the best thing to do was to keep schtum, and after a while they left me alone.

But the funny part was that not once was the subject of counterfeit dealing brought up, so I just assumed that I was only wanted for this so-called robbery they were on about, although I couldn't think of any that I might have got a pull for. I tried to hear what the Old Bill in the charge room was saying by putting my ear to the door. A bit later I was told I'd be staying for the night. I said "What for? I haven't even been charged yet," but I just couldn't find out anything. The next morning I was brought some cold fish and chips: this was about eight o'clock. I said, "When were these brought in then?" The old bill said, "Last night," so I chucked them back at him.

I was beginning to get withdrawal symptoms and started shouting out from the cell and getting abusive. This Old Bill opened the door and said, "You think you're being clever don't you? Go on then, off you go. Go on, just piss off out of it." And he held the door open for me. Now I felt better! I didn't need asking twice and out I went. I walked towards the charge room and there's another copper standing there. I couldn't believe it, it was the one I'd shoved into the swimming pool on Hayling Island. He says, "Nice to see you John." I couldn't take it in, I was totally gob-smacked. But I soon realised what it all meant: Nigel had been nicked and had grassed me up. The Old Bill here had just been taking the piss.

I was stuck in a car with four of the bastards to go back to a police station in Hampshire. Carol didn't know what was happening;

as far as she knew I was still at Peckham. Anyway, when we got onto the A3 I started to get withdrawal symptoms again. Heroin makes you constipated and your bowels start to feel loose once you withdraw. So I'm sitting there in the car and I start farting and everything. We stopped at a little chef place, or whatever it was, and they said I could get something to eat providing, once they took my 'cuffs' off, I behaved myself. So we went in the place and I sat at a table, with two on my side and two opposite me. I told them I needed the toilet and one of them came out with me. I told him there was no way he was coming inside the cubicle while I had a crap so he waited outside the door. Once inside, I saw this narrow window which, fortunately, I could now get through where I'd lost so much weight due to my habit. I squeezed through it and had it away on my toes.

I came off the main road and into some fields, ending up in the Devil's Punchbowl, a well-known wooded beauty spot in the Hampshire countryside. I hid out there for several hours until it got dark, then I made my way up to the top and passed this big house where there was a Volvo estate parked up on the driveway. It must have been only just parked there because there was shopping on the back seat and the front door was left open. I jumped in, took off the handbrake and let the car roll back and round onto the roadway, turned off down the hill and bump started the engine up, and was soon on the A3, speeding along and leaning back every so often to grab myself a bit of food from the shopping on the back seat. I was back in London within an hour or so.

There was no way I could go back home of course, as the Old Bill must, by now, have been getting the right hump with me. I went to see some of the old crew, like Billy and the lads, and they made sure I had somewhere to stay for the next few weeks. And it wasn't as if I couldn't get hold of money, there was plenty left to survive on. I'd go out with a hat and silly glasses on and stuff like that, and getting hold of the gear wasn't a problem. I'd just stay away from my usual haunts that was all. In the end though I got fed up and came home.

What I did was to hide out in this store unit we had for the club, which was in our corridor. I filled in the door to it and papered it over so you wouldn't know it was there. Then I went round to the room behind it, the kitchen, where there was a cupboard under the kitchen sink, and I knocked a hole out at the back of the cupboard so it led back into the store unit (making sure to leave a piece of white painted wood over the hole, so anyone looking inside wouldn't even know it led into anywhere else). It was a bit cramped inside the unit but it did make a good bolt hole. I timed myself so I knew, if necessary, I could get in there in fifteen seconds, and allow another ten seconds to fit the piece of wood back to cover the hole. Remember the Old Bill wouldn't be able to knock the front door down anyway, because of the alterations I'd already done which made it like a fortress.

I always remember being in the bolt hole one day when Carol was talking in the kitchen with her friend. I just had to come out as I was bursting for a piss. Carol actually thought I'd gone out, and she was just sitting there drinking coffee with her friend, the kids were playing together (they hadn't been told about the hiding place in case they opened their mouths outside) and suddenly my head appeared from under the kitchen sink. The look on her friend's face was a picture!

Around this time I decided I'd have to get myself some new ID. I already had moody driving licences, birth certificates etc and I used these to get myself a British Visitor's Passport from the Post Office in the name of Andrew Mayton. Although Billy and my other old mates had found me a place to stay in, it didn't mean that I went back to working with them because, if I had done, they'd have soon latched on to my skag problems. Any earning I did, and I now needed to earn again due to my heavy outgoings, had to be with the circle that were into heroin. I bought the keys of a council house off a geezer in Denmark Hill and moved in, taking over the rent. This was to make it easier for me to do a bit of dealing, and have the punters come to me. I got by for a time like this, keeping a low profile with the neighbours and using my new identity. I'd go and see Carol and the family three or four times a week.

One day I was chatting to Carol about my addiction. She was desperate for me to get off the shit, and I knew how badly it was affecting me. She was telling me she was at her wit's end where I'd kept promising to do something about it, but nothing was happening. There was a knock on the door, one of the kids answered, and suddenly armed coppers were swarming all over the place. I shot out on to the fire escape, climbed onto the safety rail and jumped onto the roof. I couldn't go anywhere, just two hundred metres either way; I was about forty feet up in the air. The Old Bill was running up and down the block – this was in the middle of the estate in daytime and, as I ran backwards and forwards along the roof, they're shouting out "He's up this end, he's at that end," and so on.

I had some gear in my pocket and there was this special hole I had in the sole of the leather shoes I was wearing. I knew I wasn't going anywhere so I jumped back down onto the fire escape, laid down, then took this skag out of my pocket (it was wrapped in paper) and slid it into my shoe. Then I went back inside where the coppers were waiting for me.

"Johnny Mack?" They said.

"No, Andrew Mayton," I replied.

"Come off it mate," the geezer said.

"What do you mean, I can prove it," I said and I pulled out my driving licence, medical card and twelve month passport, even some video club cards I had. They already had a picture of me but I now looked different where I'd been on the drugs.

They kept looking at this photo and saying, "It's not him!"

I told them the reason I was there was because I was having an affair with Carol. They wanted to know why I had run away. I said that when I saw some geezers in plain clothes I thought it was Johnny Mack's mates so I legged it, then came down when I realised it was the police.

They then took the cuffs off me and I began to feel good – I was about to walk. They said, "We've still got to search the house though." Carol said for them to carry on. I'd lost my own genuine passport some time before and couldn't find the bloody thing anywhere. It had a more recent photo of me than the one they'd got, so what happens next is they go and find the fucking thing. I was gutted. In comes this copper from the other room with a big grin all over his face. He was the Det. Inspector, and he says, "Nice try, John,"

So that was it. They took me first to the local police station in Peckham, then over to Croydon where I was wanted for something else according to them. This was normal practice, to do the rounds when you were pulled in, and it could take a couple of days, depending how many different areas had unfinished business with you. Anyway I was soon reunited with the Hampshire Old Bill and taken into custody. Nigel had been bailed for the moody twenties dealing and had gone off to Cambridge and done an aggravated burglary of antiques. He was now in Bedford prison. The Old Bill tried to build up a case against me for the twenties job, and took me to just a few of the various places where I'd passed them. They tried to get me to own up, but I wasn't having any. They said they could produce witnesses, which of course they could, but I wasn't about to co-operate.

I went to court and they opposed bail, but I got it. I was shocked. One minute I was doing a runner and they're searching all over, now I get bail. The Hampshire Courts seemed like a piece of piss to me – the Old Bill had even believed I came from Bristol! Anyway I went back home and didn't have to hide out anymore, it was great.

When it came time to attend Crown Court I went on my toes again. By the way, Nigel went up and got two and a half years. He also got five years for the Cambridge robbery, to run concurrently. By now my drug habit was worse than ever and I wasn't living at home – I was at rock bottom. In the end I went to see a doctor to see if I could get any help. I poured out my heart to him, told him how I'd got started on the stuff, how bad it had become and everything. (I'd already found out that I'd have to wait at least eighteen months to get into a local treatment centre in Camberwell Green). Anyway this guy, who was a locum I'd never seen before and wore a blazer and a kind of posh yachting hat, looked at me and said, "What do you want me to do?" I was carrying a rolled up newspaper and I just started to whack him with it in sheer frustration.

I came out of the place not giving a shit. Why worry, I thought, and I hit the drugs harder than ever, going on a bender. One night I got nicked and couldn't even remember how it happened. I'd obviously put myself on offer somehow but I was just so out of it I didn't have a clue. I got whisked down to Portsmouth nick and put in a cell, and from there I went the next morning to Portsmouth Crown Court on a bench warrant as the original court I should have gone to was now in recess. I managed to get by on the drugs that I'd always keep stashed away in my shoe, but I wasn't really up for fighting the case. It seemed pointless with all the witnesses they had, so I put my hands up to it.

The judge's name was Inskip, he was an old geezer who wore a patch over his eye. He asked to have a look at one of the masses of boxes that they'd got the snide twenties in as exhibits. He said that they were the best he'd seen yet. I thought to myself 'Here we go, I'm going to cop a big one here,' but fortunately I had a right result. He only gave me two years.

Chapter Twelve

PORRIDGE AND COLD TURKEY

My main worry about going inside was that I was running out of gear. I knew I'd have to declare that I was a junkie so I could somehow get off of it. When I was taken to Winchester prison to serve my sentence I was given a form asking me whether I took drugs or had a problem with alcohol, or even whether I was homosexual – AIDS was beginning to take hold at the time. Anyway, I came clean about the drugs and said how much I was on. So, instead of the main wing, I was taken to the hospital wing. The smell there was disgusting and I was chucked into this cell. I could hear nothing but calling out and shouting from other inmates – most of them were nutters and the screams were something I'll always remember. The screws were none too sympathetic either. You got literally slung into your cell and I felt too weak and lousy to give them an argument. I saw the doctor and asked him if he was going to give me anything. He said, "Yes." Then he got the screw to bring me a jug of water. He said, "There you are, drink plenty of fluids, you'll be alright."

And that was it, no medical help to calm the cold turkey. I went into withdrawal. In a day or two my body functions began to work again, including my bowels. I only had a small chamber pot and I would fill that up, and the shit would come over the sides. It was disgusting. The screws wouldn't open the door to let me empty it so I had to put up with the stink and everything. Then, after a few days, they tried to make me come out of the cell on exercise, but the light really killed my eyes because my pupils were wide open now, instead of being pinholes. Also I felt totally disorientated and told them I just couldn't handle it. Anyway I was left alone and after a couple of weeks I began to lose the withdrawal symptoms and I started to eat. And, within about six weeks, I was back onto the main wing.

The first job I was given was mailbags. I remember the sign on the wall which said 'More bags, more fags'. I did that for a while but it wasn't my idea of fun and I managed to get another job soon after. A mate used to come and visit me and bring me some gear in – but it was only hash, which was the currency you used in there. To get it in, it was first wrapped up in clingfilm, then it was put in 'Treats' sweet packets, so when it was given to you, the screws thought you were eating sweets instead of putting blocks of cannabis in your mouth. You would have to swallow it, and then pass it out, which you'd do by getting shit tablets from the medical officer. MO, by telling him you were constipated. (You'd get another con or two to do the same, so you could use their tablets as well.) That way it would come out within five hours of your visit, in your bucket in the cell. Getting it out and washing it etc wasn't a nice job but it had to be done. And that practice is still used today.

In Winchester the four wings, A, B, C and D, were based around a central point where the screws' offices were situated. Above that centre was the labour control, which was actually operated by a con although one of the screws was in overall charge. So, once I had the currency (the cannabis), I went to the labour control geezer and told him I was pissed off with sewing mailbags. I asked if he had anything available on the garden party or something similar, but he told me I couldn't do that because I was a category-B prisoner and had to work in a secure unit. Anyway, I arranged for the geezer to get a bit of my 'blow' and he asked me how I fancied a job as a barber.

I said, "Yeah, that'll do me fine," although I'd never cut hair in my life!

He said, "Okay, you start tomorrow."

The next day I went back to the labour control centre to pick up my tools from the chief PO. I told him I was the new barber. "Oh yeah?" he says and he gives me this look as if to say, 'Well at least you won't be cutting *my* fucking hair'. He pointed out my tool box. "There you are," he says. All the stuff was there – scissors, razors, shears. Then this screw, who's really just quietly taking the piss out of me, says, "We've got someone for you. He's just about to be shipped out to Dartmoor and he needs a haircut." (At the time, this was an actual rule; transferring cons to Dartmoor had to have it done, like it or not).

I went to the guy and he turned out to be a six foot six Hell's Angel who weighed about twenty five-stone and was covered in tattoos. He stank like a sweaty sock and, instead of talking, he just growled. I said to him, "All right mate?" and he just grunted and sat down in the chair. I made a start, thinking to myself I'd have to treat this just like I would cut a hedge. After about half an hour or so, just quietly hacking away, it began to look alright. No one was more surprised than me, and the fella didn't grumble or complain at all. He just went off apparently satisfied with the job. After that I just adopted my own way of cutting hair. It wasn't the professional way; it was totally wrong, but I just seemed to get away with it. Remember I was cutting about twenty heads a day so I soon got quite confident.

One day I was walking to the exercise yard with a couple of armed robbers I'd met and they were playfully taking the piss out of my barbering skills. (Neither of them, by the way, would let me touch their hair). One of them said, "We can tell that you're the barber." I asked why. He said, "Have a look down there," and he pointed down to the exercise yard in front of us where the cons were all walking clockwise in these circles within circles. (That's how they did their exercise – the fitter ones on the bigger outer circuits and the others on the smaller inner ones). And all these cons looked so similar it was weird – you couldn't help noticing that they all had the same haircuts. "They look like they're all wearing syrups," this robber was saying, "and you expect us to let you touch our fucking hair…?"

The screws would laugh and take the piss a bit as well, and it became a bit of a joke. But it was the only way I knew. And the great thing about the barber job was that, when they trusted me a bit more, I was given a category-C, which meant that I could now go all over the prison to cut hair – like in the clothing store, the kitchens, the boiler house etc., and not just stay in the centre. I had a timetable so, for example, Mondays I would go on B-wing and cut the cleaners' hair in the morning, then go on to the clothing store for the afternoon, and so on. So I began to get around quite a bit more. And, as a barber, I wasn't often searched, which meant I could deliver stuff around the nick. Even if I *was* searched, I'd already have taken the precaution of having the gear, tobacco or whatever, stuck up my arse in a tube like a cigar holder, and attached to string so I could pull it down.

Another perk I had when I began to improve in the job was the means to earn myself extra baccy. I'd say to a con (even though they were all entitled to free haircuts). "What do you want, the standard, or the quarter ounce?"

He'd say, "What's the standard?" and I'd point out some con or other who was passing and say, "Like that."

When he saw it he'd say something like, "Fucking hell. No, I'll go for the quarter ounce mate." And then I'd take that bit longer with him and give him as decent a cut as I could, earning myself another quarter ounce of baccy to add to my supply. By the way, we were only allowed to keep a couple of ounces of baccy at any one time, but I'd have loads of it spread all round the nick. What I'd do was go to see these geezers who'd just been given a short term sentence – say two or three weeks for not paying a fine, or maintenance, or poll tax etc and find a non-smoker. Then I'd ask him if he'd look after my baccy and, in return, give him a couple of Mars bars or whatever. They'd be as pleased as punch. I'd only pick people who were not likely to fuck me over; after all a half ounce of Golden Virginia or Old Holborn in those days was worth a tenner inside. So, what with the baccy and the puff I was shifting, I became quite happy in my work.

There were some Iranian terrorists in Winchester at the time in A-wing. They'd let off a car bomb in London. They'd been in Parkhurst originally but had been shipped out to A-wing (which was down in the basement) as punishment. This was the usual practice when someone kicked off in the major prisons – they'd come to this wing as punishment. I got called to come down and cut their hair. I met all sorts there, including the geezer who killed the two little girls in a quarry in a well-publicised case in the sixties. He was a total pig.

Wednesday mornings was my time to go on the 'twos' in A-wing, where there was a landing for blokes on 'Rule 43' – in other words the 'nonces' What I'd like to have done when I cut their hair was to stab the fuckers with my scissors but, where I was trusted, I knew I'd better behave. So I had a go at them by charging them half ounce for their cuts instead of the normal quarter. And, instead of taking extra time like I did for the others, I'd just chop it off any old how and call that it. To be honest, I'd wet their hair then cut it unevenly, taking a few patches and lumps off, soak it again, then comb it back behind their ears and everything, so it looked quite smart. But when it dried out it would frizz up and there'd be chunks and lumps and all sorts, and it would look fucking horrible. But at least I did treat all of them the same! And it made up a bit for having to go in there, because sometimes the bastards would even be proud of themselves and their reputations. They'd say, "Do you know who I am?" and stuff like that.

I remember one guy who had come down from Wakefield where he'd done ten years already for raping a young girl, and for murder, I believe. He started telling me what he'd done and how he'd done it and I got very angry with the fucker. I had these scissors held firmly in my hand and I was dying to stick them straight through his ear into his brain. I just had to walk out to stop myself. I went to the screw's office and said, "Look, I just can't cut this cunt's hair; he's telling me all about what he did."

The screw said, "Oh, he's not doing it again is he? Well I don't blame you mate, just leave it." I couldn't deal with evil fuckers like that, not without having a go at them.

One good thing about Winchester was that there was not much in the way of hard drugs. There was plenty of puff, and most people enjoyed a smoke, but it wasn't like Brixton where you could get anything. Mind you, I could afford most things I wanted in Winchester due to my tobacco earnings. Another little sideline I had was dirty books. Again, where I knew and mixed with a lot of people, I'd ask cons who were being released to send me dirty books to add to my little library. Lots of them would forget, but quite a few didn't and I'd take them around the nick. Razzle and Playboy and stuff like that I'd get, and I would rent them out, say seven books for a week – one a night – would cost them a quarter of an ounce. I'd also help myself to any food I wanted from the kitchen – I never went hungry.

And another perk I had was the luxury of a single cell. Mind you I had to fight for that one because they put some geezer in my cell that was only doing about three weeks, and he kept crying and getting on my fucking nerves. I had to break his bed and kick up a fuss so that, in the end, they took him out and just left me on my own – which was how I liked it.

After I'd done six months, I came back to my cell one day and a chitty had been left for me telling me I was being transferred to Dartmoor. As I was now a category-C prisoner I complained to the governor because Dartmoor was for cat-A and cat-B prisoners. Not that I was too bothered about that, but the last thing I wanted was to be shipped out of a place where I'd got things organised to suit me. The governor said he'd look into it, but I didn't expect much help from him – I was used to the system and had been palmed off before. I had a chat with the probation officer and he phoned Carol for me. She then contacted our local MP, who was Harriet Harman, and it was made clear to her that it would cause hardship and inconvenience for me to go right out to Dartmoor. Anyway, Harriet Harman contacted the governor and, in the end, the decision was changed and I ended up doing all my time (sixteen months) in Winchester, which suited me fine.

The week before I came out, I went to D-wing to cut a guy's hair. D-wing was for un-convicted prisoners on remand, who were allowed to wear civvies and had other privileges. One of these privileges was to have cigarettes and not just baccy like us. Anyway this guy paid me for the haircut with five cigarettes, and a screw caught me with them on me, so next day, I was on governor's report. The governor said, didn't I realise that the fags were contraband, and I said, "Well sir, *you* must give *your* barber a tip – and that's all it was, a tip!" But it was no good. I lost the job and a week's earnings, and just had to stay in my cell that last week at the prison. It was twenty-three hour bang-up, but I had a good book to read and what the fuck did I care anyway? I knew I'd be out in seven days.

When I got back home I made up my mind not to go back on the gear. I'd been working out in the prison gym doing weights and I felt fine. But I began to go and see Byron again. I started off having a bit of charlie but then, with seeing him more and more, I got back onto the smack. This time it was with a vengeance, worse than before. I did notice though that a few of my mates, who were dead against skag at the time I went inside, were now on it themselves. Eddie Mitchell was one.

Things went downhill for me quickly. I lost my self-esteem; I didn't give a fuck about my appearance, whereas before I'd always been very smart. I found myself in all sorts of dives and shitholes, in a trance really, mixing with scumbags and skagheads. I tried to open the club again but it only lasted a couple of days because I couldn't be bothered to go and get the booze in. Carol was at her wit's end. She'd seen me like this before and had to suffer all the aggravation. When she caught me taking the drugs I'd lie to her about what I was taking, telling her it was an antidote, and so on. Finally she told me she'd leave me if I didn't do something about the problem.

I'd got so paranoid that I reactivated the electric fence at the back of the fire escape, shit-scared that someone would get in – there were a lot of dead pigeons at the bottom which would land on the thing and get fried. Anyway, one morning I just looked at myself in the mirror. I was going out and had put on these Prince of Wales check trousers that I hadn't worn for sometime. I'd lost so much weight now that they were just falling off me. I looked like a sunken-cheeked, staring-eyed sack of shit, and I became very emotional and broke down. I knew something had to be done, I had found doom.

I went to see a friend of mine called Ian who was completely straight – he didn't do any thieving or anything and was a really genuine geezer. I told him I had to do something about my problem. He told me he had a flat that he was moving out of, that I was welcome to use for a couple of weeks to get away from everything, and to get myself straight. I told Carol what I was doing and she went to the south coast to stay with my mum and dad for a little while. I put myself into this flat and told no one apart from Ian and another geezer called Steve, who was a big-time drug dealer who I'd been best man for at his wedding. I needed someone to know where I was and keep an eye on me because I knew I was going to get in a state.

The first night I went in I took my last bit of gear, and drank a bottle of Pernod. The next morning I woke up with a bad headache and, where the booze had made me sleep a little longer, I was already into withdrawal. I began to get the shits and knew things were starting up. Within a day I was on the floor. I couldn't walk and I couldn't talk. I was in a kind of haze, not really knowing what I was doing. I had a gas fire that I'd filled up with fifty pence pieces when I went in. I came to one night, and the fire was out and I was freezing, as it was mid-winter. I managed to crawl to the gas meter and I tried to break the lock off, but had nothing with me to do the job properly plus I was weak. I ended up smashing the meter and broke off the weakest part where you insert the coins. Luckily enough the casing came off, which meant I could just click the switch up so I had a continuous supply of gas to stop me shivering and shaking.

The whole withdrawal was like a bad dream, a nightmare. I could barely move, I couldn't sleep, I didn't know what day it was, or even where the fuck I was. Although the front door was left unlocked there was no way I was going anywhere. After about six or seven days I began to feel slightly better because the hallucinations started to ease. I heard a knock on the door and it was Steve. He told me that he'd come to see how I was, but within a short time the real reason for his visit came out. He had a deal going down that night and he needed my help. He must have known by looking at me that I was in no state to help anyone. And, from my past experience at Winchester, I realised that I was within a few days of getting straight, and there was no way I was going to fuck that up for anything. But the snaky bastard didn't care about that, and he did something that proved it. The fucker actually got out a bag of skag and put it on the table in front of me. Although I didn't have much strength, I had enough to tell him to take the bag and to fuck off out of it. He tried to apologise, but I couldn't forget what he'd done. He'd proved that his deal was far more important to him than thinking about my health and our friendship.

After ten days in the flat, I had my first good night's sleep – without the dreams and the sweats I'd been suffering. When I woke up I was starving, because anything I'd tried to eat before I'd just puked up, or shit out straight away. I felt a lot better. I went round to see a friend of mine, a brilliant girl called Sue (the one who used to come to the club that I mentioned earlier). I knew I could trust Sue. She was white but mixed a lot with the black fraternity and went out with a yardie geezer. When she saw me, she served up this shepherd's pie meal for me – although it was really meant for the yardie geezer! She also gave me some of his puff which she said would settle me down.

She did her nut a bit about me not telling her I was staying nearby, because she would have brought me stuff round and looked after me. But I knew I'd done the right thing by staying on my own - to get the job done properly.

I felt really chuffed now that I was back on track and I phoned Carol to tell her I was off the shit. My clothes were falling off me, and I knew I needed to get away from the flat, so I got in touch with Carol's brother in Bermondsey who arranged for me to stay with him and his family. They knew the score, and I was fed well by his wife for two or three weeks until Carol and I got together again. I didn't want to do anything to upset Carol after all the aggro she'd had, so I decided to stay away from crime for a bit. I got myself a motor and went cabbing. But I couldn't forget some of the people who'd shat on me, as I saw it. And one of them was Steve. Big, muscular, expensively dressed, Desperate Dan look-alike. He was doing very nicely now thank you, while I was not earning anything like what I'd been used to. I'd helped him out over a job when we first met, then we'd become real good mates, with me best man at his wedding and godfather to his kids. I'd always thought of him as a decent bloke, but now I saw things a lot differently. And that could only lead to trouble.

Chapter Thirteen

PAY BACK

Steve was a dealer, a guy who looked down on users – he'd just turned to drugs as an easier and more profitable option than going out doing blags. But, believe it or not, he was the only person I've ever known who drank puff. He'd buy a quarter of 'squidgy black' as we called it, or cannabis resin, which was very soft and oily, and he'd break it up and pour boiling water and some coffee onto it in a mug and just drink it like coffee. There'd be a big film of the stuff left in the bottom that you could have taken out and smoked. He'd always mixed with his own type: armed robbers, hi-jackers and the like, and despised drug users, as many of his kind did. Just to prove what a macho (and stupid) kind of geezer he was, he named his kid Rocky because the *Rocky* films were very popular at the time. He was tied up with a little crew from Bermondsey but, even though we'd been friends, was always careful not to give too much away about his contacts.

Steve would occupy my thoughts while I was doing the cabbing, and, now that my brain was beginning to function a whole lot better now, I began to think how nice it would be to use him the way he'd tried to use me, so I could get back on my feet and back with Carol and the kids. Remember, I was still sleeping on the floor at my brother-in-law's place and wasn't earning big money. Now that Carol had decided to leave the inner city environment once and for all, I'd had to get rid of the club, so there was no extra income to come from that now.

I'd done Steve a few favours in my time and the bastard didn't know how much he'd hurt me by throwing that bag of skag on the table when I was at my most vulnerable. And he wanted me to get up and make contact with some people I knew, that he didn't, to do his drug deal for him. Steve's name was at the top of a list I made out, a list of scumbag dealers who I felt had taken advantage of me in the past. They were low-life fuckers most of them that I wouldn't have spat on if they were on fire, but I'd had to treat them with respect and, yes, even grovel to them at times, just to get my gear.

A few weeks after my cold turkey session I still looked thin and drawn and I still had the yellow complexion. This actually suited me because, as part of the plan I had in mind, I wanted people to think I was still dabbling in the drugs. I started to mix on the circuit again and visit places that I knew Steve went to. I knew that Steve had only told a couple of people about me trying to get straight, so no one was that surprised that I was still on the scene. I would make out that I was still having a line here and there just to make it all seem kosher.

When I saw Steve he was, at first, a bit offish with me because he was expecting some sort of reaction after our little falling out. But I just acted as though I had forgiven and forgotten it all. I let him think that all I was after now was the chance to get out there and make a nice few quid from the drugs. But what I really had in mind was doing my best to set the bastard up.

An old mate from my earlier days as a burglar, Johnny Salter, was my accomplice in the scheme. When I was, for example, having a beer with Steve, Johnny (who Steve didn't know) would come in and throw a bag full of money over for me to check. I'd take the money out and there'd be, say, four big wads of notes wrapped in elastic bands, each wad being about five grand. At least that was what it would look like – really they were just paper with twenty pound notes wrapped around the outside. Steve soon got the impression that I was doing alright for myself and the bastard began to change his attitude – he couldn't get enough of me now. The hook was out and he was starting to take the bait.

Not that he wasn't a shrewd operator. This particular night, in a club where you could snort cocaine on the tables, Steve offered me a line but I noticed that he didn't take one himself. I gave him some money to go to the bar to get a drink and, when he turned to go, I made a snorting noise but brushed the coke off the table with my hand. He had wanted to loosen my tongue and was trying to find out more about how he could get into the operation that he thought I had, so he could rip me off. But he wasn't the only one scheming and I was determined to get the better of him.

When he came back from the bar I told him that I was in a position to get hold of some nice gear, and he said that his people should be able to move it. We agreed that he should have a chat with them and that I'd speak to my 'people' so a deal could be worked out. He had no idea that I was living in Bermondsey with Carol's brother and I decided to go on nights for a spell, with the taxi driving, so there was no way he could get in touch. There were no mobile phones then, and he couldn't contact me through the club anymore. I did a week of nights, so I could send some money to Carol, but I knew somehow that Steve would manage to track me down.

At the weekend I was sitting in the Close Encounters club in Forest Hill, with Johnny Salter, when he came in. I just couldn't help but smirk and said to Johnny, "I told you he'd be back."

Johnny said, "Yep, he's bitten mate"

"Where've you been then?" Steve wanted to know. "I've been looking everywhere for you."

I told him that I'd spent a few days dealing in Amsterdam. He swallowed it, because it was what he wanted to hear. He treated us to drinks that night and even wanted to talk business there and then.

I said, "Come on, you know the score Steve, we can't talk here. We'll need a proper meet in private." We agreed to meet the next day at his place.

I went over to Steve's alone because Johnny was keeping in the background as far as the business side was concerned. Steve told me that he wanted five kilos of heroin. We agreed on a price of fifteen grand a kilo, which was very cheap. I knew that he'd try and rip off his own people for some of the money at this sort of price by telling them it was eighteen grand a kilo, or whatever. Plus, they would be paying him for making the deal. So the carrot that we dangled for him was a big one.

A few days later we had another meet and Steve said that his guys wanted a sample. For this you needed to give, say, half an ounce – it was no good giving just a line, you had to show you had plenty of gear, otherwise the buyers would get suspicious. I didn't have the money to go and buy half an ounce of gear so I had to think of some other way, and I told Steve I'd be in touch. When I discussed it with

Johnny he came up with a classic. "How many dealers have you dealt with this last year?" he asked me. I told him quite a few. He said "How many of them are still operating?" I said most were. He said "There's your answer then – we'll get some off them!"

We decided to hit a guy who was an Irish dealer and user who lived on Dog Kennel Hill in East Dulwich, in an old tenement housing estate where Charlie and Eddie Richardson once lived. Johnny checked the geezer out and came and told me he was still operating. He'd just bought a new Mercedes, Johnny said. He and his missus had all the expensive clothes and jewellery to go with it, even though they both still managed to look exactly what they were – the scum of the earth.

I went to see a user I knew, who used this geezer, taking with me this bag full of a light-brown mixture of instant coffee and marvel that had been ground right down to make it look like skag. I asked him if he knew anyone who might want this 'gear', which I told him was Persian – Persian gear being that same shade of light brown, and free of all the glucose and other shit that made skag look dark. This guy was impressed with what he saw and said, "Yeah, I know someone who'll have that." I couldn't go direct to the Irish dealer because he'd supplied me in the past and would have smelt a rat.

So it was agreed that this user would go to him to discuss a deal. We arranged to meet the following day, and this was when the user told me that our dealer friend was keen. In fact he'd do it straight away, I was told, the only stipulation being that the dealer (me) had to be there, and because there was no way that he was going to just give the money to a user (him) on trust. This of course was understandable. So we arranged the deal for the next day at the user's place.

I arrived early and went inside with the user, but made sure to leave the door on the latch. This was so Johnny could get in shortly after and hide himself in the bathroom. Then the user asked if it was okay to give himself a fix, which he did right there in front of me. Remember it was only a few weeks since I'd got clean and when I saw the geezer injecting himself I felt this terrific rage come over me – I could have stuck the fucking needle straight through his eye. But, of course, I had to control myself.

Then there was a knock on the door and this Irish dealer/user came in. He looked a right fucking mess. He had expensive shoes on which were all scuffed up, expensive trousers which you could see he had been sleeping in every night, and an Yves St Laurent shirt that stank to high heaven. His skinny, bony hands had gold and diamond rings on which were almost falling off where they were too big for him. You could see that he'd made an effort to try and look the part. He sat on an old pouffe. I was sitting on the edge of the user's bed and the user was on the floor.

This Irish dealer guy looked at me as if to say 'I fucking know you don't I?' but I never said a word. I just plonked the 'gear' on the table and said, "There it is, then." Then we put it on the scales that the user had there, and it came to twenty nine and a half grammes, allowing one and half grammes for the plastic wrapping on it. So, the guy was happy that he had his ounce – now he wanted to try it out. I said, "Okay, sure, you try it." I was looking at the door behind him as he undid the wrapping. Then Johnny came creeping in – he was such an experienced burglar that he could be in the same room as you and you wouldn't know he was there. The user was well out of it on the floor after taking his fix.

Johnny came up behind the Irishman and I sat well back on the bed – not wanting to get splashed! Then Johnny's baseball bat whacked the geezer round the side of the head. As he hit the floor Johnny and I jumped on top of him. The one thing I knew about dealers who were also users was that they always carried their stash with them at all times (except when at home, where they would hide it away). Sure enough the guy had it on him. And it was this stash that we needed to use as a sample for the Steve deal. (If he *hadn't* been carrying, our plan was to take him back to his place, and make him tell us where the drugs were).

Fortunately for us, as well as his drugs he was also carrying his money – about fifteen hundred quid. It wasn't a fortune but I was grateful for anything at that time. We also helped ourselves to his rings and jewellery. We then tied him up, along with the other geezer, and we left them there. One thing I did do though was to make sure that the other geezer (the user) got something for helping us to set up the deal. He was face downwards on the deck with his hands and feet tied together behind him, bondage style. I took a teaspoonful of skag from the dealer's stash and put it on a piece of paper, then placed it in front of him on the floor. There he was, shoulders pulled back where his hands were tied up behind, straining to get his nose down to the floor to have a sniff. The next bit I couldn't believe. The poor sick bastard, looked up at me, and he said, "Thanks!"

We shared the money out between us and I let Johnny keep the 'tom'. And, of course, we now had the skag to use as a sample. Johnny was well pleased and up for doing this every day! I contacted Steve the next day to arrange a meet, met him later on that day, and gave him his sample (which I'd already checked out, and there was no doubting that it was good stuff.) The fact that I never asked for a deposit on the half ounce I gave him made it look as though I had shit-loads of the stuff, and I could tell by his manner that he really thought he was on to a mega earner here. I doubt whether he gave his people the full amount anyway – knowing him he probably kept half of it back to cut and then sell on the Albany estate where he lived. It didn't take him long to get back to me after that anyway. He was all over me to make a deal, he couldn't wait.

His next thing I did was to make contact with a guy I'll just refer to as Jack. Jack was the diamond geezer who I've already mentioned I served time with in Brixton prison. When we were there we had both mixed with Charlie Wilson, the great train robber. Jack was what I'd call a real gentleman villain – you knew you could rely on him a hundred percent and there weren't too many like that in our game. He was a very clever man and lived in the Chelsea area, but I'm not going to go any further than that about his identity. Jack had access to quite a few properties because he used to take over houses by sending people in to squat them, and then, once taken over, he'd rent them out. At that time the council used to take about six months to get people out through eviction orders, and this was a nice scam.

I went over to Chelsea to see Jack and I asked him if he had a place I could use to do a bit of business in – somewhere there wouldn't be any comebacks over. He asked whereabouts I needed it. When I told him, he said he could fix me up with one just around the corner from Dog Kennel Hill. Jack gave me the key to this place, a council maisonette with not much in it apart from an old sofa. Johnny Salter and I cleaned the place up a bit, put a TV and some other stuff in and generally made it look as though it was lived in. I invited Steve over to the place to talk business, and to make it appear as though that was where I was living now. I had my dog Bullseye, a Staffordshire bull terrier, with me as well to make things look even more kosher. Steve wasn't stupid and did mention that the place looked a bit bare, but I told him I'd only just bought the rent book and moved in so I hadn't had much chance to do a lot. He seemed convinced by this. Anyway, we agreed we'd do the deal two days later, here at my 'new home'.

The block which my maisonette was in could only be accessed by car from one direction, so it happened that if you wanted to park up and not look too conspicuous, then you had to use this particular car port at the entrance to the estate. At that time the Special Patrol Group would patrol the area and, if there were two or more blokes in a car together, then they'd be likely to get a tug. So Steve, especially if he was carrying a lot of money with him, would be anxious not to make himself conspicuous. Johnny and I had done our homework well and we knew you could see this car port from the window of the maisonette. We also knew that the estate had an escape route out, which you could use if you were on foot.

On the day I was ready in the place and, from my window, I saw Steve get out of a car which had two other guys in it. He was carrying a bag which, obviously, had the money in it. He came in the direction of my place, but when he made to come in to the under side of the flats, I lost sight of him. I knew how long it should take for him to come up the four flights of stairs to the balcony and then walk along to me. What should have taken about half a minute took him four minutes, and I knew then what he was up to. Not only was he out of my sight for those four minutes, he was also out of sight of his two guys in the car. This meant to me straightaway that he'd told his people that the skag was to cost more than I was actually charging him - now he was ripping them off by taking the balance of cash out of this big paper carrier bag he had and stashing it away on the stairs, his pocket or wherever.

When Steve came into my place, he looked around a bit suspiciously. I said, "Look Steve, there's no one else here, it's just you and me. We're mates, aren't we? There's nothing to worry about." He asked if I had the gear. I said, "Yes, I've got the gear, Steve, but not *here*."

"Where is it then?" he said.

"It's no more than five hundred yards down the road with my people, in the car," I said.

He told me he wasn't happy with the arrangement.

"What do you want me to do Steve? I've only got to go out the back way – your people aren't going to see me go, then I'll be back in a few minutes with the stuff. But my people won't part with that gear until they see the money." I said.

"I don't like this… I don't like it," he said

I told him that it was up to him – if he didn't want to do it, to go back and tell his people the deal was off. Then I said, "Think about it, my people don't know you. They're not going to just part with five kilos at this price without the cash. Think of the street value of the stuff compared to what you're paying for it." In the end I convinced him. He handed me the carrier bag. He had this sad look on his face. He said, "I've got a bad feeling about this."

"Look Steve, the only bad feeling you'll have is if you take this bag back to them and tell them it's off," I said.

I knew, in the end, the greed would get to him. And I knew also that he had a few debts of his own, so the last thing he wanted was to lose out. He reluctantly let go of the bag. I said, "I'll be five minutes."

"Okay, okay," he said.

I went out the back way and the dog followed me. I left Steve with the TV going and the kettle on for him to make a drink. When I got to the agreed place, Johnny was in the car waiting for me and the dog jumped straight through the open window as if to say, 'Let's go boys!' I got into the passenger seat. Johnny said, "Did you get it?"

I winked at him. "Spot on, mate," I said.

He started to shout out, "Whoa, what a fucking result –we've fucking done it." And away we went.

We split the seventy-five grand between us, Johnny and I, Johnny went his way, and I took a trip down to the coast. I met up with Carol and she was delighted that not only did I have plenty of money for the family now, but also that I was clear of drugs. After a few weeks with Carol and the family – spent buying essentials, plus a few treats like a new motor for me – I went back to London. Steve seemed to have disappeared altogether. My best guess was that he had taken what money he'd put aside from the deal for himself, got his wife and kids and fucked off somewhere, because there was no way that the two guys in the car would have stood for being ripped off, and he daren't have gone back to them. But I never saw the geezer again so I'll never know what he did. Even Johnny's discreet enquiries led nowhere.

I asked Johnny how he felt about doing a bit more work together. He was well up for it. I then got hold of Jack to see if he could fix me up with another place (by the way I had slipped him a grand for his help with the last place, and he'd been well happy with that). I told Jack I wanted something just on a temporary basis and he found me a nice two-bedroomed place in north Dulwich, near Dulwich College. It was definitely a better class area – Margaret Thatcher had a place not too far away. Nobody knew I was living there – not even Johnny. This, I decided, was going to be my base.

I also decided that I was going to do some chauffeur/cabbing – not locally but in the West End, now that I had a nice car. I only worked about five hours a night but I'd pull in about a hundred and fifty quid. The cabbing was also good because I looked on it as part of my rehabilitation from the drugs. And, of course, it was a way of keeping my head down. I couldn't go out socialising because of what I'd done to Steve, word would have got round that Johnny Mack was about and there might have been one or two faces that'd had a stake in his drug operation who would want to put a bullet in me. So I kept to the West End, where I wasn't well-known, and this nice quiet place I had in north Dulwich. Mind you, that didn't mean that, during the day, Johnny and me didn't meet up and do our plotting for more scams.

I loved Johnny – he could be a bastard if he was your enemy but the pair of us got on like a house on fire. He came up with an idea that we should do the Irish dealer again. I said, "We can't use the same scam again, mate," but he said not to worry – we'd use a different one this time. I argued that the geezer had probably learned a bit from last time. "The fuckers never learn," he said, "Come on – let's do it."

So, what we came up with was this. After digging out some old search warrants I had (the Old Bill always gave you a copy when they searched your house) we took one and tippexed out my name and the officer's name. Then we photocopied the form, so we had a nice new looking one, and put the Irish geezer's name and address on it. We got hold of a Metropolitan Police card, cut the symbol off and put this on another card with a moody photo and details, so that it looked like a genuine warrant card. Then we went out and watched the Irish guy, from a distance, for a couple of days – this was quite easy on the estate. And we didn't have to watch all day or anything because, like most skag heads, he didn't get out of bed until about two in the afternoon. He would start dealing about five, then at nine he'd lock his door and flake out for the evening. We'd watch people trooping in to get their gear and estimate how much each had spent – twenty here, twenty there – 'Mmm, that one could be a hundred', and so on.

Then it was time to put the plan into action. At about eight one morning, both dressed in long black macs, we went to his house. It had a solid door with a spy hole. We put a bit of tape over the spy hole and banged loudly. We could hear a lot of scuffling about inside – people getting up, doors banging. An Irish accented voice shouted "Who is it?" I said, "It's the police". More scuffling around. We could picture them, the dealer, and his missus, stashing their gear away. Then he came to the door, tried to look through the spy hole but couldn't see, and asked for our warrant, which I shoved through the letter box. Putting on a fake accent I said, "If you don't open the door it will be broken down." The door opened but the chain was left on as the dealer tried to squint round to see us.

Johnny didn't hesitate. His foot crashed into the door knocking it back to smash the Irishman on the head. He fell backwards and I saw that he was bleeding. Johnny jumped on him and dragged him up the three or four steps to his living room. There was a mattress on the floor with a filthy old duvet on it and, under that, an ugly old tart with no clothes on. The place stank to fuck. The geezer couldn't look at us because he was concussed, the claret still running into his eyes. I said to the old tart that she was under arrest, and that she must tell us where the drugs were, otherwise we would take the place apart. She mumbled something about not knowing what we were talking about. To me something was definitely wrong. Skag heads would not normally get undressed to go to bed like ordinary people. They sleep in their clothes and just doze.

By now the Irishman was face downwards on the deck, blood running out of his head, Johnny was standing beside me, and the old tart was still lying there. I just picked up the end of the mattress and yanked it upwards. The old tart rolled backwards down it and hit the wall behind her. Underneath the mattress was this pile of notes – fivers, tenners, the lot. Johnny started scooping it all up, while the woman just lay there against the wall. At this point the geezer staggered to his feet. He said "Just a minute – you're not Old Bill!"

"No, we're fucking not. And you didn't take any notice of what you were told last time either." I said. (I'd warned the prick last time that he'd better move out of the area, because there were too many shit-heads like him around polluting the place). I said to him, "This time we're going to take all your money *and* your drugs. But we'll be back, and if you haven't left the area by then we'll just fucking shoot you." The message seemed to get home.

"I'll leave, I'll leave," he said.

I asked him where his gear was. He said, "I ain't got any." I looked at Johnny and he looked at me. I turned to the geezer again.

"I'm going to ask you just one more time, and that's it. Now – understand what I'm saying to you. Just *one* more time. If I get the wrong answer he (I indicated Johnny) is going to do something terrible to you. Now (I spoke very slowly, emphasising each word) – *where is your stash*?" I said. He gave me the same answer. Johnny opened up his mac and he produced the biggest machete you've ever seen. He walked straight at the Irishman, brandishing it, and the guy, his face already covered in blood, screamed out, "No, the toilet, the toilet."

We found about six ounces in the cistern. We took that, and the money of course, but the guy begged us to leave him just enough skag to get himself straight on. I looked at Johnny and he said, "Well, we've had a good result, so why not?" We gave him some powder, maybe a couple of grammes, and he actually thanked us – much the same as had happened with the user we'd tied up before. Again, I could see the funny side of this. But I certainly felt no pity for the prick.

So we walked out of the door with about five grand, plus the powder. I had to get rid of the skag, because I didn't want the fucking stuff near me – that was how I felt about it now. So I told Johnny to take it and get the best deal he could on it. The cash we split straight down the middle just like before. I went down to the coast again for a couple of weeks to give things a chance to quieten down and Johnny managed to cash in on the skag.

After this I returned to my place in north Dulwich. I was beginning to feel quite good by now – my health was definitely improving and I was doing some gym work, and had a punch bag fixed up at home. I was eating well and also taking protein supplements and so on. I began to feel like the old Johnny Mack again. Soon I contacted Johnny Salter and he gave me half of what he'd made from selling off the skag.

He said to me, "Who are we going to do next then, mate? There must be plenty of other dealers out there." I told him, yes there were, and asked him, out of interest, which he'd done business with to move this last bit of gear. It came out that he'd sold some of it to this student in Camberwell. Johnny said the guy was quite well connected as the stuff was going into colleges. I suggested it might be worth paying him a call, as he didn't know me from Adam. Johnny agreed. The guy had only had a couple of ounces from us but it had been good stuff, so the geezer's dealer had probably cut it, made a good profit, and would be keen to get hold of some more.

Johnny went to see the student and suggested that the guy's supplier might like to buy another lot of gear. The student agreed to make contact and, a couple of days later, he told Johnny yes – his man was interested. The guy wanted half a kilo, Johnny learned. So, again we knocked up our little mixture of coffee and Marvel, and we put it in two plastic bags which were vacuum packed and sealed with a heat wire to look like proper bags of heroin. We arranged a meet at the student's place and we got there early and waited in the car so we could see the other guys turn up and go into this tower block. Sure enough the student arrived and went in; he had an Asian guy with him who wore a turban.

After a couple of minutes Johnny and I went into the block and up the stairs. The place was nearly all bedsits for students. We knocked on the door. The student answered. Johnny introduced me as his supplier and the student said his man was inside, and for us to come and meet him. Inside was just like a normal bed-sit with kitchen, and the guy in the turban was sitting there. He nodded and we just quickly said hello. I asked him if he had the money with him and he said, "Yes, have you got the drugs?" I could tell that they weren't used to this sort of meeting – I was dealing with amateurs here. There was a bit of an awkward silence and no attempt was being made to produce any money.

Johnny wasn't an amateur though and he knew when to take over. He slapped the student hard across the face with the flat of his hand. "What's going on," he demanded, "are you trying to fuck us about or what?" The guy with the turban made to leave but I stood in front of the door. I said, "Where the fuck do you think you're going?" He started to protest, saying he didn't want to do the deal. They hadn't met the likes of us before and were obviously just used to dealing with students. Johnny came over to the Asian guy and started searching him. All he had on him was about thirty quid.

I began to think that maybe we'd been invited there just to get skanked. I turned up the volume on the radio that was playing, to drown out any sound, and then me and Johnny started to push the Asian guy around a bit. But he wouldn't tell us where the money was or what was going on. All this time the student was sat there quietly on the bed after being told to shut up or else. Then Johnny pulled out this two pound club hammer and biffed the Asian guy on top of his turban. The turban cushioned the blow, but it cushioned it a bit too well. There was something wrong, I could tell. I yanked the turban off of his head and there was a pile of notes underneath. Johnny half laughed at this. "Nice one," he said, "What a fucking place to hide it!"

The Asian guy sat with the student on the bed as we started to count the notes up. Only half of it was there. What the fuck was going on here, I wondered. I said to the Asian, "What were you going to do then, only buy half the gear?"

"No, no," he said.

I was starting to get pissed off. "What's all this fucking 'no, no' – what *was* your fucking plan then?" He recoiled onto the bed while we intimidated him. Suddenly I noticed, on the headboard, this line of what I thought was cotton. And this line went to the window, which was only about a foot away. I was suspicious and pulled at it. It wasn't cotton but fishing line. I pulled up the window that it led to and then tugged on the line. Up came this bag and in it was the other half of the money. The Asian's face dropped. When Johnny had finished bawling him out, I said to him, "Look, I'll tell you what I'm going to do with you. You're a slippery bastard and you don't deserve to get treated right, but I'm going to give you a chance. Now, how fast can you run?"

"How fast? Run?" He didn't understand at all. I said, "Right then, here's your gear." And I threw it straight out of the open window and down into the street. He was off the bed, out of the door and down the stairs like a shot from a gun. He had a long overcoat and you could hear him almost tripping over it on the stairs as he dashed down. We went out behind him, got in our car and off we went, still laughing our bollocks off.

I went back to north Dulwich and lay up for a couple of days. Even Johnny didn't know my address and, while we were in this game, that was the best way to keep things. Johnny was a diamond I know, and he could be trusted, but if you had your head screwed on, you stuck by the tried and tested code that the likes of us all lived by. Friendship was one thing but it paid you to keep your privacy when it came to where you were shacked up.

Johnny, of course, was all for doing some more earning together. Like many of the big villains of the time, he fancied getting a caravan at Leysdown, near Margate. It was the place to be, except for those who were on the run from the law, of course, and most of them were in Spain. I never really knew that much about what Johnny got up to when we weren't working together but I knew that he wasn't short of a few bob, and I knew that he looked after his family well.

So, even though Johnny was keen to do some more dealers, I gave things a few more weeks to settle down. After all, these people were not stupid and, once the word had got around about what was happening, you'd be silly to push your luck too far. Eventually I got hold of Johnny and told him there was one guy in particular who I'd like to get a payback on. He was called 'Irish George' and, as it happened, he was another geezer who lived on Dog Kennel Hill. I'd known Irish George since before I got started on the gear and, in those days, he was very intimidated by me – I could literally order him about and tell him what, and what not, to do. When I got on the gear though, the tables turned and he took full advantage of the situation. I remember selling a lot of my furniture to him for silly prices to get drugs.

I also remembered going to Utrecht with him once to a car auction – he wanted me there as I knew about cars – and him bidding for, and getting, a Mercedes. We brought the car back on the ferry and I showed him how to get through customs without paying import duty – it involved taking the bumper off and sending it by post.

When we came back via the Hook of Holland we missed the boat and had to wait twelve hours for the next one. I ran out of gear, and it was too far to go back to Amsterdam to get some. So, I had to sweat it out on the ferry and go through a spell of cold turkey - because George said he didn't have any drugs. By the time we got on the train from Felixstowe to London I was in a bad way. But George, who had as big a habit as I did, was fine. So I knew that he must be getting himself sorted by chasing the dragon when he went out to the toilet. As long as he was okay the slippery bastard hadn't given a fuck about how I felt. So, for this alone, I reckoned I had good reason to take revenge. And I also wanted revenge on his suppliers, a Jamaican crew who had blokes like George all over south London selling their powder.

I warned Johnny that we would have to be extra careful on this one and, as it turned out, I had every reason to be cautious. When I told him about Irish George, he surprised me by telling me that he actually knew the geezer. I said, "Alright Johnny, the best thing is for you to stay on the sidelines. As long as you're handy in the car, somewhere close, when we do it."

I went to see Irish George at his lovely big house near Tulse Hill. George had kids, and a nice little Irish wife called Mary. One thing I did notice though was that there was no carpet anywhere in the house. I went upstairs to the kitchen and the first thing I saw was that the cooker was missing – it turned out George had sold it. They were cooking on a three bar electric fire which they had on its back. There was a saucepan balanced on its fucking grill – I couldn't believe it. Mary, who had been quite a stocky little ginger-haired woman (one I'd always liked because she was very sweet and inoffensive), was now as thin as a rake. I guessed George had got her on the gear now, and I asked her about it. She admitted she took a bit to steady her nerves. The man was a complete pig to her and his kids. And it was his heroin habit that was to blame for it all. I could see now what I didn't (or didn't want to) see before – that the fucking stuff was evil. I hated it and I hated people who dealt in it.

I told George I could get him some powder and I gave him a sample of a couple of grammes which we'd kept back from our last scam. Straightaway he went and tested it. I told him I'd be in touch in a couple of days to see if he wanted to do some business. I hoped that his people would give George the money because he already knew me well, and I hoped that we could do a nice, easy exchange between just the two of us. But things didn't work out to plan on this one.

George came back to me and said that they wanted ten ounces, which I agreed to let them have. This time we didn't use the coffee and powder mixture that we'd used before, but I got hold of some stuff from a fella in Essex who I'd been banged up with. He'd been working on a similar scam to us. This stuff was a vegetable extract powder which looked exactly like skag. When it was laid on a silver foil you could 'chase the dragon' by smoking it through a tube. The powder would turn to a dark brown, almost black, oily substance and you'd then turn the foil over and smoke it again. You could get maybe five or six 'runs' out of it by keeping on turning it around. The only way it wasn't similar to heroin was that you didn't get a buzz by smoking it.

I said to Irish George that I didn't want to be directly involved with the black geezers who supplied him. My reason for this was that they could have known, or even been partners of, the Asian guy I'd ripped off. Or, come to that, of Steve. The deal we agreed on was that Irish George's suppliers would bring the money and hand it over to him in his kitchen while, unbeknown to them, I'd be in the spare bedroom, where George would then bring it in to me so we could quietly do the exchange. What I didn't know was that I was not the only one who was trying to do a double-cross.

When the day came I was in this spare bedroom in George's house, as arranged, and I heard this team come into the house. There were three black guys and this girl who, for some reason, they took around with them. She was a user and also an 'old tom'. I stood there with the door slightly open and I could hear them all talking downstairs. George's kids were there by the way and had to listen to all this going on. After a while this bird's voice started to get louder and she was having a right go at George, accusing him of ripping her off. I couldn't make it out at first and wondered what was happening but, suddenly, I began to realise what it was all about.

The fuckers were putting this on for my benefit. George had already told them that I was in the house. And, to make it seem as though George was innocent of any double dealing with me, they were pretending he'd skanked them for some money over something else so they could make out to beat him up, search round the house for the money, discover me, then take my gear instead of the money.

The next thing I knew, this black geezer came through the door into the bedroom. I knew the fucker, his name was Winston. He said, "Alright, John?" I was a bit surprised to see him because he was only a petty, small time crook when I knew him, nothing special. But he and the two others had turned into a fierce little crew from what I'd heard. He said, "Is it you that's got the skag then?"

I said, "That depends..." realising I'd got a tough situation to try and talk my way out of now. We both went downstairs to the kitchen on the first floor. The other two guys were aggressive and saying things like, "George has fucked us for the money, man. He's had our girl's money. We want it back and we want it now – you got to give it to us. You're doing business with him so *you* owe us the money."

I looked at George in disgust – he was trying his best to look scared and even Mary, his wife, was putting on an act. I said to these black guys, "Don't worry, you'll get your money, there's no need to get upset about it." The black geezers then produced these big, pointed, fuck-off knives – like chef's knives without the serrated edges. "Give us what we want," they said, really meaning business now. "Give us the fucking gear." I didn't have the vegetable extract powder on me, it was in my car just round the corner, and Johnny was in his car at the bottom of the road. They started to hold the knives against my throat, and one was at my back. Winston told the other two to be careful of me because he knew I could be a bit tasty. He was trying to keep in with me and saying things like, "Sorry, John, but it's all because of that fucking George, he shouldn't have taken the money off her."

Another one of the black guys was the opposite, he fancied himself a bit. I could feel myself getting a bit angry because I knew that, now I was clean and back on form, I could probably have taken all three of the fuckers – if they hadn't had knives. But I realised also that it would have been pointless hammering them, because the bastards clearly hadn't brought the money with them anyway. I decided to play along and went outside with them to my car, which was probably some twenty or thirty yards up the road. When I went to the boot of the car they were very nervous, thinking I might have a gun. "Watch him, watch him," they were going. I was quite calm. I said, "It's alright, nothing to get frightened about – it's under the carpet here where the spare is." They lifted the carpet and there was this packet with the vegetable powder in.

I could see their eyes and their teeth gleaming in the dark as they excitedly got hold of it. They thought they'd got a mega result. They then backed off with the knives and I said, "You know what you've done there, don't you? You've fucked off the wrong people – they're going to come for you – they're going to fucking kill you."

Off they went in their car with a big roar and a skid. I went back towards the house and I could see, by now, Johnny had got out of his car and was on his way towards me. I went inside to Irish George and I said to him, "You cunt, you think you're fucking clever don't you?" I knew what was about to happen when the black guys, thinking they'd got ten ounces of heroin, discovered they'd got ten ounces of vegetable extract. I said to Mary, "Take the kids, Mary, and get out of here now!" I gave her fifty quid and told her to get a cab down to her Mum's place. George started to protest and run off at the mouth a bit so I smacked him one, putting him over. I said to him, "You're the biggest fucking waste ever. You fucking scumbag."

By now Johnny had joined me in the kitchen and wanted to know what was going on. I said, "This cunt has tried to skank us." Johnny was all for doing him over well and truly and I had to force him downstairs. "Do him, do him," he was going and I had to literally barge him out of the door, saying, "Leave it, just leave it, Johnny." We both got into our cars and made an arrangement to meet up at the end of the road. When I got there Johnny was still ranting on. "What the fuck are you playing at, John?" he was saying. "Why didn't you do him?"

"Just shut your mouth," I said. "Watch this, and learn!"

Fifteen minutes later, this car came speeding past us and screeched to a halt outside George's house. Sure enough, the three black geezers got out and they kicked his door down. Mary and the kids had gone by now of course. The black geezers now thought that George had set them up, and we knew he was now getting his comeback. Eventually they rushed out, and I said to Johnny, "Are you satisfied now?"

He said, "I see what you mean!" He asked me what I reckoned these guys would have got out of Irish George.

I said, "Probably about half a kilo of turnip powder!! Does it really matter?"

Looking back, I suppose it was callous of me to leave then, but that's what I did. And, in any case, the last thing I wanted was to be caught on the premises with a bloke in the state he must have been left in – for all I knew at the time he could have been dead. Before I left Johnny, I told him that this was the end for me as far as this particular scam went. We'd both had a good run for our money and I'd got my own back as far as Irish George was concerned now. Not only that but I'd had enough of drug dealers, and was quite happy to steer well clear of them now. I went back to the coast that night, and I never saw Johnny Salter again. I was told he eventually killed himself in gaol by taking an overdose, after he'd been nicked on a big burglary.

Anyway, looking back, I feel that I did the right thing by cutting out when I did. I made a fair bit of money, got the paybacks I was looking for and quit while I was still ahead. And remember, it could all so easily have gone wrong – as it nearly did in the case of Irish George.

Chapter Fourteen

PRIZE FIGHTER

After the Irish George episode I decided it was best now to keep a low profile. I had no regrets about what I'd done; I suppose it was my way of making amends to myself for letting these scum bags treat me so badly, still, I only have myself to blame for getting into the drug scene, a lesson well learnt. But I fully realised that there were people about who wouldn't be looking at things the same way. I'd rocked the skag boat big time and my old haunts were best steered clear of.

A lot of my time was now spent down on the coast with Carol and that was where we built up our new home. The kids were found decent schools and I thoroughly enjoyed being around them and Carol a lot, as opposed to living on my wits back in the smoke, and having to look over my shoulder all the time. Of course, from the money point of view, I knew that although I'd managed to stash a bit away it wouldn't last forever, so I still returned to London and did bits and pieces – mostly cab driving in the West End like before, but avoiding my old stamping grounds south of the river. I still had the useful 'safe house' in North Dulwich to operate from, which I'd made a point of keeping on.

Now that I was clear of the 'evil shit' and not smoking or drinking, I began to put in some serious training down on the coast. I'd always loved boxing and I started to do lots of road work, weights, and punching the bag. But getting all that crap out of my system didn't mean I lost weight. Where the drugs had made me underweight before, all skin and bone, I was now starting to pack on some solid muscle and it wasn't too long before I was a fit fourteen and a half stone. And I felt the benefits of my new regime mentally as well as physically. It was good to get the aggression out of me and being in condition had this nice calming effect on me.

As mentioned, I made no effort to get in touch with any of my old contacts as of yet. As far as they were concerned I'd disappeared off of the planet and that was how I wanted it. When I looked back at the geezers from Peckham, and the nearby areas, that I'd mixed with, it became clear to me that a hell of a lot of them were now either dead, mysteriously vanished without trace, or serving long prison sentences. It also occurred to me that I was well lucky to be shot of that lifestyle. (At least that's how I was thinking at the time anyway, but you never know what's around the corner, do you?)

My love of boxing and my newly acquired fitness meant that I would visit local clubs on the south coast and do a bit of sparring with the seniors, as well as help out with the juniors now and then. I got talking to a geezer in one of them called Barry Knocker (of all names) who tried to persuade me to take up the game professionally even though I was, by now, not exactly a youngster. I had no intention of exposing my past to the geezer – which I'd have to do, if I applied for a licence – so I just palmed him off by saying that I didn't really have the dedication for it now. But he didn't let it drop and one night he asked me how I felt about getting into unlicensed prize-fighting.

Of course I'd been to unlicensed fights in the past and knew that the Queensberry rules often flew out of the window in these contests. Head-butting and kneeing in the bollocks were all part of the game – it was street fighting, and that was something that I'd had plenty of experience of. The idea seemed reasonable to me and, of course, the money would be welcome. Barry said he could arrange to get me a couple of fights against local pikeys. I decided not to tell Carol about this offer because she too knew what these fights were like and had seen them at first hand. Now that she had a fully fit, muscular husband making love to her regularly, as opposed to a spaced out druggie scum bag about once every six months, I reckoned she wouldn't be too keen on the thought of some pikey jumping up and down on my nuts and trying to kick my head in, just so as I could earn a few quid extra.

I went along to one of the local pikey sites with Knocker and he introduced me to the head guy, a big red-necked Irishman called Mick. You were never likely to get a surname out of these geezers, they were either 'Mick the Brick' or 'Terminator Pat' or some other silly name which you'd never see on a tax return. Mind you, their caravans were like palaces inside, some of them, it was unreal. Anyway this Mick, who seemed a decent enough geezer, said he'd got a couple of show bouts coming up and that he was looking for someone to take on one of his fighters. The attraction for me about these fights was that if you used your brain and you bet wisely with the bookies, you could easily treble your purse money. For example, the pikeys didn't know anything about me, but Knocker had seen most of them perform in the ring and he knew those I could handle and those who would put up a hard fight.

Of course the pikeys made a lot of money themselves, often by bringing in fighters who were below the form of the 'home fighter'. Then, after coming to an arrangement with their man, they would bet on what round he would finish the outsider in. Most of the fights were kosher – the blood, the pain, and the broken bones were all real – but it was all about betting odds and money not about the sport.

For my first fight I went along to this pikey site near Southsea one Saturday night. I was fighting an Irish guy who'd had half a dozen fights, won four, and lost two. It wasn't bare knuckle; we wore bag mitts weighing about four ounces. They suited me; I preferred them to bulkier eight ounce gloves. Before my fight I watched some of the other bouts. What surprised me a bit was how the fighters stuck to the Queensberry rules (more or less) for about the first three or four rounds, and then you would start to see the dodgy stuff creeping in – the butting, treading on toes, elbowing, gouging etc.

These geezers were not the sort to have trained in the type of clubs I was used to. They had beer guts, some of them, and I had to laugh at one particular geezer who was actually standing at the bar drinking pints of lager before his fight. When he got into the ring he copped a right uppercut to the belly straightaway, and then started to spew his guts up while the other guy pummelled him.

For my fight I was to receive £600 for a six-rounder. The ring was marked out with four six-inch posts hammered into the grass and surrounded by these thick naval-type ropes which were not too kind on the skin if you had your back on them. We had a ref and a bell etc and we fought on the grass which was part marqueed by the refreshment area where the drinking and the betting took place.

My opponent, Brendan, came into the ring. He was a bit shorter than me, very dark with curly hair worn in no particular style, and with a slight growth of beard. He had tattoos in Gaelic all over him and this big, fuck-off ear ring. He looked quite menacing. The ear ring interested me though because it wouldn't be a big help to him if things got a bit dirty in there. And the chances were they would.

Knocker was in my corner and he told me that Brendan would come rushing straight in, so to sidestep him, keep my boxing up, and not get too involved, while I assessed the situation – particularly to see how much stamina he had. I knew I had the fitness where I'd been doing my roadwork. True to what Knocker had said, the geezer came rushing straight at me when the bell went. I sidestepped and he ended up going clean through the ropes. There was uproar outside the ring when his mates starting slapping him about, trying to encourage him and pushing him back inside. As he was getting through the ropes I rushed over and kneed him in the kidney, sending him sprawling back outside the ring again. I began to get angrier as the crowd got noisier and I found myself half in and half out of the ring stamping on the guy. His trainer came over to help pull me back into the ring and off of his man.

Once I was back there, Brendan, who'd been done more damage outside of, than inside, the ring, charged back through the ropes, well pissed-off by now. As he came at me I caught him with a perfect one-two, left- right, combination. Bosh! As he hit the deck he seemed to skid and his chin left this small channel in the mud where the ground was so soft. The crowd were going mad; there must have been a hundred and thirty to a hundred and fifty people there. Just to top it off I went over and gave him another kick in the kidneys. The ref pulled me away. Up gets Brendan, covered in mud, looking angry as fuck and off we go again. And remember, he's hardly even laid a glove on me at this stage. But now he managed to force me over to the ropes, and my back got cut on one of the big steel staples supporting the wooden corner post. I could feel the blood running down in my shorts and onto the cheeks of my arse. And he was now getting in some good shots, pummelling me in the guts. The guy could punch and he was really hurting me.

Now I started to get very angry and I was using my knees to try and get him off me. One particular effort caught him square in the bollocks, making him bend forward and drop his guard in the process. I swung a terrific right uppercut which caught him bang under the chin and he just went. Knocked spark out. End of contest. His trainer tried to revive him by throwing water over him. For a horrible moment I thought he might not get up but fortunately he was okay. I went over to Knocker and, when he'd had time to recover, we were joined by Brendan. Mick was furious with Knocker who he thought had given him misleading information about my ability. "You focking cunt," he was going, "Why did you say it would be an even match up?" Knocker just said that he'd only seen me in the club training, and helping the kids, and didn't know how I'd perform for real. Remember many of these fights were not fair, even match ups, but rather bouts between blokes with ability and 'outsiders', conned into fighting, so the pikeys could bet on their blokes and make money.

I wondered whether there might be any problems getting my purse money, to be honest, but there wasn't. They told me I'd done well, and Knocker had put on some side bets and given me half his winnings, so I came away with my six hundred quid, plus almost as much again. I wasn't especially marked up and I never told Carol what I'd been up to, but we just put the extra money away in our little stash. As long as I came home alright Carol didn't ask too many questions.

It must have been a couple of months after that fight that the pikeys approached Knocker again and asked would I do another fight. I knew that they would have a stronger opponent for me this time now that they knew what I could do. They came up with a fee of a grand for this one. Bearing in mind that I didn't know the ability of the fighters these pikeys were producing, I had a word with Knocker to see what he could find out about this latest geezer. I learned he'd had quite a few amateur bouts and hadn't lost many. Also he wasn't a knee-er, gouger or biter, but he could bang. I held out and said a grand wasn't enough. If the bloke could bang, what was to stop him changing his ways and putting the boot in if he got me on the deck? They came back to me again and offered fifteen hundred quid. I accepted.

This time the fight was at a site in Fareham. Many of the same characters who'd been at the other venue were there as spectators. The first thing I noticed, and this was a surprise to me, was that the odds about my fight were even money, take your pick. For the first one I'd been the underdog – that's why we'd done so well on the betting. But this told me that the odds makers must have been quite impressed by what they'd seen.

This one was an eight-rounder as opposed to the six we agreed on at Southsea. And I approached it differently in the opening rounds, sticking more to my boxing and forgetting the dodgy stuff. It was jab and move – jab, jab with the left, sidestep, the occasional clinch, all the time keeping my hands high. Routine stuff that you'd see in most amateur rings. My opponent must have been about thirty-five to thirty-eight. He had quite a big gut on him; again he was heavily tattooed, all round the arms and the shoulders – but not in Gaelic this time. His head looked just like a potato, only one made out of rock. He was a tough character and could certainly take his share of punishment.

I sussed out that his main priority was to go 'downstairs' – to my stomach, kidneys (and bollocks if he could get away with it). Still, the first couple of rounds were fairly even, with us both boxing more or less within the rules and even touching gloves at the end of the rounds. I was enjoying myself. Then came the fourth round and the guy simply let loose. This must have been the round his backers had forecast him to win in, and they were out to collect now, him and his mates.

I fought back and we both went at it hammer and tongs, neither of us prepared to take a step backwards. I felt my nose go – it had been broken before and I knew the feeling – he did this with his head. Towards the end of the round I could sense he was tiring though because his arms were getting lower and lower and he was starting to gag for breath. I saw my opportunity and let loose with a three or four blow combination to his gut, followed by a butt to his head and a final right hander which caught him flush to the side of his temple. Down he went, but he managed somehow to scramble back to his feet. Now his legs had gone though and he was doing a silly walk that I can only describe as like the one that Trevor Berbick famously did when Mike Tyson nailed him in their heavyweight title fight. The geezer now lurched back into the ropes and, as he stood there, I rushed in and smashed probably the hardest right hand I've ever thrown to his jaw. He hit the deck, this time completely out to the wide. It was 'Goodnight all'.

When I came home to Carol this time I was well battered and bruised. I remember she had to take my shirt off for me, my ribs ached like fuck, my nose was busted and my bollocks had really been given a right good seeing to – it was a wonder I could produce sperm properly after that. But I felt good about winning, and I felt that the fight had somehow got a lot of negative crap out of me. Mind you, Carol did go ape-shit when she found out what I'd been doing, and told me I didn't have anything to prove.

I promised her I wouldn't do any more fights on the pikey circuit and for a while I carried on splitting my time between the coast and my Dulwich place, from where I'd do the cabbing and chauffeuring. I was still careful to avoid my old haunts as I wasn't sure whether any of the drug business stuff I'd got up to had finally got around to, and upset, certain faces.

I remember taking Carol once to see the place I had at north Dulwich and she couldn't believe how clean it was. This was because I was a right messy bastard at home, and left all the cleaning up to her, but I did keep this place spotless. Now and then we'd go back there, just using the place more or less as a holiday retreat, and we'd breathe in the London air again and nip out and have a pie and mash, which we both loved, just like in the old days.

I got to hear that the cinema in the Old Kent Road, the Astoria, had been taken over and been turned into a joint called 'The Mad Dog Bowl' where, from memory, they had some sort of skateboard set-up. But it was the set-up upstairs that I was more interested in. It was the headquarters for the newly formed National Boxing Council, run by Joey Pyle, a legendary figure who knew all the 'faces', past and present, and who was well respected at the very highest levels in the world that I was a part of. When Joey spoke, everyone listened.

I decided to go along to one or two of these shows and met some old faces from the past. I was a bit apprehensive about this, but I found, to my relief, that none of them seemed to know anything about my more recent exploits – the attacks on the dealers and so on. The shows themselves I enjoyed watching– it was eight-ounce gloves, good referees, and all pretty kosher stuff. There was a bar and bookies, and you could have a drink and a flutter watching the contests. I'd actually take Carol up with me, and we'd have a pleasant evening there before getting in the car and going back to the coast. We both enjoyed going back to south London but I must admit that I, particularly, missed the atmosphere up there big time. The atmosphere, the pie and mash, the liquor, everything.

One time, when I was doing one of my regular stints up there driving a cab while based at my Dulwich place, I went into this club I used to train at in Vauxhall, called St Anne's. I asked if they would like me to help with training the youngsters there, preparing them for upcoming amateur championships, ABAs and so on. They agreed and I'd go in there two nights a week, just to keep my hand in and to give me something to do really. But I felt good at this stage in my life. I enjoyed working with the kids, I was fit, I wasn't drinking or smoking, and I certainly wasn't taking drugs. I wasn't thieving, or getting mixed up in anything hooky. I felt content with my life.

Anyway, one day –when I was back on the coast, as it happened – I got a call from the trainer of the club in Vauxhall. He said he'd got a couple of tickets for an all ticket show at the Mad Dog Bowl, and would I be interested? I said yes, and I took Carol up to the show. It just happened, at that particular time, my money was running down a bit, and I said to Carol that I quite fancied having a shot at fighting there myself the next time they had a bill. As she could see that the fights were well run, and that there were proper rules and so on, she did not put up any argument.

There was a guy topping the bill there this night called Harry Starbuck. Harry was in his forties, a big geezer who you could tell *had*

had a very muscular physique. But it was now beginning to go, because it didn't matter how hard you trained at that age, everything would always end up going south a bit. He had a 'teddy boy' haircut, with a quiff, and duck's arse, or 'DA' at the back. I remember he had a pub in the Catford area. But it wasn't so much Harry who took my eye that night as another geezer, an Irishman called Barry, who was in one of the supporting bouts. This geezer was a fucking animal. They put him in with an ex-ABA middleweight champion, a smart boxer who was much taller than Barry's five-eight. He jabbed Barry's head off for the first few rounds but Barry just soaked it all up. Then, in round four or five, Barry came out and really went to work. He decked the geezer, and then started to put the boot into him.

That's when it all kicked off. Chairs got chucked around and fights started outside the ring. Joey Pyle's guys managed to restore some order in the end. Remember this was the last thing Joey was after – bad publicity. He was trying to expand his National Boxing Council, not get it closed down. And, of course, this fight being on the under card, they hadn't yet had the main bout, which most of the betting was on and where the big money would change hands. They certainly didn't need the Old Bill charging in and bringing the show to a close. Carol wasn't too impressed either. After me telling her I wanted to fight on one of these bills, and how nice and organised it all was, here we were, with the women being herded off to the loo out of harm's way, and the bar shutters coming down and everything.

Anyway, as I say, they managed to restore some order in the end and the main fight went on with Harry Starbuck. After the fight, which Harry won, I went up to the bar to make my approach to Joey Pyle. Joey, a short, thick-set fella with not much hair, listened while I explained my situation –I'd had experience, and would like a try-out on one of his bills. He wrote down my phone number. "Alright son," he says, "give me a week or two and I'll get back in touch with you." About two weeks later I got a call to go over to Shoreditch, to the Masonic Hall. When I got there I was given a medical, and everything was arranged so they could give me my licence to fight in the NBC. While I was there I was waiting in this room with five or six other fighters when who should turn up but this Barry, the Irish geezer who'd started the riot at the Mad Dog Bowl. I soon realised that he must have been fighting illegally at the time I saw him, but at least now they were making sure he was brought on board so everything was kosher. It wasn't that easy for them to recruit fighters – you had to have a lot of bottle when you didn't know who you might get put in with next. What you had to remember about the organisation was that most of the guys behind it had shady pasts, and things like fight fixing and rigging the odds were just par for the course.

After I got my NBC licence I started to train a couple of nights a week at the famous gym at the Thomas a Becket pub in the Old Kent Road. A lot of the top fighters had trained there; I suppose Henry Cooper was the best known. In my time there I'd see the current heavyweight challenger, Billy Aird, being put through his paces. And I made a point of taking a couple of the lads from St Anne's boxing club along with me as well. I'd also see Eugene Maloney (who I've already mentioned elsewhere in the book) and his famous brother Frank. It was a magic place really, full of history for a fight fan like me. Danny Holland, who used to be Henry Cooper's 'cuts man' at ringside, ran the gaff. In fact the Old Kent Road itself was a bit of a fighter's shrine – the Wellington pub down the road got taken over and renamed the Henry Cooper, and I believe Terry Downes owned another pub there called the Prince of Wales.

Shortly after getting my NBC licence I got a call asking if I was up for a fight in a few weeks' time. They told me my payment would be a grand, but they didn't yet know who my opponent was to be. This made me a bit suspicious straight away. Anyway, I said I'd do it. Although it was for an eight-rounder I knew the money was quite good because I'd heard that some of the other geezers there – the new comers anyway – were only paid five or six hundred quid for their first bouts. And I treated it very seriously by training every day and getting myself into good shape. I was doing my roadwork with the trainer at St Anne's, and he'd also help me in the gym with some weight training, sparring and so on. This was good because, in case you feel tired and you get a bit unfocussed, you really need someone behind you all the time giving you that motivation and I found it worked out well.

I started to get a bit concerned about who I was going to fight though. Posters began to appear, going up around the place advertising Harry Starbuck to top the bill on the particular date that I was supposed to be fighting. I knew from experience though that, about a week before the actual show, full posters would have to go up which would include all the under card fighters such as myself and details of who was fighting who. The ridiculous thing was that I didn't have a contact number for the NBC anymore – I hadn't bothered to get one because I'd just assumed that they would keep in touch with me anyway.

Eventually I got a message on the phone at my North Dulwich address, from where I'd been doing all my training (and doing some cabbing as well, with money getting tight, while Carol was back on the coast). Anyway, they wanted me to fight this Barry bloke. I just said to the geezer, "You've got to be fucking joking!" Bear in mind that at this time I'd been possibly getting a bit carried away with dreams of success and fame, and all that stuff, with this NBC. Now these dreams were being totally destroyed because, instead of the proper boxing and proper rules I'd been preparing and training for, they were offering me mayhem by putting me in with a fucking animal who would think nothing of kicking, biting, gouging, butting and anything else he could get away with. Anyway, Joey Pyle's guys tried to convince me, saying, "No, you'll be alright, don't worry," and all the rest of it, and eventually I said I'd consider it.

A couple of hours later they were back on the phone offering me more money – and that made me more suspicious. Next day I consulted a couple of fellas I knew and asked them what they thought. They said more or less the same thing. "Think about it John. You're going to go into the ring and fight one way and he'll be fighting another. Before you know where you are you'll be taking the gloves off and it will be total war. And this bloke is a complete fucking nutter – anything could happen. He wouldn't know the Queensberry rules from his arse. Give it a miss, mate, it ain't worth it."

I felt very frustrated by the situation. Here I was having done all this real boxing training, and hoping to put it to good use in a proper, fair fight under proper, fair rules. Also I could have done with the money on offer. What was I supposed to do now – take a chance, waste all my training and come out of it possibly maimed for life, just so people could make themselves a lot of money betting on the other geezer? After talking it over with Carol, I told them no, I wasn't prepared to take that chance, and I was just not interested in their offer.

They tried a couple more times to persuade me, but my mind was now made up and I wasn't having any of it. I'd felt a bit belittled, to be honest, to think they were trying to take me for a mug. But that was the way these people operated – recruiting mugs then cashing in on the betting. I had to admit to myself now that the secret dream I'd always had of becoming a genuine boxing contender was never going to happen. If I'd gone about it differently, with an established promoter, and so on… who knows?

Funnily enough I did go to this particular promotion at the Mad Dog Bowl – purely as a spectator. And, would you believe it, they were still trying to con me into fighting on that same bill on the very day of the fight by offering more money, and promising me a dead easy fight next time with some other geezer, also pointing out that I could have a flutter on myself when this happened and, with my winnings *and* my purse money, I'd really clean up. I still said no.

I later watched Barry come out and muller some poor fat-gutted, ginger-haired bastard that they'd dug up from somewhere. He lasted about two rounds and at the finish his face was cut to fuck, his ear holes were bitten, and he was limping and holding both hands gently to his injured bollocks. To be honest I think there was more fairness and respect shown between fighters at the pikey camps. This lot should have been renamed the National Bullying Council. Or perhaps the National Betting Council.

Although I would keep up my training, when I was living at north Dulwich, I did not fight anymore. I'd occasionally go down to the coast to see Carol and the kids but I liked to have some money in my pocket when I did so. And, although there was a bit left in my stash that I had buried, it was now dwindling fast. I decided I'd got to go back to work. Boxing was not going to earn me a decent living. Getting paid a grand was okay but remember that had to last me for about six weeks until the next promotion came up. And I had to pay rent on two places, north Dulwich, and the family place on the coast. So, back to work it was, and I expect you know what I mean by that word.

I went back to the coast for a spell while I planned things out, and then I got in touch with my old friend Byron. It amuses me to think of it now but, when he answered the phone and heard my voice, I could sense the shudder he gave – it seemed to come right down through the line. You could hear him thinking 'Oh, fucking hell, not him – what's he come up with this time!' I arranged to go up to see him in London. Byron was still into the drugs, still supplying the rock stars and so on. But what I wanted from him was to make contact with certain people who I thought might be able to help me execute a little plan I'd had in my mind for some time now. It involved turning over a certain well-known gaming establishment in the suburbs.

Chapter Fifteen

THE PHANTOM HEIST

What I had to do first when I spoke to Byron was to convince him that I was back to my normal self now, and free of the gear just like the Johnny Mack he'd known when we first met inside Brixton. I explained to him that I'd had this particular bit of work on my mind for some time now and really wanted to see it through. From the information I'd been given, the job should have been good for fifty to sixty grand, minimum, a lot of money back then, and certainly enough to set me up for a good time to come. Byron was interested when I mentioned this and we agreed to meet up near Chelsea Bridge.

When I saw him he still wore the same old coat but looked healthier now. He was off the gear and on a special methadone programme. He kept looking at my pupils to make sure that I was off of the stuff, but could also see from the muscle I'd put back on that I was now in good shape. I explained to him about the job. I'd had a look at it – what was involved was removing two safes from this gaming establishment. Originally I had wanted to steam in the front door with a shooter but now thought I knew a much easier way. But this would involve getting the help of a good team because the place was 'belled up'. In other words these infra-red beams went from one wall to another, protecting the place, and they'd have to be bypassed somehow so a good team with knowledge was required. There was a substance available that you could use from a spray can that would detect exactly where the beams were when you squirted it over the area, anyway I told Byron I'd got a good plan laid out. What I wanted from him was help with getting hold of some decent army walkie-talkies and electronics gear. Byron knew a lot of people and these were things you couldn't always get hold of in shops – you wanted ex-military stuff really.

To be honest I looked on the plan as my last score, my 'Eldorado'. I'd already uprooted and disappeared in effect, with no one knowing where I was, now all I had to do was to make one last big score. And I wanted Byron with me because I trusted him. Also I knew that, to a degree, I could make him do things my way. If it had been someone else, someone more independent-minded, then there might have been problems and arguments over who was in charge and so on, and that was the last thing I wanted. Byron wasn't a burglar or an ideal 'muscle man' but it was him I wanted with me.

I showed Byron the job. This partly involved entering the premises (when it was open for business, of course) so as he could see the lay-out for himself. The building itself was very secure but the two safes were pre-war ones and, given the time, you could just peel the backs off of them or use a diamond grinder or whatever. But I intended to literally lift them out of the premises. The safes could be picked up using a sack barrow. The door leading to the safe room was alarmed and there was a pressure mat and door sensor behind it, so if the door was forced it would set off the alarms. And if anyone got past that point they would set off the alarms anyway as soon as they trod on the floor in the office – all this was inside information I had picked up from a geezer I knew.

My plan was for us to visit the premises on a regular basis as punters, so we could find ourselves a little bolt hole down in the basement where it would be possible to hide out for a few hours. We managed to get this spot where we could get above the pipes and we tested it to make sure that, even when someone came into the room, they didn't know that we were there, hidden above them. We would wait until the security staff had done their inspections, locked up and fucked off for the night, then we would drop down out of our little cubby hole and set the alarms off. Then we'd jump back, up above the pipes again, and wait for the police to come round to do their checks, the owners to come down after getting called out, and all the rest of it. It was amazing just to be perched up there while the Old Bill walked around below us, completely unaware we were there.

We went through this routine five or six times, over a period, until the Old Bill wouldn't even bother to respond because they just assumed there was some kind of malfunction there. What I was after was the security of knowing that, should things go wrong on the night and the alarms were set off, then at least we'd have the extra time we'd need to get away and, hopefully, there'd be no response at all from the authorities on the basis that it was just a faulty alarm system. After all, the owners had now been called out several times, the alarm people had checked things out and couldn't find the 'fault', so it had to be virtually written off as one of those annoying blips you just had to live with.

Another thing we did when using the premises as ordinary punters was to bring in and hide various tools, like a big borer (brought in two pieces), coal chisel, hammer, and so on. All this took time and, over a period of weeks, we got very familiar with the place – always keeping a look out, of course, for any new alarm or security systems that might have been installed. Once we had all the tools we needed in our overhead cubby hole, the last thing to think about was how we were actually going to get the safes out and away. I found a Fiat Caravanette with a side loading door and we stripped out the interior and built a little ramp that could be attached to the side door to extend to the pavement. When we drove up to the emergency exit of the premises, where the safes would be coming out, it would be only a matter of about four feet to get them into the van via the ramp, because you could park up really close and, luckily, it was a really dark street as well. There was no CCTV at the time either. I worked it out that, from the time we opened the emergency exit doors, it would take us no more than three minutes to get the safes across the pavement and safely into the van.

I hadn't really intended to involve anyone else on this job but, as it happened, I'd met this guy, a young Belgian or French geezer I think he was, who'd done a bit of work with some people I knew. He was what you'd call a 'yes man' – he'd just do what he was told and I decided to use him as a driver and look-out.

On the night of the heist the place was teaming with people. I don't want to be too specific about things like dates – the reasons for this will become apparent as the story unfolds. Anyway, just before closing time, Byron and I nipped downstairs to the cellars and our little cubby hole. The place was like a maze down there, with boiler rooms and lagging pipes all across the ceilings – you're talking about an old building. The only reason anyone would have had to disturb us or to find our tools would have been if a pipe had exploded right in the spot we had them hidden.

Our driver was outside in the specially adapted van, in contact with us by walkie-talkie. It was like something out of 'Mission Impossible'. It was just what I wanted because, the way I saw it, there was no need to go charging in with shooters, holding people up. You just needed that bit of extra patience to earn your living. But, believe me, the adrenaline was still there, along with the excitement. After we had checked out the radio with the driver, who was in place across the road, we waited for the establishment to close for the night. Then, sure enough, the guard made his usual, final check round the place – we could see him below us. As he went out of one of the escape doors at the back he clicked on the alarm switch. This particular door had extra protection, which made us curious. It had a chain and a big fuck-off padlock contraption whereby he could slide out of the door but it would still be, in effect, locked. Then he could put his hand round, click the security circuit on, and then shut the door. It was a lapse in security really, because what should have happened was that the guy should have gone out through the front door. Not that I was a security expert or anything - I'd just get the names of systems, then get advice from old burglars, and the like, on how was the best way to crack them.

When we heard the geezer finally go we got down to action. We'd had these wooden blocks made and we had two scaffold boards with rope handles which we walked along to the main foyer from our hiding place. We knew where the beams were that would set off the alarm in the foyer – they were about one foot above ground level, although you couldn't actually see them unless you sprayed them with this substance we had with us (which I won't mention). Anyway, by stepping over the beams, then setting up the blocks and laying the boards across them, we could literally walk over where the beams were. By this means we got as far as the office where the safes were.

We countered the security system by only taking out the main part of the door and leaving what was just an archway in effect. This meant drilling hole after hole after hole until we'd taken out a doorway within a doorway, and left just the outer frame, with hinges, lock etc in place. Once inside the office we used the board and block technique again to step over the pressure mat, immediately inside the door, that we knew would have set off the alarm if we'd touched it.

The two safes themselves were not connected to anything – there were no alarms on them. This was where the security was so lax. What we had to do was manhandle them onto the board, and that was where the physical work came in. I knew that it was going to be a bit too much for me and Byron alone, especially getting them up and over the pressure mat, so I had brought in a rope tackle to help, and I rigged that up in the first place so that it just meant pulling on it and dragging the safes across, one at a time. We got them through the archway in the office door and out to the foyer floor outside. We now had to move them with the aid of the sack barrow to get them over the beams.

This was taking forever – we must have been at it for about four hours. It was fucking hard work and we were both sweating like pigs in there, working our bollocks off. But I looked on it as honest toil because we weren't hurting anyone, and it was all covered by insurance anyway. And it was to be our last bit of work!

Even so, I began to get a bit worried about the fact that Byron was wearing all these chains and watches etc like he always did do. Where the work was so heavy lugging these fucking safes, there was a good chance one of them would come off and drop us right in the shit if found. By this stage we were beginning to have major arguments. There was no doubt that Byron was tired – he was totally knackered and was all for giving up. He wanted us to grab what loose change was lying around and call it for the night. But, the way I saw it, we were almost there now and had the prize within our grasp. Why the fuck should we give up now?

In the meantime we're taking so long that this driver outside keeps talking to me on the walkie-talkie. Half of what he's saying is in English, the rest in fuck knows what, and I can't really make out what he's on about. "For fuck's sake, just wait will you?" I'm saying. We'd arranged to try and maintain radio silence and do the job in military fashion. I didn't have a clue who might have been listening in on us or what frequency we were on. For all I knew we could have been going all over the fucking CB radio waves. So, what with all this going on in my ear and Byron moaning and saying that he wished he'd never met me and so on, things got very tense, still we worked. Worked and sweated.

After about another two hours we actually got the two 'peters' (safes) over to the double doors near where the exit was. We both just sat down, totally knackered. I knew I had to cut the two chains on the doors. But, bypassing the infra-red switch was the dodgy thing – would it break the circuit and set off the alarms? We decided to allow ourselves a breather, and have a fag. Byron was so hoarse that at one stage I thought he was going to have an asthma attack and die on me. There was a tap nearby and I kept filling up this old cup to make sure he had plenty to drink – I'd never seen anyone sweat like he was doing. Of course we'd got our gloves on, even our hats, so that made us even worse.

I made a start on the cutting work with these bolt croppers. They were too small to do the padlock so I had to work on the links of the chains. While I was doing this I suddenly heard it. It was a noise from the other side of the building, like a door being slammed. Byron and I looked at each other. We hadn't really explored that part of the building it seemed to be coming from – only the parts necessary to hide out, store our tools, and, obviously, pick up the safes. I said to Byron that we'd have to investigate.

We now moved to where we thought the noise had come from, torches in hand. I took the lead, with a crowbar at the ready. The corridors were concrete – it was an old pre-war building – and there were these rooms at the sides with heavy, vault-like doors which were difficult to open. I went into several of the rooms, which had no windows even. Nothing there. Byron kept talking nervously and I had to keep telling him to shut up because I needed to listen out. If there was a night watchman or someone around, then he would have to be tied up because, as far as I was concerned, we'd nearly pulled it off now and I wasn't about to have the job fucked up at the last minute.

I came across a small stairway which led to another corridor with several more of these doorways. I thought to myself that whoever was there must be in one of these rooms. I called Byron up to me. I whispered to him, as quietly as I could, that if anyone should manage to get past me, he was to stop them by giving them a clout with the hammer which I now passed to him. I stressed not to hit them on the head. I didn't want him to kill them – just stop them from getting away before I had my chance to jump on them. Byron wasn't too happy and started to protest. "I don't need all this shit…" he was saying when, out of the blue, we heard one of these heavy doors opening. There was no mistaking the noise. Then we heard footsteps coming down the corridor.

I waited there, just around the corner, with my crowbar at the ready. Byron was right behind me, and our torches were turned off. Then, as suddenly as they'd started, the footsteps stopped. I turned the corner. I could not believe it – there was no one there! I looked into the rooms along the corridor. Not a thing, just the same concrete, windowless rooms measuring about twelve feet square. What the fuck was going on, I thought. I'd heard it, Byron had heard it. What the fuck was it?

I came back to Byron and, as I put the torch on him, noticed he was as white as a sheet. "This isn't right," he was going. Next thing, he went firing down the stairs, and away. I started to chase after him. I couldn't believe what was happening. I'd gone through all this hard graft, not to mention the mental pressure, and now here I was being run out on by my mate, just as it looked like we were reaching the finishing line. And I'm shouting out, "Stop Byron, stop you cunt," and at the same time I've got the walkie-talkie going with this French geezer shouting "Hello, Hello… it's mee!"

Byron got as far as the fire escape and, in his panic, started cutting the chain himself. "This is not normal," he was going, "The place is haunted." I pleaded with him to come back to have another look at the building. "I'm not going back there for anyone," he said. He was literally crying with fear. I said to him, "Look you cunt, if you don't come back I'll smash you right in the boat, you fucking waste of space, with this jemmy." Eventually he followed me back. The last thing I wanted was for him to try to make his own getaway, the state he was in, and drop everyone in the shit.

We made our way back to the corridor where we'd heard the footsteps. Well almost – however much I threatened him, Byron wouldn't come up the last flight of stairs with me. I went into one of the rooms and Byron, hearing the noise of the door opening, thought it must be whoever, or whatever, had made the noise before, and immediately had it on his toes again. Again we had the same pantomime – me chasing, calling him back, and, at the same time, shouting at the driver on the walkie-talkie. When I got to Byron this time he was completely fucked. He was adamant that he wouldn't stay any longer, he didn't want to know. He said he didn't care if I hit him, kicked him, maimed him or what – he just couldn't go on. It didn't matter to him that we were nearly there, nothing mattered to him except getting out – and that was it!

To be honest I didn't really know what to do at this stage. I liked Byron in spite of everything and didn't want to hurt him. And I'd been a bit scared myself, of course I had. After all there had definitely been someone up there, and I'd checked all the places he or she could have come from. Something just wasn't right. In the end, disastrous as it seemed to me, I had to go along with Byron's wishes, and call it a day.

I cut the chains, bypassed the circuit, opened up the fire exit, shut the door behind me; the alarms did *not* go off. As I shut the door I knew I couldn't get back in and I knew that, about six feet behind that door, were two safes that could have been my passport to an easier life. We walked to the van. Byron was now tailing behind me, and he kept saying, "I'm really sorry, I really am." When we got into the van the driver wanted to know what was going on. I told him a load of bollocks about a problem inside and that I'd contact him the next day. I felt so gutted I could hardly bring myself to speak.

When we got back to where we were staying, our two women were there waiting – my Carol and Byron's Nicky. When Byron saw Nicky he just burst into tears. He was still as white as a sheet, and really fucked-up after the experience. The pair of them, unbeknown to me, had already arranged to travel to the continent the next day. Now, of course, things were not going to be so easy for them because they didn't have the dough they were expecting to have. The only one of the four of us who didn't let it affect them too badly was Carol.

Believe it or not her reaction, when she heard what had happened, was to nearly piss herself with laughter. She just couldn't get her head around this 'supernatural' business. And the thought of the place being haunted, with Byron (and even me, if I'm honest) being shit scared, just made her throw her head back and laugh out loud. So there we were – Byron crying, Carol crying with laughter, and me shaking with anger and sheer frustration.

Anyway, the next morning, around dawn, I met the driver, who was having a kip in the van, and told him to dump the vehicle. When I got back to the house Byron was still a bundle of nerves and full of apologies. It's difficult to say how I really felt. I was fucking angry still, yes. And, to be honest, I was so gutted that when I saw Byron take his methadone (where he was still trying to get off the gear) I felt like going on the gear again myself. When I thought about all the effort, the planning and money I'd put into this job – all for fuck all – perhaps it wasn't surprising.

I felt so bitter about it all that, later on, I couldn't even bring myself to buy a paper or listen to the news for word of any repercussions. I suppose you could say I was in denial. So that morning was the last time I saw Byron. He just repeated his position that he was sorry but he couldn't have gone on, also that he was still trying to get himself straight, and so on. He told me about his booking to the continent for that day. We all shook hands and hugged each other goodbye, they fucked off, and that was it. I never saw them again from that day to this.

Chapter Sixteen

JOEY'S DOWNFALL

Although Carol kept seeing the funny side of the Byron incident, the poor bastard had obviously had some sort of deep spiritual fright to make him go that shade of white; it left me pondering what to do next for the best. We decided we'd go back to the coast to let the dust settle and think things through. At one stage I did consider going back to the smoke to do another drug dealer, but I knew Carol wanted me to steer clear of that sort of crap and, to be honest, deep down I'd had enough of that game myself. And I didn't really want to get hold of Johnny Salter again either, because to be seen around with him could cause more possible aggravation. In the end it came down to what I knew would keep me going – a bit more of the cabbing 'up west.'

I did about four days a week while based at the North Dulwich drum and then I'd have a couple of days or so back on the coast. It was while I was working up west that I just happened to bump into a geezer that I knew, that was to lead to an unusual and also hilarious situation. Let me explain; although I was, at the time, trying to steer clear of any major villainy, it just happened that one day I'd dropped off a fare near Forest Hill and was doing a three-point turn in the road when I clocked these three geezers I knew, coming out of a club. One was a geezer called Joey, who I had not laid eyes on for a long, long time.

Joey was a con-man and a good one too; he'd started off forging Post Office books, cheques etc, then he'd got bigger ideas and bought a laser printer, which in those days were as big as a fridge, and he'd copy postal orders and giro cheques. He was a real clever bastard, but he was also a snaky cunt and I'd heard, via the grapevine, that he'd upset a certain respected face who was a good friend of mine, and this face was out to get some payback. He'd made the mistake of conning his own kind instead of just sticking to ordinary punters. Anyway, I got to thinking about Joey and the more I thought, the more I realised that bumping into him could give me just the opportunity to make a nice few quid that I'd been looking for.

At that particular time Joey would have been about thirty-eight to forty, a tall, good-looking geezer, well-dressed (except if he was 'playing the part' to act out a different role in order to con somebody). He was, I suppose a would be James Bond-cum-Walter-Mitty, what with his different IDs and passports etc – all courtesy of his great forging skills. But he was also a very convincing and cunning con-man. He could mix in the company of business people and the like, and he'd sound and look the part. One day he'd be a 'Mr Hargreaves', the next day he could be 'Detective Constable Smith' or someone else, he was that good. He was an unbelievable character, but no one trusted him in our area, I suppose for obvious reason; he never worked much in 'the manor' but would operate in the suburbs and the like.

I first met him when I was about sixteen and I'd nicked half a dozen post office books. I was told that a bloke in Bermondsey would buy them off me for a fiver each. So I went round and I met Joey and, sure enough, got my thirty quid off him – not bad money at the time for a sixteen-year-old. Anyway, I got to know him quite well and I watched him at work. He would buy in all sorts of nicked books with government stamps on, like benefit, pension, Post Office books etc. Then he would get a piece of greaseproof paper, put it over the blunt end of a pencil, hold it there, and then rub it quite hard against the official stamp in the book. The friction caused by this would replicate the official stamp on the greaseproof paper. Then he would transfer it to, say, a paying-in book that he'd recently obtained (there were various different types of stamps in use at the time – for example, one to pay in, one to take out, one to close your book down etc), make out an entry for, say, a hundred and fifty quid, again, the amounts were always entered in ordinary handwriting in those days, so writing the amount in was no problem (I would like to point out that this method is now obsolete).

Joey did show me another way to replicate an official stamp. This involved using, of all things, a hard boiled egg. He would roll the egg round onto a stamp in the book, making sure it was the right temperature to get the job done, but the only trouble with this method was that the result would come out very faint. Also, when it came to taking the books into Post Offices', they might ask for some ID but if it was clear and dark they wouldn't make a big fuss about it. Anyway, Joey would send his little gang out to withdraw cash at various Post Offices' around South and North London and they would return with several hundred quid plus, of course, withdrawal stamps on their books, which he could use.

When you considered how lax things were back then, it wasn't difficult to see that Joey had a nice profitable little business going. But he was always an ambitious kind of geezer and it wasn't too long before he branched out into more major stuff. For example, he decided to go into property as an up-market landlord and he developed a great scam which went down really well. He would go into an out of town estate agency in Surrey or Sussex by pre-appointment, and he'd be immaculately suited and booted, with a limo, on the pretence that he wanted to rent or buy an up-market property, a suitable property which had to be some distance away from the estate agents itself. It also had to be an empty property. There were quite a few of these at the time because it was the eighties and things were pretty tight, what with repossessions and high mortgages.

Once he'd decided on something suitable, Joey would arrange a viewing. He'd mention casually to the estate agent that he was an executive in the music business or some other credible business and, when the agent saw the smart suit, the briefcase, the BMW parked outside etc, he'd be taken in. Joey would make a point of being friendly, and work on building up trust. When it came to looking at the property, he'd make out that he was over the moon about finding it. He couldn't wait to discuss it with his wife; he thought it was a terrific price for something so good – all this sort of bollocks. Of course the agent would be well chuffed at hearing it, it was music to his ears and he could almost taste a fat commission. On the rare occasions that Joey sensed that the agent might smell a rat, or was too rigid in his methods, he would blow him out and not take it any further; he was shrewd like that.

Joey would then find out when the agent was available, so he could, as he said, 'bring my wifc along to view the property'. He'd also find out when the agent *wasn't* available, so that if, for example, the agent said, 'I've got to go out on Tuesday but I could squeeze you in the morning first thing', Joey would say okay, that was fine – what time did the guy have to be out of the office that day? The agent might say ten thirty or whatever, and so they'd make the appointment for, say, nine thirty at the house. Then, just before the appointment time, Joey would phone. 'Sorry Mr Brown', he'd say 'I'm afraid I've been unavoidably delayed, I can't get there for another couple of hours. It really is so disappointing; my wife was so looking forward to seeing the place'.

Faced with this dilemma, the agent would, in nine cases out of ten, say, that would be okay – just pop in and collect the keys from the office and drop them back after you and your wife have viewed the house. Joey would then collect the keys have them cut, and drop them back to the office where he would tell the receptionist, or whoever, that they were 'thinking about it.' And remember, he might have several of these cons on the go at one time. Anyway, at this stage in the operation, he'd keep the agent sweet with a lot of spiel like 'Don't let anyone else see the property, I'll give you a definite answer by Friday, I've just got to finally persuade her – I'm sure she's coming round'. Then, as arranged, Joey would phone on the Friday and, to the agent's delight, he'd confirm that he wanted the place. This call would be made just before the office closed on the Friday evening, leaving Joey a clear weekend with no competition from other buyers, a few empty houses, and several nice new sets of keys.

Meantime he'd put advertisements in the classified section in the local papers. People would see there was, for example, amongst other offers, a 'four-bedroom house, unfurnished, for rent. Or possibly a 'Georgian four-bedroom house, with swimming pool.' Bearing in mind that the areas that Joey picked out were always prosperous ones, mainly around the stockbroker belt, there was never a shortage of potential tenants. And he would already have tenancy agreements made up (copied from existing agreements), rent books, the lot. And they would all look completely kosher.

The adverts in the local paper would quote the phone number of an isolated phone box, usually one in a lay-by, where Joey would park up all evening, take calls, and arrange viewing appointments. And, of course, he'd have other people as well helping him out when it came to showing potential tenants round the other properties which he'd have on the go at the same time. These other gang members (helpers) would all know exactly how to play it and what to say. They'd make out that they were in a bit of a hurry to get to their next appointment, when people came to view, and come to the point quickly saying, "I think you would make great tenants, could you manage to get cash for this? You can? Excellent, you can move in on the 22nd," or some other moody date. The tenancy agreement and keys would be handed over; the punter would be over the moon. Occasionally, if the customer lived locally, they could be persuaded to go and get the cash out while the gang member went with them.

Joey's favourite types of customers were foreigners and he and his gang would do their best to get as many as possible by picking up their accents when they phoned. He considered they were more likely to be baffled by the tenancy agreements, and all the rest of it, and of course this was only natural if they hadn't been living here long. And the other thing with them was that they were more likely to deal in cash. There were a fair few illegal immigrants around even then, and they would not, of course, have bank accounts.

But Joey was a greedy man and he certainly didn't limit himself to taking money off of foreigners. Well-off English people were just as attractive to him, and this was the reason that he found himself and his racket in serious trouble one day. One of the people that he conned, unbeknown to him at the time, just happened to be the daughter of a pretty tasty, big-time South London villain. The daughter was married to a completely straight, professional accountant, with no connections to the underworld, so Joey could not have had any clues about her background or who she really was.

Just to give a picture of the scene you'd have to imagine this woman – and possibly even her husband as well, because he wouldn't have been the only professional to be taken in by Joey – meeting Joey at the house. Joey would pretend to be acting for the agent or landlord. "I am just his nephew," he'd say, "and I'm acting on his behalf. Unfortunately I can't be hanging around all day – I'm in the music business actually and I've got a meeting in Holland, so I've got to be on a plane from Gatwick later on." So this woman, like many before her, would be pressured to cough up the cash quickly if she really wanted the place. Joey would take the cash, promise to drop the keys round to them later on – which he'd do – and then tell them when they could move in – say a week later. He'd even take them through a decorating program, asking what colour they'd like this room or that wall, and so on. And they'd happily pay out hundreds of pounds to him. Multiply this by the number of 'clients' Joey had on that particular day and you begin to get an idea of how much money he'd rake in. And, of course, his gang would be on a percentage, with Joey himself taking the lion's share.

One thing Joey would always make a point of doing was to make sure that he'd set the same date and time for moving into a property for all his victims. So, if you can imagine the scene, it would be chaos with, say, four or five different families turning up at ten o clock on a Saturday morning in their removal vans arguing, often in foreign accents, and waving their rental agreements around. Why did he do it? I couldn't say, but he just thought it was hilarious.

But Joey wasn't especially respected in the criminal fraternity. This was mainly because he was a 'white-collar villain' who you would never catch getting his hands dirty by doing armed robbery and stuff like that, or putting himself at risk physically. He was an out and out con-man just like his father before him, who'd been involved in the black market in the war years. And, from what I could gather, most of his family were well at it too.

Anyway, as mentioned, it was the rental con that caused a big-time fall out with a particularly dangerous villain whose daughter got taken in – and then ran home to Daddy when it came on top, feeling very peeved indeed. So, by around the time I met Joey when I was cabbing, I had heard via the grapevine that there was a 'price' out on him. And, to be honest, my need to collect at the time was far stronger than any particular liking I had for Joey. I didn't feel I owed him anything and certainly wasn't going to pass up a chance to make a nice few quid for myself and my family.

As I said, there was a 'price' out on Joey and, in normal circumstances that would have meant he would get a right good hammering or possibly worse. And, by the way, that might well be what happened to him eventually, I really can't say. But, because it was this villain's intention to avenge his daughter and he wanted to make an example of Joey, it was decided that Joey, apart from anything else he might cop, must be put through the same ordeal as the villain's daughter had suffered. And, once I'd had a chance to contact the face, this is where I came in.

I arranged to meet Joey at his local pub not too far from my place at North Dulwich on the pretence of doing a bit of business. He was a fairly good-looking geezer, always immaculately dressed, about six feet tall, and he turned up in a convertible sports car and, in his usual way, instead of drinking beer, he drank something ridiculous like crème de menthe from this special glass he insisted on having. Oh yes, and there were always couple of young birds hanging round him, impressed by his style – or, of course, his money.

It was his habit to come into the pub and throw this big bunch of keys he carried, onto the stage, which was right next to his table. The stage was used for the go-go dancers that performed there. If the idea of leaving your keys out seems strange to younger readers I should mention that it was an enormous bunch and, in those days the fashion was to wear slim fitting trousers rather than, say, baggy jeans etc, and you just couldn't get that sort of thing in your pocket. Anyway, I met Joey a few times and, following orders from the villain, one night I managed to nick the keys, which was really quite easy in a busy pub. I passed them to a geezer who I had waiting outside specially and he got another set cut.

It took him about an hour to bring them back but, before he'd had the chance, Joey missed them. There was a bit of a panic but, fortunately, when the guy returned them to me, and while some other people were looking around on the stage for them, I managed to sneak them back. I got up on the stage with the others and then said, "Oh look, they've fallen down behind the speaker." Joey was delighted because he had all sorts in the bunch – including shop keys, because he owned some video shops as well.

Once we'd got the new set of keys I thought that I would be asked to rob the shops. This would have suited me fine and I was well up for it. But that wasn't what the villain wanted, he wanted Joey to know how his daughter, and the other poor fuckers, Joey had conned, really felt. Mind you, the villain did let me take the shop keys and I was extremely grateful for this and made good use of them. After all, videos were the new thing at the time and you could make yourself a nice few quid out of them.

One of Joey's habits was to spend a weekend in Amsterdam on a regular basis. He enjoyed a bit of puff and he certainly enjoyed sex. He would take a couple of young girls with him when he went – whether he took them for swapping weekends or what I don't know, but there was plenty of action to be had in the clubs over there, that much I do know. It also happened that the villain's friend's wife had a travel agency that Joey used, and so therefore the villain knew just when Joey would be going away for a weekend.

A plan was put in place whereby Joey's apartment – a flash, plush job, right in a prime spot, with all mod cons, security door, camera, etc – was advertised for rental in exactly the same way that Joey's scam operated. And, of course, it coincided with a weekend that Joey was away. I did not get involved in this side of things because my task was to, believe it or not, witness the scene on the day in question, and, from a safe distance, take photos! The villain was adamant that this was all he wanted from me in return for the nice profit I got from Joey's videos, plus the price which Joey had earned himself from ripping off the villain's daughter.

On the day in question – which was the Monday morning that Joey got home from his weekend flight to Amsterdam – I watched from my car, which was parked on the brow of a slight hill, and could see that all the people going into Joey's place were of foreign appearance – there were no white faces to be seen. Indians, Cypriots, West Indians, the lot, trooped in but not an Englishman in sight. No sooner did one group of Turkish Cypriots arrive in their van and start carting stuff inside than a Jamaican geezer got out of his van and started to argue with them – followed by an Indian family who parked up and started to try and stop the others by waving their piece of paper at them. More Cypriots turned up and there was pushing and shoving and plenty of swearing in different languages.

After the arrival of a couple more groups things got to the point where the Old Bill had to be called and, shortly after their arrival, who should turn up but the man himself, Joey. He was going mental trying to get everyone out of the way so he could get indoors. Remember his gear was in there –although I don't know how much of it was still there by then because the villain had probably already helped himself to most of it. Anyway the whole business must have been investigated by the Old Bill and, of course, Joey was well in the frame, because of all the other reported, unsolved cases of the same scam which had been pulled outside the manor. He perfectly fitted the description they'd got of the geezer behind it all. To be honest I didn't wait around to find out what happened to him – I'd got my dough and that was good enough for me.

I did of course give the camera back to the villain and, by the way, was sure I noticed a lot of Joey's stuff in his place when I went there. He was totally creased up by what had happened and laughed his bollocks off. It was the first time I'd actually seen the geezer laugh. But I don't think that Joey's troubles would have ended there. This fella wasn't about just having a laugh. If you crossed him – or his family of course – then you were in the shit. And if Joey did end up inside I know the villain had people there who would have got at him. Either way, Joey would remember what must have been the biggest mistake of his life – conning a perfectly innocent, hard-working young woman whose old man just happened to be one of the tastiest villains in South London.

After this episode I went back to the coast to be with Carol. I'd done well out of it, especially by clearing out Joey's shops because the gear I'd got was easy to get rid of – a geezer I knew agreed to buy it all for a knockdown price which still left me with a nice few quid. But I knew I'd need to make some changes in my life now. Peckham was beginning to get too risky now and I knew Carol wanted me to get out of the villainy. And I'd just about had enough of it all if I'm honest. I was pushing twenty-nine and I decided to take an ordinary straight job on the coast. It was silly money, nothing like the amounts I was used to. But for a while I was happy. What I didn't know then was that my life was about to, again, spiral out of control big time. If I thought at that stage that I had already gone through the worst spell of addiction I'd have to suffer, then I couldn't have been more wrong. Unfortunately there was worse to follow. But that's another story which – who knows – I may get a chance to share with you sometime.